Innovation, Science, Environment

Innovation, Science, Environment

Canadian Policies and Performance, 2006-2007

Edited by

G. BRUCE DOERN

Published for
The School of Public Policy and Administration
Carleton University
by
McGill-Queen's University Press
Montreal & Kingston · London · Ithaca

© McGill-Queen's University Press 2006
ISBN 13: 978-0-7735-3062-1   ISBN 10: 0-7735-3062-2 (cloth)
ISBN 13: 978-0-7735-3072-0   ISBN 10: 7735-3072-x (paper)

Legal deposit first quarter 2006
Bibliothèque nationale du Québec

Printed in Canada on acid-free paper that is 100% ancient forest free
(100% post-consumer recycled), processed chlorine free.

McGill-Queen's University Press acknowledges the support of the Canada
Council for the Arts for our publishing program. We also acknowledge
the financial support of the Government of Canada through the Book Publishing
Industry Development Program (BPIDP) for our publishing activities.

Library and Archives Canada Cataloguing in Publication
Innovation, science, environment: Canadian policies and performance,
2006-2007/edited by G. Bruce Doern.

ISBN 13: 978-0-7735-3062-1   ISBN 10: 0-7735-3062-2 (cloth)
ISBN 13: 978-0-7735-3072-0   ISBN 10: 7735-3072-x (paper)

1. Technological innovations – Government policy – Canada. 2. Science
and state – Canada. 3. Environmental policy – Canada. 4. Research
institutes – Canada. 5. Technological innovations – Government policy.
6. Science and state. 7. Environmental policy. I. Doern, G. Bruce, 1942–
II. Carleton University. School of Public Policy and Administration

GE190.C31552006   352.7'45'0971   c2005-906343-2

This book was typeset by Interscript in 10/12 Minion.

Contents

Preface

This is the first edition of a planned annual volume of commentary and assessment of Canadian and related comparative innovation, science and environment (ISE) policies and institutions. It has emerged initially out of a broader body of research and teaching at the Carleton Research Unit on Innovation, Science and Innovation (CRUISE) and the School of Public Policy and Administration at Carleton University. Aimed at an audience of interested and informed Canadians involved in, or affected by, this crucial realm of Canadian policy, politics and governance, the book examines the ISE policy priorities of the federal government. Chapters are also devoted to broader areas of federal-provincial and cities/communities involvement in these fields as well as the crucial international and comparative dimensions which impact on Canada.

We are especially indebted to our roster of contributing academic and other expert research authors from across Canada for their insights and for their willingness to contribute to this inaugural edition. The book is structured on the basis of a general call for chapters in the ISE field, a number of which were then selected for inclusion by the editor. In this volume and in later ones our aim is to involve academics from a variety of disciplines as well as doctoral students from across Canada doing advanced research in the ISE field and also knowledgeable practitioners from the public and private sectors.

Thanks are also due to Robert Johnson and Kimmie Huang at the School of Public Policy and Administration for their excellent research and technical support and to Joan McGilvray and her colleagues at McGill-Queen's University Press for their always-professional editorial and publishing services and expertise. The research support of the Social Sciences and Humanities Research Council (SSHRC) is also appreciated, two of whose grants underpin three of the chapters in the book and other related work that is underway.

None of this work would have been possible without the continuing support and scholarly stimulation provided by my colleagues at CRUISE, in the School of Public Policy and Administration at Carleton University and in the Politics Department at the University of Exeter.

G. Bruce Doern
Ottawa
November 2005

Innovation, Science, Environment

1 The Martin Liberals and Changing "ISE" Policies and Institutions

G. BRUCE DOERN[1]

Innovation, science and environmental (ISE) policies and institutions are nominally only a small part of federal (and provincial) responsibility. Compared to social welfare policy and health policy, ISE policies involve relatively small amounts of money and modest amounts of a government's regulatory capacity. Nonetheless, ISE policies and institutions are linked to each other. At the technical level the key environment issues are scientific problems that demand scientific, economic and social innovation. Organizationally, environmental issues and the application of science reach across industrial sectors and into the nooks and crannies of virtually every other policy field and human activity.

ISE policies and institutions also have different political constituencies from those of other major policy fields. Science policy is much more a subject of interest by elites and science itself does not have a vocal interest group structure although it does have lobbies via universities and via technology-centred business associations. Non-governmental organizations (NGOs) have some interests in science issues (e.g. northern science and technology) but usually do not have well funded or continuous access to decision makers. Neither innovation nor science policies are typically "top of mind" issues for voters and public opinion. On the other hand, environmental policy (with the related notions of sustainable development as discussed further below) is routinely a popular and continuously expressed concern by Canadians and reinforced by numerous activist NGOs and consumer groups. Some businesses are also keen practitioners of sustainable development (SD) and sustainable production (SP).

Figure 1 provides an initial glimpse into the growing links in the ISE realm. ISE policies have a core definitional meaning but they also have slippery and disputed changing boundaries as government's change their descriptive labels for debate (and political communication) and as underlying dominant theories evolve and change. *Science* policies involve support for basic research and for the education and training of highly qualified s&t personnel in various scientific disciplines in the natural sciences, engineering, and the social sciences. They also involve government science, both research and development (R&D) and Related Science Activities (RSA) to facilitate governmental policy, and regulatory and monitoring roles carried out in the public interest. Science policies are partly underpinned, certainly for purposes of communication, by the notion of a *linear model* or continuum whereby basic research and R&D are seen to lead to applied research and development and then to innovation in new products and processes and which ultimately leads further to actual commercialization in Canadian and global markets.[2]

Innovation policies are targeted more at the development of new products and processes, and place a greater emphasis on indicators such as rates of patenting and the creation of spin-off companies. The above noted linear models for science policy were eventually seen as an overly simplified view of what happens in dynamic economic and technical settings. Later and most current innovation policies see the underlying dynamics as being non-linear and thus lead to a changed policy debate through concepts and ideas such as national systems of innovation, local systems of innovation and clusters as complex multi-directional interactions among firms, universities and governments and their variously networked s&t personnel.[3]

For its part, *environmental* policy was first broadly cast as "end-of-pipe" clean-up of pollution from various sources relating to air, water, and land. It was later augmented in the latter half of the 1980s by the paradigm of sustainable development (SD).[4] SD focuses on the need by present decision makers to leave the environment and eco-systems in at least a good a state for the next generation as it was for the current generation. There was also a greater recognition that one had to distinguish between pollution and emissions. Not all emissions are polluting but still some emissions must be controlled and managed with science-based limits and mechanisms. SD therefore implies more preventative approaches rather than just clean-up. It is also defined by governments and business more loosely as "the triple bottom line," in short, as policies and approaches where decision makers explicitly take into account the economic, environmental and social consequences and effects of their decisions. In the broadest sense, SD identifies a normative goal towards which ISE policies must strive, and a framework within which its successes and failures can be assessed. In almost all that it does, environmental policy needs science, technology and innovation to assess effects, monitor pollution, model and understand complex ecosystems and habitat and create new ways of producing and consuming that are more sustainable.[5] SD therefore points to an ambitious and complex transformative agenda where changing patterns of production and consumption decrease the loading imposed upon the global environment.

Figure 1.1
The ISE Policy Realms at a Glance

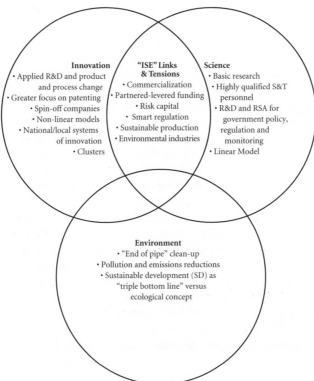

The overlapping or cross-over points in Figure 1 give selected examples where some integration and tensions are occurring. As we will see, this includes more focused policies for commercialization, in short, successfully getting new products and processes to market. It also includes ideas and practices regarding sustainable production, environmental industries as an industrial sector itself, smart regulation, and incentives to provide risk capital for firms in knowledge-based enabling industries such as biotechnology, nanotechnology, and information technologies. It also includes numerous program mechanisms characterized by levered and partnered funding arrangements (as discussed further below) linked to new organizational forms and networks. As indicated above, these are only selected examples.

A fuller account of areas of linkage can be found in policy realms such as infrastructure and the cities agenda where there are environmental tie-ins to the funding and also in policies affecting health and consumer issues as well as programs supporting bio-remediation and overall environmental technologies.

For these and other reasons examined in this book, ISE policies and institutions need a more focussed, linked, and continuous scrutiny regarding both policy intent and aspirations and institutional results and performance. In an overall sense, ISE policies must ultimately be judged through various kinds of performance data of varying quality and clarity. Appendices I and II of the book supply a sample of some of the basics in this regard. Appendix I shows that Canada still lags behind other countries in terms of gross domestic expenditures on R&D as a percentage of GDP, business enterprise expenditure on R&D as a percentage of GDP and levels of patenting. As chapter 3 shows, the federal government aspires to take Canada from 15th to 5th in these global league tables but there is a very long way to go. On the other hand, Canada leads on higher education expenditure on R&D as a percentage of GDP, a result that is directly attributable to major federal spending in the past seven years cast broadly as "innovation" policy but most of which went to universities (see more below).

Appendix II draws on Environment Canada's environmental reporting and shows a very mixed picture of actual environmental performance. Some areas such as acid rain and protected areas are improving and others such as greenhouse gas emissions and non-hazardous solid waste are deteriorating. Still other areas show neither progress nor deterioration, the situation in realms such as air quality, and the ozone layer.

Within these larger performance backdrops and ISE policy realms, we examine current federal policy. In the current Martin Liberal minority government period of national politics, the dynamics of ISE policies and institutions are especially problematical as they fight for space, funding, and political attention at a time when staying politically alive is the primal urge.

This chapter's overview of ISE changes and dynamics proceeds in four steps. First, we look at Martin Liberal government policies and priorities in the ISE realms. Second we locate these changes in the context of past ISE trajectories of change and inertia including changes initiated by Paul Martin when he was Minister of Finance from 1993 to 2002. We then preview the chapters and views of our authors. Their chapters examine a range of ISE policies and institutional dynamics including: S&T and innovation overall as seen through the National Research Council's response to changing federal agendas; Canada versus UK innovation strategies; federal sustainable development (SD) strategy approaches; two of the federal S&T granting bodies (the Natural Sciences and Engineering Research Council, and the Social Sciences and Humanities Research Council); a case study of the mining and supply service sector ripe for the application of the innovation strategy but one in which there has been little progress; environmental industries and the role of the Canadian Environmental Technology Advancement Centres; source water protection and innovation in local government and multi-level governance contexts; and information disclosure as an environmental policy instrument.

Conclusions and final observations on future ISE prospects and constraints are then offered. These centre on: the serious continuing weakness of industrial investment in R&D in Canada; the challenges regarding the significant gaps in the federal sustainable development strategy process; the dilemmas and potential dangers of efforts to get universities to become more commercialized; and the continuing need to experiment with any number of partnership-based networked approaches to funding, regulation, and information disclosure.

"ISE" IN A MARTIN MINORITY

While this section focuses on the past two years of Paul Martin as Prime Minister of a Liberal minority government, there is a very real need on matters of ISE overall and especially on innovation and science to consider the de facto Martin ISE era as a decade long story. Martin as the Chretien Government's Minister of Finance played a major ISE role advised by his Deputy Minister, Kevin Lynch, both when the latter was DM of Finance and earlier when he was DM of Industry Canada. Later in this chapter, we will see more of this larger and earlier trajectory of changes in science and innovation, including the spending of $13 billion on S&T and innovation from 1997 on. But it must be noted at the outset of this section that many of the science and innovation policy challenges that Martin faces as Prime Minister are the products, for good or ill, of the decisions he made as Minister of Finance. The good part of these earlier changes was that there was a needed boost to S&T funding mainly for universities. But the commercialization agenda was needed earlier and was not pursued in a focused way.

Our look at Martin minority government ISE policies, priorities and linkages of the last two years involves three elements of analysis. First we summarize overall Martin priorities. Obviously, the prospects for ISE depend greatly on where it sits in the larger priorities and in the bidding war over money and political attention spans, most notably in a raucous and uncertain minority Parliament situation and a pending early 2006 federal election. In that context, we then highlight the Martin Liberal's science and innovation policies and its movement towards a greater commercialization focus captured earlier in Figure 1. Finally we look at their environmental and related sustainable development policies. Among the ISE realms the closest longer term links have been between the "I" and the "S" aspects of policy. But again, as Figure 1 suggests, the "E" aspects have always had important links to innovation and science policy but these are deepening to an ever greater extent.

The Martin Liberals' Overall Priorities

The Martin Liberal's 5 October 2004 Speech from the Throne (SFT) opening Canada's 38th Parliament was largely built on its June 2004 election platform but mediated by second sober thoughts arising from its unaccustomed position as a minority rather than a majority government. Reiterating that Canadians wanted the new minority Parliament to succeed, the SFT made specific announcements and commitments under the broad headings of: a strong economy; the health of Canadians; children, caregivers and seniors; Aboriginal Canadians; Canada's cities and communities; the environment; and a role of pride and influence in the world. Interspersed under these various headings were promises such as: (ISE-related initiatives are highlighted in italics)

- reduce the debt-to GDP ratio to 25 percent within 10 years;
- implement its Learning Bond as an innovative savings vehicle;
- *initiatives to turn more of Canadian's bright ideas into new businesses including improved venture capital to promote such commercialization;*
- fundamental reform of the Equalization program as a part of continued support for regional policy;
- the Ten Year Plan to Strengthen Health Care; (signed with the provinces in September 2004);
- put in place the foundations of a national child care program developed with the support of the provinces (agreements already signed with several provinces);
- do more to ensure that Canada's prosperity is shared by Canada's Aboriginal people;
- *develop the New Deal for Canada's Cities and Communities, including offering a portion of the federal gas tax, growing over five years;*
- *new investments to commercialize new environmental technologies funded out of the proceeds of the sale of the Government's Petro Canada shares;*
- *respect its commitment to the Kyoto Accord on climate change;*
- invest more in Canada's military by increasing Canada's regular forces by 5000 troops and our reserves by 3000.[6]

The 23 February 2005 Budget Speech by Minister of Finance Ralph Goodale provided the second major opportunity for the Liberals to set out their promises and priorities for Canadians, but this time with some fiscal flesh on the STF policy bones. Crafted even more warily with an eye on voter wishes, internal Liberal cohesion, and the views and tactics of the three opposition parties, the Budget Speech laid bare a budget that amounted to the largest spending increases seen in decades. Among the key features and provisions of the 2005 Budget are: (ISE-linked initiatives are highlighted in italics)

- new spending of $42 billion over five years;
- $11 billion cut from existing spending through the work of the new Cabinet Committee on Expenditure Review to be reallocated from lower to higher priorities over the next five years;
- real economic growth forecast at 2.9 percent in 2005 and 3.1 percent in 2006 (based on average private sector consensus forecasts);

- based on the Health Plan, federal cash transfers to the provinces and territories will increase from $16.3 billion this year to $19.6 billion next year, thereafter escalating by 6 percent annually, reaching $30.5 billion in 2013–14;
- balanced budgets projected through to 2009–10;
- $12.8 billion increase in defence spending over five years;
- an annual $3 billion contingency reserve, to be applied to debt reduction if not needed to meet current budgetary commitments;
- $5 billion over 5 years to introduce an Early Learning and Child Care initiative, $100 million of which will be for First Nations on reserve;
- *Share of $5 billion in federal gas tax revenues will go to cities and communities over 5 years rising to $2 billion in 2009–2010 and continuing thereafter indefinitely;*
- a tax cut achieved through raising the tax exemption level on incomes to $10,000 by 2009 (currently $8, 150);
- a lowering of the corporate tax to 19 percent from 21 percent by 2010;
- *$4 billion over five years to meet Canada's Kyoto Protocol commitments plus $1 billion for a Clean Fund;*
- *An acceleration of capital cost allowances for firms investing in efficient and renewable energy generation equipment;*
- $1.6 billion for heritage, the arts and sports.

After the federal budget speech, the Liberals were pressured into a further $4 billion in spending following a deal with the NDP, which helped save them from defeat in the House of Commons. The NDP package included one environmental initiative. While ISE policies and initiatives do show up in the Liberal game plan (see further discussion below), they are dwarfed by other fields in the biggest burst of federal spending in four decades.

Innovation and Science and Related Commercialization Policies

In its first post-2004 election Throne Speech and in other statements the Paul Martin Liberal Government said that it was going to focus on a commercialization policy or strategy as its central micro-economic policy for Canadian prosperity in a 21st Century knowledge-based economy. In 2005 there was increased speculation as to whether "commercialization" would be the overall label used to describe the strategy or whether it would be subsumed under the label or competitiveness or even productivity. Nonetheless, an explicit mandate to develop a commercialization strategy was assigned by the Prime Minister to Industry Minister David Emerson, the newly elected MP from British Columbia. Early in 2005, he appointed an advisory committee to advise him on the nature of such a strategy. As an economist, a former Deputy Minister of Finance in the government of British Columbia, and, most recently, the CEO of Canfor, a major forest products

company, Emerson brings to the commercialization strategy task an interesting and informed background and analytical capacity. Early in his ministerial tenure, Emerson observed: "Think about the level of R&D in the
United States compared to Canada. Think about the productivity performance in the United States compared to Canada. And then stand back in a
world of global supply chains and think about investment decisions at the
margin. And you're in Canada or you're in China or wherever you are and
you are going to make an investment that is designed to serve the North
American market if not the world market and you have to choose between a
Canadian location and an American location."[7] Emerson then went on to
argue that Canada has to attack these issues by having "a very hard-nosed,
comprehensive, and aggressive attack on competitiveness ... the reality is we
will succeed in this country if we can be a leader in developing and applying
and commercializing technology and if we become a world leader at developing and applying the human capital that's required to efficiently
manage ... technology ... [8] Citing his experience with Canfor, he went on to
argue that it is "not so much an issue (whether) this factory is an efficient
factory or (whether) this particular cost factor is lower than it is in the
United States. The real formula for quantum moves – and we need to make
a quantum move- is ... we're going to have to look at the entire supply
chain. We're going to have to look at industrial clusters that hang together as
integrated collaborative economic partners."[9] Emerson then went on to
stress that the Canadian private sector under invests in R&D compared to
major competitor countries. He pointed out that the Government of Canada had stepped into the breach in recent years with over $13 billion in-
vested mainly in universities and public institutions. So his next question,
which he stated bluntly, is "how the hell do you get it back out and get it
commercialized and infused into the economy so that it spreads widely and
creates growth momentum and efficiency throughout the economy?"[10]

Some aspects of this commercialization focus was earlier revealed in the
5 October 2004 Speech From the Throne (SFT). It set out a commitment to
"strengthen Canada's ability to generate and apply new ideas." In particular,
it stated that:

The next challenge is to turn more Canadians' bright ideas into dynamic businesses,
great jobs and growing export earnings. To that end, the Government will ensure a
supply of venture capital, particularly for early-stage businesses – for example,
through the venture-financing arm of the Business Development Bank of Canada.

The Government will develop policies to foster Canadian capabilities in key enabling
technologies – such as biotechnology, information and communications, and advanced materials – which will be drivers of innovation and productivity in the 21st
century economy.

Providing "smart government" – the third element of our economic strategy – aims to make it easier for business to do business in Canada.

Smart government includes a transparent and predictable regulatory system that accomplishes public policy objectives efficiently while eliminating unintended impacts. This can be a competitive advantage for Canada. That is why the Government welcomes the just- released report of the External Advisory Committee on Smart Regulation.[11]

These key parts of a commercialization agenda had been previewed in the 2002 Chretien government's *Achieving Excellence* innovation agenda paper, under a subsection of the report on commercialization.[12] It stressed that while Canadian firms had increased their R&D in the previous decade, adopted new production technologies, and 26 percent of Canadian manufacturer's firms were first to innovate nationally (and some internationally), the commercialization performance was still markedly below other competitor countries. The report then went on to discuss factors that influence levels and degrees of commercialization including the need for greater venture capital as well as the other aspects itemized in the Throne Speech.

Later aspects of federal thinking were highlighted in Emerson's statements on Industry Canada's priorities, the department Emerson heads and the department with the overall lead role in S&T and innovation policy. Three strategic outcomes were emphasized in this statement:

- A fair, efficient and competitive marketplace;
- An innovative economy; and
- Competitive industry and sustainable communities.[13]

Emerson, went on to state his view that, "These three strategic outcomes are mutually reinforcing … successful businesses combine with thriving social enterprises and a sound environment to form the sustainable communities that attract investment."[14] Thus commercialization themes are central to Emerson's view but links are also drawn with the environment both directly and through the federal cities agenda cast as sustainable communities. But these environmental links still deal with only a narrow range of issues affecting the natural environment which are the larger central concern of environmental NGOs and many voters.

Dr. Arthur Carty, the newly appointed National Science Advisor to the Prime Minister (and formerly president of NRC) pointed to some other recent decisions that were also a part of a commercialization focus.[15] One was a Budget 2004 item of $270 million for risk financing. The Prime Minister's Advisory Council on Science and Technology recommended further funding for the 2005 Budget. These and other proposals from industry did not materialize given the above noted social policy and other priorities. It was decidedly not an S&T

budget or a commercialization budget in any serious or focussed way.[16] Budget 2005, however, did contain, as we see below, some commercialization funds for developing the best new ideas for environmental technologies. A private sector Task Force on Early Stage Financing also has reported to federal and provincial deputy ministers of innovation. It recommended a number of measures linked to tax policy, the SR&ED tax provisions (including incentives for angel investors). Other work in the federal government on biotechnology and the biohealth sector has also focussed on the risk capital needs of the many SMEs in this key sector, most of them new in the last 5 to 7 years.[17] In addition, Environment Canada had established four industry sectoral environmental competitiveness tables to advance innovation and environment initiatives and discussions.

On the other hand, in the early Martin moves on science and innovation governance, there is a quite mixed set of messages. The Office of the National Science Advisor (NSA), as chapter 3 shows, has been minimally funded and looks pretty slim compared, for example, to its UK counterpart. The NSA was established to help integrate the government's in-house science and technology activity. Arthur Carty brings considerable credibility to this task but he has not been given the needed resources to do the job. In December 2003 Martin scrapped the then existing junior minister position of secretary of state for science, research and development and replaced it with a non-ministerial parliamentary secretary for science and small business who reported directly to him. Then in the July 2004 Cabinet shuffle, this new position was left vacant. As a result, the industry minister, who already has a massive department and portfolio, no longer has ministerial-level support for science and innovation policy.

Environmental and Related SD Policies

The Martin Liberal government has sought to make more explicit and systematic the links between economy and environment and innovation through greater targeted commercialization policies. This has been evident in Environment Minister Stephane Dion's early speeches as minister, in the 2005 Budget, and in the 2005 federal Kyoto plan, in which an immediate environment-innovation link was drawn.

Dion's discourse on environment and innovation has centred on Environment Canada's Project Green, the overall name for a bundle of federal initiatives. At the very outset of one key speech, Dion stressed that: a "heightened environmental effort is needed to ensure not only our quality of life and that of our children and future generations, but also the very competitiveness of our economy. Indeed, it is becoming increasingly clear that in this new century, the most cost-effective technologies are very often the least polluting and the least resource wasting. We are seeing the intensive search for greener production methods pay off in a new cutting-edge form of entrepreneurship and a very dynamic market."[18] In his House of Commons speech on the 2005 federal Budget, Dion began with a story of his meeting that day with representatives from a small Canadian Aboriginal firm with new technological ideas regarding waste management emphasizing again the environment-innovation link. Thus again, Dion went on to assert that the 2005 Federal Budget "is the greenest one since Confederation."[19]

While there is some normal political hyperbole in these claims and while previous Environment ministers have certainly made the environment-economy-innovation link, the 2005 Budget and other developments such as the Kyoto plan, suggest that the Martin Liberals do have a deeper ingrained or internalized view about these close linkages than previous governments and are prepared to talk about them and act upon them (though the latter is much more difficult). Thus the 2005 Budget begins by asserting that the Government of Canada believes "that a healthy and sustainable environment is an integral part of economic growth."[20] The 2005 Budget committed a further $5 billion package of measures over five years by

- "Addressing climate change by promoting reductions in greenhouse gas (GHG) emissions and encouraging the development of environmental technologies.
- Building on existing tax measures to encourage Canadian businesses to invest more in efficient and renewable energy generation.
- Investing in public infrastructure to encourage more efficient use of energy as well as the remediation of brownfield sites.
- Protecting our natural environment, including the Great Lakes, oceans and national parks."[21]

More specific budgetary measures were itemized under these various categories of the package. Later in April 2005, Dion announced the updated and expanded Kyoto Plan which committed still further budgetary resources over a longer period.[22] It consisted of approximately $10 billion to be spent over seven years to meet Canada's commitments to reduce greenhouse gas emissions to agreed targets.[23] The $10 billion figure was much larger than the earlier estimated costs revealed in the 2005 Budget Speech largely because the Liberal plan had to rely more on buying change than regulating or compelling the change.[24] This shift to a greater spending component was due partly to the opposition of the business community to a direct regulation-focused strategy for implementation of the Canada's Kyoto commitment but it was also due to deep-seated Liberal timidity (and dithering) on their Kyoto file as a whole.[25]

Thus when Dion was making his above mentioned speech on the federal budget, he was able to draw attention to the combined new budget and Climate Change initiatives. In particular, he drew an immediate link between environment and innovation by stressing the new Climate Fund announced with the Climate Change plan. An initial $1 billion was committed with increases up to $4 billion by 2012. The "cash for tonne" Climate Fund, in Dion's view "will make it possible for progressive companies to find funding if they manage to reduce greenhouse gases in the municipal, industrial or residential spheres."[26] Under Dion, the Liberals have also launched sector sustainability tables under a new Competitiveness and Environmental Sustainability Framework (CESF). Four of these have been established in the forestry, mining, chemicals and energy sectors.[27]

The adequacy of these Liberal environment-innovation plans are of course subject to numerous criticisms by the opposition parties in a minority Parliament and also by business associations and environmental NGOs. This has especially been the case over the Kyoto plan. We will see more about the recent historical context for these criticisms in the next section. But as a starting point, it is still possible to see that the Martin Liberal's are increasingly convinced about the need to pursue a tighter environment-innovation link.

ISE POLICIES AND INSTITUTIONS IN BRIEF HISTORICAL CONTEXT

If the above statements and aspirations capture the current Martin era views of the ISE realm overall, how do they sit in a larger historical context both in policy terms and institutional terms? Such a context-setting portrait proceeds in two stages. First, we look broadly at change in the nature of Canada's overall ISE policy and institutional system, looked at through two time periods. Second, we summarize broadly the nature of the environmental and related SD institutional debate but with a focus on evolving views about the extent and forms of government intervention.

The Changing ISE Institutional System

The evolution of the Canadian ISE Institutional System can be characterized by looking at the two periods of change.[28] Table 1 summarizes the two time period lists of agencies, bodies and/ programs. Period I refers to the ISE Institutions established historically until about the late 1980s. Period II refers to a second tranche of institutions established in the late 1980s to 2005 period. It must be stressed from the outset that the two periods cannot be characterized only in relation to ISE issues and forces. They also are characterized by changes in general approaches to governance and public administration where increasingly the focus has been on how to reduce traditional hierarchies and enhance client-focussed and flexible delivery of services and better systems of public and stakeholder engagement.[29]

Table 1
The Changing ISE Institutional System

Period I: Early Institutions to the Late 1980s

Geological Survey of Canada

Agriculture Experimental Farms and Laboratories

National Research Council (NRC)

Atomic Energy of Canada Ltd. (AECL)

Atomic Energy Control Board (AECB)

Defence Research Board

Industrial Research Assistance Program (IRAP)

Defence Industries Productivity Program (DIPP)

Medical Research Council (MRC)

Canada Council (initially included social science grants)

Natural Sciences and Engineering Research Council (NSERC)

Social Sciences and Humanities Research Council of Canada (SSHRC)

Program on Energy Research and Development (PERD)

Canadian Space Agency

Science Council of Canada

Economic Council of Canada

Environment Canada as lead federal environment agency

Federal S&T Laboratories and agencies engaged in R&D and Related Science Activities (RSA) (evolved and now in several science-based departments and agencies such as NRCan, Environment Canada, Health Canada, Department of National Defence, Fisheries and Oceans Canada) Industry Canada (telecommunications)

Scientific Research and Experimental Development (SR&ED) Tax Credit

Concepts of "sound-science" embedded in Canada-U.S. free trade agreement

Period II: The New ISE Institutional System – The 1990s to 2006

Networks of Centres of Excellence (NCE) (linked to NSERC and SSHRC)

National Roundtable on Environment and Economy (NRTEE)

International Institute for Sustainable Development (IISD)

Commissioner for Environmental and Sustainable Development (CESD)

Program on Energy Research and Development (PERD) (reduced funds but more multi-departmental and competitively networked)

Technology Partnerships Canada (TPC)

Canada Foundation for Innovation (CFI)

Canada Research Chairs

Millenium Scholarships and Trudeau Scholarships

Canadian Institutes of Health Research (CIHR)

Table 1 (*continued*)

Genome Canada

Canadian Biotechnology Advisory Committee (CBAC)

Canadian Biotechnology Secretariat (CBS)

Sustainable Development Technology Fund (SDTF)

Canadian Foundation for Climate and Atmospheric Sciences (CFCAS)

Climate Change Action Fund: Technology Early Action Measures (CCAF-TEAM)

Climate Fund

National Advisory Board on Science and Technology (NABST)

Advisory Council on Science and Technology (ACST)

Council of Science and Technology Advisors (CSTA)

Office of the National Science Advisor

New institutional requirements for ISE built into international conventions and agreements signed by Canada (eg. climate change; biodiversity, endangered species; SARS, BSE)

Federal S&T Laboratories and agencies engaged in R&D and Related Science Activities (RSA) (further evolved through greater requirements for revenue raising, fees, and commercial contracts, as well as intellectual property licensing and encouragement of formation of spin-off companies; also influenced by concepts of smart regulation, citizen engagement and international regulatory cooperation and harmonization)

The two periods are first characterized very broadly in order to highlight their differences. As we progress, however, some of these differences necessarily have to be de-emphasized or analytically relaxed. Some agencies in the second period are replacing predecessor bodies but are functioning according to new ideas and pressures. Many institutions exist in both periods but again under the different ISE policy ideas and pressures.

Period I encompasses an array of entities forged across more than a century of ISE policy development but when the "E" in the equation was only beginning to emerge. Some of the institutions in Period I functioned before Canada had explicitly stated "science policies." It includes very early bodies such as the Geological Survey of Canada and the agriculture experimental farms and research labs. These bodies were unambiguously tied to Canada's then resource dependent economy. A somewhat later tranche of entities flourished in the context of World War II and the post-war era including: NRC (formed in 1916 but which grew mainly in the context of World War II); AECL, AECB, the DRB, NRC-IRAP, and (after the cancellation of the Avro Arrow) DIPP. The key granting bodies, the MRC, NSERC, and the SSHRC were reforged and spun out of earlier bodies in the 1960s and 1970s and were centred on peer-reviewed grants to researchers and also support for graduate students. The Canadian Space Agency also emerged from its roots in the NRC.

The federal s&t laboratories and agencies trace their roots to the already mentioned early resource-centred science but by the late 1980s they included an array labs located in key science-based departments, each needing R&D and Related Science Activities (RSA) to underpin their growing policy, regulatory and monitoring responsibilities.[30] Environment Canada was of course a part of this mix when it was formed in 1970. By the late 1980s, the Canada-U.S. free trade agreement was in place giving rise to more evolved notions of the role of "sound science" in trade disputes involving health, safety and the environment. Last, but not least, in this list is the SR&ED Tax Credit administered by Customs and Revenue Canada which provides refundable tax credits for smaller, largely Canadian owned, firms as a complement to normal R&D tax deductions which are available to larger often foreign-owned firms.

Period II shows the emergence of a melange of bodies and funds established in the late 1980s, 1990s and the period up to 2006. This regime is most associated with the cluster of mainly post 1997 entities such as the CFI and SDTF, which were established as foundations (so-called third-party bodies) in federal budgets when Paul Martin was the minister of finance. Their funding (the eventual $13 billion figure noted earlier) was made possible by the slaying of the federal deficit and the emergence from 1997 on of healthy surpluses. Often lumped in with these are the CIHR (the evolved successor to the MRC), the Canada Research Chairs, and CCAF-TEAM and also the recently announced Climate Fund referred to earlier in the chapter. Other institutions were also created during this period which added further to the "E" in the ISE mix but most of which were simultaneously involved in both the innovation and science aspects as well, especially since they brought the growing concerns about sustainable development with them as a part of their mandates. These new bodies included the Commissioner of the Environment and Sustainable Development (CESD), The National Roundtable on Environment and Economy (NRTEE) and the International Institute on Sustainable Development (IISD).

However, another feature of Period II is the general notion of networks and competitive partnered leveraged funding. Programs such as the Networks of Centres of Excellence Program, the Program on Energy Research and Development (PERD) and Technology Partnerships Canada (TPC) were central here. The Networks of Centres of Excellence Program in many ways pioneered the concept of virtual networks, and competitive network bidding processes. PERD was a similar pioneer in internal governmental determinations of R&D priorities in the energy field through competitive processes among several departments with energy-related mandates. The TPC, which grew out of abortive efforts to cancel the DIPP program in 1995, also involved competitive processes for investing in firms with provisions for repayment.

It is useful to also consider broadly what core ideas governed the support for innovation and science (and s&t) in these two periods and also to relate the shifts that occurred to the nature of public budgets and fiscal policy, to the ideas about reinvented government and governance, and other macro political-economic imperatives. The conceptual idea which most governed the largest part of Period I was the previously noted linear model of the spectrum of scientific activity. The broad presumption of this model was broadly linear in nature. It essentially suggested that basic or pure research, broadly drove the *later* applied research and development phases and this in turn then led to inventions and ultimately to innovative products sold in markets to consumers. To this day, the federal government still partly diagrams its own sense of its innovation and science policies and institutions by locating specific bodies, programs and funds at approximate points along this kind of continuum. Thus, this linear model still has some relevance in terms of basic policy communication.

Nonetheless, as noted earlier, this linear presumption has been challenged by other evidence and experience which shows that s&t and r&d and innovation and commercialization interactions are much more complex, and indeed with causal links being often reversed and much more subtle. In short, the pathways to real innovation are multiple and complex. The new institutional linkages and partnerships between industry and universities were partly forged on the basis of this broad new understanding of the nature of innovative activity.

In addition to shifts in core ideas in the two periods, there have also been key impacts from fiscal policy and budget cuts, from the way new approaches to competitive levered funding occurred and from general ideas regarding reinvented government and concepts of *governance* as opposed to just government.

Science budgets and the number of scientists supporting federal policy and regulatory functions were cut quite severely in the last 15 years as a whole, particular under the impetus of the 1995–96 Program Review, cuts whose impacts extended until the end of the 1990s.[31] Cuts to both science-based departments and agencies (sbdas) and to the federal granting bodies were large, often as high as 30 percent, particularly for the sbdas.

However, in the late 1990s, when the federal deficit had been vanquished and surpluses re-emerged in the public purse, some selected aspects of science budgets have grown or been re-kindled in different ways (e.g. the cfi was generously funded; the granting councils had both cuts and then some increases or adjustments to provide more stable funding). But by this time, more that simply the ideas of innovation and clusters were taking hold. Concepts of budgeting tied to notions of reinvented government or the New Public Management (npm) were also influencing how the new ISE institutional system would work and how funding would be offered and managed. The new system was characterized much more by the notion of competitive government and leveraged partnership funding. To get money one had to bring money. The competition for budgets was also built into an ever more explicit bidding process. This is where some of the institutional learning curve can be attributed to the initial Networks of Centres of Excellence Program and also to changes in PERD when its funds were cut severely in the 1990s from its mid-1980s levels. The formation of the Canada Foundation for Innovation (CFI) in 1997 then added further to this innovation-cum-budget reform model by bringing in the delivery mechanism of a foundation, which quickly was given the label of a "third-party" delivery mechanism. Paul Martin essentially established the CFI when he was Minister of Finance in the Chretien Liberal government and its form was partly defined by a desire to get surprisingly high year-end surplus funds into an organizational form, the foundation, which would not be easily reached by other parts of the government with different priority demands. To some, including the auditor general of Canada, this was the unaccountable "parking" of funds in a way that was contrary to the core notions of accountable Cabinet-Parliamentary government.

A logical further question to highlight again here is whether the current ISE institutional system constitutes an internally integrated system. At one level, it partially is in that some broad rubric of policy ideas has guided their development and evolution. But at another level it is not internally integrated in that the constituent units or entities have their own origins, histories, values and links with their communities and client groups. While a key feature of Period II is the more explicit recognition of complex networks, Period I also had networks well before this concept was an explicit managerial fashion (e.g. the NRC, its institutes, and the IRAP program). Thus, as suggested from the outset in this chapter, there are points of integration and also considerable tension in the ISE system overall.

The net effect of these later changes in ISE policies and institutions was that by the time the Martin government came to power in 2004, the Chretien Liberals, with Martin as Minister of Finance for most of those years had poured over $13 billion into S&T and innovation. But by far the largest part of this funding went into the universities (and related health and hospital) sector rather than to firms. This funding was badly needed but it still left the issue of actual commercialization by firms as a mainly unfulfilled part of federal policy.

Environmental and SD Policy and Institutional Evolution

Environmental and SD policies and institutions are, of course, a part of the overall ISE institutional story portrayed above. Particular new bodies and competitive funding arrangements and pools of money were geared to the environment and SD realm or formed aspects of bodies such as the CFI. Newly created programs such as the Martin Liberal's Climate Fund will have to find their place in this already complex mix of funds and agencies. However, overall environmental and SD policy and institutional evolution is not just a history of a myriad bodies and funds. It is also a struggle over how interventionist governments should or can be in trying to produce better environmental and sd outcomes in specific ecological and pollution and emission-reducing situations, sectors and trans-boundary contexts. This account of views about intervention is best seen as having evolved in three phases.[32]

In the first phase from the early 1970s to the mid-1980s environmental policy was dominated by "end-of pipe" approaches and "command-and-control" regulatory approaches. Firms were regulated with something close to a "one size fits all" approach. In some key sectors distinctions were made between old and new production systems and firms were required to adopt the best available environmental technology when they invested in new plant and production processes. Otherwise old plants were allowed to pollute while firms sought to pay off the costs of these past environmentally inferior investments. In the political and regulatory battle between environmental groups and business, the politics in this period was largely one of conflict and a zero-sum view of change.[33]

From roughly the mid-1980s to the mid-1990s, clean-up focused environmental policy became melded with sd with the latter emerging as a central discourse following the publication of the report of the Brundtland Commission in 1987. The federal government and most provinces joined the growing international club of countries and jurisdictions, which formally announced that they would practice sd. In the case of the federal government this sd focus was centred on the requirement that federal departments develop and publish sd strategies (see chapter 4) and that these would then be audited by the newly created Commissioner for Environment and Sustainable Development established as a Parliamentary Officer within the Office of the Auditor General of Canada. By promoting the aforementioned "triple bottom line" approach, sd brought some focus to an important paradigm and policy concept. However, it left acres of room for both constructive and inertial ambiguity as various interests interpreted its exact meaning in particular situations. During this period, which included the Mulroney Conservative's early 1990s major Green Plan initiatives, there was certainly increased discussion and debate for greater integration between environment and the economy. Within the environmental and sd field, and more widely in regulatory reform debates, there was also increasing pressure from business, now functioning in a free trade era but also a recession and high fiscal deficit context, that regulation needed to be more flexible and incentive-based. In short, in environmental and other ways, firms did not face "one size fits all" situations, but rather diverse and changing situations in their investment cycles, in the nature of the pollutants and emissions they had to manage and reduce, and in how they plan and phase in new greener production processes. Business and environmental groups were still immensely suspicious of each other's motives and agendas but there was a tendency in this period to do more listening and learning rather than zero-sum posturing.[34]

In the latest period from the mid to late 1990s to the present, the environmental and sd agendas have continued along this same trajectory but with related spurs to debate, discourse and action. There is still a complex mixture of environmental clean-up and sd to reckon with but in this latest period they are increasingly overlaid with new international environmental agreements and protocols in areas such as the ozone layer, endangered species, biodiversity, and, most centrally, climate change where energy policy and environmental policy interests both cooperated and collided as they searched for the proper global and national mixes of rules and incentives and also investments in technology and innovation.[35] For Canada, a growing economy and continuous fiscal surpluses from 1997 ensured that resources and political will were more readily available to deal with these issues to a greater extent than they were in the two earlier periods traced above.[36]

Also crossing over the environment and sd realms in this period have been changes in how regulation and innovation were viewed. Here the changes and debates were two-fold in nature. The larger trend was the shift in federal policy towards a "smart regulation" discourse.[37] This was an attempt to argue that Canada's regulatory system (in all fields) had to be more capable of continuous innovation so that market access for new products and processes and the protection of health, safety and environment could *both* occur more quickly and seamlessly. This view also meant that Canada had to pursue more aggressively its efforts to practice regulatory cooperation, especially vis-à-vis the United States. The second trend was the more robust defence that good tough environmental regulation and rules would themselves lead to environmental industries and to sustainable production technologies.[38] Moreover, environmental groups during this period were increasingly practicing their own form of market-centred rule making and environmental labelling. No longer content to wait for sluggish governmental regulatory approaches, environmental NGOs were establishing codes of practice, standards certification and disclosure approaches and then relying on market forces themselves to pressure firms through consumer choices not only about products but also about the processes through which products are made (see chapter 10 on disclosure policy as a policy instrument).

There are of course numerous other discrete individual elements of environment and sd policy that our summary above scarcely does justice to. But overall, this broad pattern of change (and some continuities) is important as a context for the current Martin era ISE policies overall. There is now a more deliberate and integrated discourse among the environmental and sd policy and institutional realms and the s&t-innovation-commercialization realms.

This does not yet mean, as we have already shown, that performance and desired results easily follow or that they can even be easily and convincingly measured or otherwise demonstrated to Canadians. Both integration and tensions in the ISE realm remain. A preview of the chapters that follow further draw out these issues.

AN OVERVIEW OF THE CHAPTERS

DON DI SALLE, JAC VAN BEEK AND N. BRUCE BASKERVILLE examine the insights and challenges associated with the National Research Council's NRC's evolution from a traditional science organization to one that adopts a systems perspective to address enduring issues and achieve results. The authors show that this evolution has taken place in an environment where federal commercialization policy is uncertain, financial constraints are a reality, and performance management expectations for science organizations are high. The chapter argues that performance management of science activity is greatly affected by the underlying logic and approach of the organization and that in Canada, this logic and approach is undergoing fundamental change. Canada's innovation system is evolving towards greater connectivity in response to an increasingly uncertain and turbulent environment and ongoing technological convergence. A networked architecture is needed to connect the many players of that system to allow for flexible and effective contributions by science and technology to complex, evolving issues and economic opportunities. Performance management is critical to success as organizations seek to connect largely self-directed individuals to the broad goals of their organizations that, in turn, will operate within networked environments. The authors argue that the issues are not exclusive to any one organization and one could safely argue that the present level of experimentation taking place in NRC bodes well for a robust and well-considered approach to running our public institutions. Federal government science organizations will be greatly affected and likely very different, if we are successful in challenging assumptions and embracing the learning of fellow travelers in the frontier environment described in the chapter. The outcome could provide a model for how nations with limited resources might contribute effectively to addressing enduring societal issues in part through effectively managed cooperative science.

MICHAEL ROSENBLATT AND JEFF KINDER analyze the most recent innovation policies of the Canadian and the UK governments. They show that both strategies lay out similar ambitious goals and objectives and set out some reasonable measures attached to them to determine performance success or failure. The main differences between the strategies are found in the governance structures, particularly in the degree of supporting mechanisms and resources. The UK has a better-funded and clearer role for their chief scientific advisor. The chapter also shows that each used different targets and metrics to measure otherwise similar goals. The authors argue that preliminary results of the Canadian strategy are mixed, with some notable improvements in areas such as taxation, Masters and PhD admissions, access to learning opportunities and broadband access but also some shortcomings in areas such as investment intention and R&D spending.

FRANCOIS   BREGHA examines the federal Sustainable Development Strategy (SDS) process. In 1995, the federal government established five key SD objectives, which were intended to serve as a common starting point for the SDS's system of decentralized departmental strategies, and to serve as a foundation from which additional and more concrete commitments can be established. The chapter shows how this incremental process is no longer enough. Bregha argues that the SDS process is now at a critical juncture and that either the next generation of strategies due in December 2006 address the major deficiencies noted in this chapter or the whole exercise risks becoming increasingly ritualistic. In spite of their names, SDSs have not become the strategic documents they were intended to be: rather than setting the government's SD direction, they have in many ways become communications vehicles for initiatives developed elsewhere or for other reasons. Timid, under-funded, and without an overarching vision, these strategies have become shopping lists of actions that do not greatly challenge the status quo. It is now clear, if it was not earlier, that a combined "plan-implement-audit" process is not enough to support a transformative SD agenda.

DÉBORA   LOPREITE explores the Natural Sciences and Engineering Research Council (NSERC) and its longer trajectory of change from the late 1980s and early 1990s to the present, particularly under the impetus of policies regarding the "so called" knowledge-based economy (KBE) and related notions of competitiveness, later under the federal innovation strategy and now under the Martin era effort to forge a commercialization focus in S&T policy. The chapter also examines NSERC in terms of the actual dynamics of the KBE and competitiveness-innovation as they affected markets, which increasingly made new demands on universities, and hence on NSERC's support for research, for the development of highly qualified persons, and also with respect to how it delivered its research funding. Three main themes or arguments are developed regarding NSERC's evolving role. The first is that while NSERC's granting function remains at the core of what it does, it is clear from its own discourse and activities that its competitiveness-innovation roles are ever increasing both in terms of resources and its own sense of itself. A second argument is that NSERC's relative success in recent years in garnering more resources for its overall role means that it is, in effect, creating its own future demand for yet further resource needs. As well, growing demands are also emerging on NSERC from the other increased investments in related aspects of federal S&T such as CFI investments and the Canada Research Chairs program. But as these demands increase, there is no guarantee that budgetary resources will in fact be forthcoming from the Martin Liberals to meet these demands. The third key theme is that the Martin Liberals want to see NSERC play a more overt commercialization role and to persuade universities about the value and legitimacy of such a role for universities and also to become demonstrably more of an overt national body rather than just a federal body by enhancing its regional presence.

RUSSELL LAPOINTE probes the current issues and processes regarding the effort by the Social Sciences and Humanities Research Council of Canada (SSHRC) to transform itself from a "granting council" to a "knowledge council." The chapter shows how the Council justifies the movement to a *knowledge* council, a council that better disseminates and relates knowledge to society, by pointing out that how research is conducted has evolved with changes in technology, with heightened concerns for ethical issues and by demands by both the public and government that there be greater accountability for the public money that funds research. The Council sees the movement to a knowledge council as being an opportunity to enhance and demonstrate the importance of research in the social sciences and humanities to wider publics, users, and beneficiaries. Three main arguments are developed in the chapter. The first is to agree that there are indeed changes in the research process that justify the broad direction of change being pushed by the SSHRC but also that there are significant contradictions and tension points in the new SSHRC. The second argument advanced is that the SSHRC was already becoming a knowledge council, defined in its own terms, well before the change in name implied in the current granting body to knowledge body exercise. The third argument is that these changes conform to the larger pressures and world views that the federal government has of all the granting councils and of science and government in general but that this view contains the considerable danger of requiring researchers to be the servants of too many masters in such a way that they may satisfy few or none of them very well or as well as they could.

DAVID ROBINSON examines the mining supply and service cluster in Sudbury. It is used in the chapter as a test of whether the Canadian innovation strategy as a practiced regime will support "changing horses," shifting from resource dependency to a reliance on innovation. The chapter reveals a troubling inability at both the federal and provincial level to act on an obvious opportunity. The analysis examines two recent strands in economic theory as well as the relationship between such theory and public policy. To explain why progress has been so slow in one of the few sectors specifically identified by a key Michael Porter report in 1991 it is also examines the convoluted process through which theory has gradually but very belatedly been translated into programs.

BERT BACKMAN-BEHARRY AND ROBERT SLATER focus on the process of fostering the commercialization of environmental technologies through networks via the Canadian Environmental Technology Advancement Centres (CETAC's) established over ten years ago by Environment Canada. The chapter shows how the Centres, established in Ontario, Quebec and Alberta as not-for-profit, private sector corporations, with private-sector oriented management and their own Boards of Directors, work in cooperation with provincial governments, environmental industry associations and the private sector but operate at arms length from governments. The authors argue that they fit in a unique space in the public-private sector model of arms-length governance and operations. They argue that an industry sector focus has been critical to the CETAC's success in facilitating small businesses to commercialize technologies. Further, the value added of the CETAC approach to the commercialization of new technologies is that it is practical, non-bureaucratic and client-based. It demands experienced management, strong industry networks and an appropriate governance structure. There are practical lessons to be learnt from the application of this network-based model in the environmental sector

CAREY HILL's chapter compares and contrasts two cases of source water protection in Canada. It examines local innovation and multi-level governance in the area of surface water sources[39] including the source of Toronto's water, Lake Ontario, and the three watersheds located in the Coast mountains that provide water to the city of Vancouver. The chapter argues that source protection is an important and vital component of drinking water protection but that it must be viewed in the context of a broader multi-barrier approach. It highlights two innovations with respect to source water protection, Vancouver's protected watersheds and Ontario's proposed source water protection legislation. The author argues that innovation as a policy field or concept typically focuses on the development by industry of new products and processes and that cast in this light it can readily be linked as well to sustainable development concepts and in particular to sustainable production by firms. When the issue of multi-level regulation and governance is added to this initial view of innovation, one of the commonplace reactions is that innovation is more likely to occur if layers of regulation can be reduced. The chapter shows, however, that in the area of source water protection, and arguably in environmental protection as a whole, innovation and multi-level regulation, take on more complex meanings and realities. First, policy innovation can mean simply but importantly sustained improvements in protection through a series of legal, regulatory and technical steps and practices. Second, the reality of multi-level regulation can either support such innovation or constrain it and thus there is no automatic assumption that multiple levels of governance harm it. Indeed, multi-level regulatory cooperation is highly likely to be needed.

STEPHAN SCHOTT AND COADY WING examine the use of information disclosure as an environmental policy instrument. Analyzing both Canadian and comparative disclosure approaches through their suggested typology and framework, the authors argue that information disclosure is crucial for effective, fair and appropriate regulation of polluters. They argue that such disclosure does not need to be perfect or complete to make a useful contribution along with other instruments. The increasing ease of information disclosure and dissemination via the Internet, and increasing rewards for firms that voluntarily disclose, help reduce the need for mandatory programs. Only in cases of insufficient industry-wide information do governments perhaps need to encourage disclosure with incentives, the supply of partial information about the industry structure, or temporary mandatory schemes. The chapter concludes that information disclosure not only benefits the public, but also helps individual firms realize how they perform in relation to other firms. This in itself is a very valuable effect, because it can encourage other firms to disclose and might induce under-performing firms to change their business practices. The chapter shows that the operation and implications of information disclosure programs are complex: their outcomes are affected by the behavior of multiple actors, and depend on public perception, information asymmetries, government incentives, and industry structure. This makes it difficult to predict what changes information disclosure programs will bring. As a result, disclosure strategies are most applicable to situations where it is difficult to agree on specific targets, there is insufficient information available, and where victims are entitled to pollution compensation determined by courts.

CONCLUSIONS, PROSPECTS AND CONSTRAINTS

Several conclusions and observations emerge from our account. These centre on: the serious continuing weakness of industrial investment in R&D in Canada; the challenges regarding the significant gaps in the federal sustainable development strategy process; the dilemmas and potential dangers of efforts to get universities to become more commercialized; and the continuing need to experiment with any number of partnership-based networked approaches to funding, regulation, and information disclosure.

As stressed earlier, the Martin era policy announcements and discourse are making the environment and innovation links ever more closely. The difficulty will be in determining whether actions can match these aspirations and also whether non-governmental players and institutions can do their part as well. The Martin government's effort to focus on commercialization shows up in both its nominal science and innovation agendas and in its environment and SD agendas. In a sense, federal S&T and innovation policies have always been attempting to achieve greater commercialization but now the need is more urgent and compelling. Chapter 2's focus on commercialization in the context of NRC's approach and experience, shows both what the state can and cannot do. It also reveals how dynamic and interactive the roles of key players have become. Chapter 8's account of the CETACs also points to some of the kinds of "on the ground" work involved in assisting technology transfer and development. The comparison of Canadian and UK innovation strategies in Chapter 3 shows the positive extent to which more specific performance targets are being set.

However, it is more than obvious that it is the private sector that must ultimately do much more R&D than it has been prepared to do historically. There has been some improvement in private sector S&T and commercialization and in the adoption of sustainable production practices by some firms, but overall industry's performance gap has been arguably much greater than that of government. Canadian firms have to invest more in R&D and in commercialization. Whether governments have got all the incentives right to create the climate for such investments is always disputed. The regulatory system and tax policy along with incentives aimed at improving risk capital and financing are important. Governments are pressured by business interests who see these systems in purely competitive-commercialization terms but they are also pressured by other interests who do not see tax and regulatory change only through this policy prism.

A second issue yet to be faced by successive federal Liberal governments centres on chapter 4's analysis of weaknesses in the federal sustainable development strategy and process. The Bregha analysis is not optimistic that major change will come soon to help overcome the excessively decentralized and incremental process that has been allowed to drift, trapped in its own bureaucratic inertia. This is also a central feature of Robinson's analysis in chapter 7 about the institutional inability to respond to often obvious opportunities, in this case in implementing innovation strategies but ones which also have sustainable development links. But in a broader sense a federal SD strategy with greater leadership from the Prime Ministerial centre will also have to confront the fact that the "triple bottom line" definitions of SD are simply too broad to allow for an environment-focused form of SD to emerge in any credible way. It is also simply too easy for governments to assert that SD is occurring simply because they say that they are considering the economic, social and environmental impacts without necessarily actually acting on those impacts in any substantive way, particularly environmental and ecological impacts. Part of the practical political dilemma regarding SD is also that SD may be most judged by how the implementation of the Kyoto commitments are carried out or fail to be carried out. The difficulty is that Kyoto implementation is quite literally both of the pollution clean-up and emission-reduction kind of environmental policy and also, potentially at least, the preventative inter-generational SD and technology transformation kind of green project. But SD is far larger than Kyoto. Thus the federal SD policy has many mountains to climb both in levels of public understanding and in actions by governments, firms, and communities.

The chapters on the two granting councils, NSERC and SSHRC, both show how these two traditional granting bodies have, at different times and in different contexts, been transformed. They both, along with the Canadian Institutes for Health Research (CIHR), form the core arms-length support for the funding of peer-reviewed research in Canada but they have had to take-up other policy missions linked variously to competitiveness, innovation and the knowledge-based economy and society. As chapters 5 and 6 have shown, these changes in core tasks have also been caused by some changes in the underlying structure of s&T, in the changing structure of scientific disciplines and interdisciplinary work and in how knowledge is produced. Both chapters also show how important these agencies are to the development of human capital or highly qualified persons (HQP), constraints for innovation, the environment, and ultimately to commercialization.

The changes examined in these chapters mean that commercialization is ever more linked to universities. The trend is visible in Canada and in other OECD countries as well. Universities are being encouraged and pressured to be commercially entrepreneurial. There is room for considerable concern, however. An excessive emphasis on commercialization may undermine the university system's larger role in producing public goods knowledge and science in the public domain. Businessman Mike Lazaridis, President of Research in Motion also warns against a culture of commercializing university researchers. Instead he argues that: "Commercialization happens when we educate the next generation of students with the best cutting-edge technology, the latest cutting-edge tools, the latest cutting-edge techniques and processes. We inspire them by having them study under and do projects with the very best researchers. And then when those students graduate and go help build the industry and the society of the country, that is commercialization. That happens every year" (quoted in Lougheed, 2004, 3). Universities in Canada are the recipients of large amounts of taxpayers' money and hence there is legitimate and growing pressure on universities to demonstrate that they provide value for money. Commercialization is one potential measure but it will be a controversial one.

Last but certainly not least, the analysis in several chapters highlights the need to see how ISE initiatives can and will emerge from any number of sources, sometimes occurring despite supportive policy. Robinson's analysis of the Sudbury area mining and services sector or cluster shows initial bottom-up innovation occurring in a local context without much national or provincial policy support but he also suggests how much better the outcomes can still be if national and provincial support actually reinforced these local changes. Hill's analysis of source water protection also shows diverse sources of leadership and multi-level governance actions in the two case studies of Vancouver and Toronto. The model and the assessment of information disclosure by Schott and Wing shows clearly why it is important never to dismiss policy instruments which to some may appear too soft and non-interventionist when in fact they can help produce, induce, and even indirectly compel new desirable changes of environmental and other kinds of behavior. In the demanding range of ISE endeavors, the full tool kit of governing instruments and governance structures must be creatively mobilized.

Our examination of ISE policies and institutions in the Martin era and in the last decade reveals the complex process through which a government apparatus reshapes itself to achieve more complex objectives. New theories, new language, new jargon, and new institutional forms are emerging in practice. Progress may be constrained by the realities of a minority government, especially one facing an uncertain early 2006 election. The huge Martin era financial commitments for the foreseeable future, both for itself or for any other party that succeeds it in power, means that even with future budgetary surpluses potentially in the cards, ISE issues and advocates will have their work cut out for them as many interests and regions compete for tax dollars. Meanwhile, on the regulatory side of ISE issues and governance, experiments will certainly continue, partly under the rubric of smart regulation but also under the continuous pressure of business groups and environmental NGOs. It remains to be seen how successful the many small and large innovations in the governance system will be, both separately and as parts of an overall system.

NOTES

1 I wish to thank my colleagues, David Robinson, Glen Toner, James Meadowcroft, Michael Prince, Bob Slater, Susan Phillips, Frances Abele, Jeff Kinder, Francois Bregha, Jac van Beek and Don Di Salle for very constructive and useful comments on an earlier draft of the chapter.

2 See Canada, *Federal Science and Technology: The Pursuit of Excellence: A Report on Federal Science and Technology- 2003* (Industry Canada, 2003) and Bruce Doern and Richard Levesque, NRC *in the Innovation Policy Era: Changing Hierarchies, Networks and Markets* (University of Toronto Press, 2002).

3 See Charles Edquist, "Reflections on the Systems of Innovation Approach," *Science and Public Policy* 31, 6, 2004, 485-490; Rebecca Boden, Debora Cox, Maria Nedeva, and Katherine Barker, *Scrutinizing Science: The Changing UK Government of Science* (Palgrave MacMillan, 2004); David Guston, *Between Politics and Science* (Cambridge University Press, 2000); and Chris Freeman and Luc Soete, *The Economics of Industrial Innovation* (Pinter, 1997).

4 See Bruce Doern and Tom Conway, *The Greening of Canada* (University of Toronto Press, 1994).

5 See Glen Toner, *Sustainable Production: Building Canadian Capacity* (UBC Press, 2005) and Neil Carter, *The Politics of the Environment* (Cambridge University Press, 2001).

6 Canada, *Speech From the Throne*, October 5, 2004.

7 Quoted in Vancouver Sun, "The World According to David Emerson," *Vancouver Sun*, 30 December D5.

8 Ibid, D5.

9 Ibid, D5.

10 Ibid, D5.

11 Canada, Speech From The Throne, 4.

12 Canada, *Achieving Excellence* (Industry Canada, 2002) 34-50.

13 "Ministers Message" in Treasury Board of Canada Secretariat, *Report on Priorities and Programs 2005-2006: Industry Canada* (Treasury Board Secretariat, 2005) 2.

14 Ibid, 3.

15 See Arthur Carty, "Envisioning a World-Class Commercialization System for Canada," Presentation to the Research Money Conference, Ottawa, November 9, 2004.

16 See *Research Money*, "*s&t*'s Lacklustre Performance in Budget Reflects Unstable Political Environment, Lack of Commercialization Strategy," *Research Money*, 19, 4, March 9, 1-2.

17 See Canadian Biotechnology Advisory Committee, *Biotechnology and Health Innovation: Opportunities and Challenges* (Canadian Biotechnology Advisory Committee, 2004).

18 Stephane Dion, "A Greener Canada." Speaking Notes for Speech at Carleton University, February 15, 2005, 1.

19 Stephane Dion, "Notes for an Address to House of Commons Debates on Federal Budget Bill," May 17, 2005, 2.

20 Department of Finance, *Budget 2005*, Moving Towards a Green Economy, 1.

21 Ibid, 1.

22 See Canada, *Moving Forward on Climate Change: A Plan For Honouring Our Kyoto Commitment* (Government of Canada) April 2005.

23 See *Globe and Mail*, " $10 billion Kyoto plan tabled in Parliament," *Globe and Mail*, April 13, 2005, 1 and Canada, Moving Forward on Climate Change: A Plan For Honouring Our Kyoto Commitment (Environment Canada, 2005).

24 See Douglas Macdonald, Debora VanNijnatten, and Andrew Bjorn, "Implementing Kyoto: When Spending Is Not Enough," in Bruce Doern, ed. *How Ottawa Spends 2004-2005: Mandate Change in the Paul Martin Era* (McGill-Queens University Press, 2004) 175-97.

25 See Bruce Doern, ed. *Canadian Energy Policy and the Struggle for Sustainable Development* (University of Toronto Press, 2005) Chapters 1 and 13.

26 Stephane Dion, "Notes For an Address," 1.

27 Environment Canada, "Launching Sector Sustainability Tables." Discussion Paper (Draft) (Environment Canada, 2005).

28 For further analysis see Bruce Doern, " The Changing Federal s&t Innovation Institutional System: An Exploratory Look." A paper prepared for Industry Canada and Environment Canada. Carleton Research Unit on Innovation, Science and Environment (cruise), 2003; David Wolfe, ed. *Clusters Old and New* (McGill-Queens University Press, 2003); John de la Mothe, " Ottawa's Imaginary Innovation Strategy: Progress or Drift?" in Bruce Doern, *ed. How Ottawa Spends 2003-2004: Regime Change and Policy Shift* (Oxford University Press, 2003, 172-86; and Jeff Kinder, "The Doubling of Government Science and Canada's Innovation Strategy," in Bruce Doern, ed. *How Ottawa Spends 2003-2004: Regime Change and Policy Shift* (Oxford University Press, 2003, 204-20.

29 See Peter Aucoin, *The New Public Management: Canada in Comparative Perspective* (McGill-Queens University Press, 1997).

30 See Bruce Doern and Jeff Kinder, *Government Science: Changing s&t Labs and Agencies* (submitted to University of Toronto Press, expected publication fall 2006).

31 See Gene Swimmer, *How Ottawa Spends 1996-1997: Life Under The Knife* (Carleton University Press, 1996).

32 For further discussion of this history and key phases in Canada and in comparative terms, see Doern and Conway, *The Greening of Canada*; James Connelly and Graham Smith, *Politics and the Environment: From Theory to Practice* (Routledge, 1999); and H. Pellikaan and Robert J. van der Veen *Environmental Dilemmas and Policy Design* (Cambridge University Press, 2002).

33 See Doern and Conway, *The Greening of Canada*.

34 See Debora VanNijnatten and Robert Boardman, eds. *Canadian Environmental Policy: Context and Cases* (Oxford University Press, Second Edition, 2002).

35 See Douglas MacDonald, Debora VanNijnatten and Andrew Bjorn, "Implementing Kyoto: When Spending Is Not Enough," in Bruce Doern, ed. *How Ottawa Spends 2004-2005: Mandate Change in the Paul Martin Era* (McGill-Queen's University Press, 2004) 175-97.

36 See Glen Toner and Carey Frey, "Governance for Sustainable Development: Next Stage Institutional and Policy Innovation," in Bruce Doern, ed. *How Ottawa Spends 2004-2005: Mandate Change in the Paul Martin Era* (McGill-Queen's University Press, 2004) 198-221.

37 See External Advisory Committee on Smart Regulation, *Smart Regulation: A Regulatory Strategy For Canada* (External Advisory Committee on Smart Regulation, 2004).

38 See Michael Porter and Claas van der Linde, "Toward a New Conception of the Environment-Competitiveness Relationship," *Journal of Economic Perspectives*, 9, 4, 1995, 97-118.

PART ONE

Macro ISE Policy Issues and Institutions

2 The Innovation Challenge and the National Research Council Response

DON DI SALLE, JAC VAN BEEK
AND N. BRUCE BASKERVILLE

The National Research Council (NRC) as Canada's lead national agency for research and development has evolved over the last several decades to respond to the changing innovation and commercialization environment. This chapter provides a case study of how NRC has responded to that constantly changing environment. To set the context for the case study, the chapter examines Canada's repeated attempts at creating and implementing science and technology (S&T) policy and how a federal research organization has sought to respond to, and aligned itself with, the evolving policy. In addition, the authors discuss the role of performance measurement and evaluation in shaping strategy as well as the increased accountability focus of the government to demonstrate results from science. NRC is challenged to not only generate knowledge but to transform knowledge into a variety of public goods, social benefits and wealth creation. The analysis demonstrates how NRC has employed sophisticated models to allow it to contribute to a larger process that involves partnerships to address complex problems.

The chapter presents a recent historical account of Canada's policy development efforts in the areas of innovation and commercialization as well as the new results-based management policies and the focus on broad outcomes from science organizations. This changing environmental context is creating a new frontier for managing science and technology. The chapter study then examines how NRC is responding to an environment that demands systems thinking, greater connectivity, and shared accountability.

CANADA'S APPROACH TO INNOVATION
AND COMMERCIALIZATION

The announcement of Canada's Innovation Strategy by the federal government in 2002[1] and the formation in May, 2005 of a new panel of experts to advise the federal government on the commercialization of new ideas is built on a long history of attempts at federal s&t policy implementation.

The 1980s and the 1990s were a period of unclear s&t federal policy. Debates concerning innovation and the commercialization of intellectual property into goods and services were peripheral or were elements of other policy discussions.[2] For example, the Macdonald Commission[3] of 1985 argued for a national approach to s&t. However, the extensive studies on Canada's economic and social circumstances and the importance of s&t for international competitiveness were superseded by the government's focus on free trade, the commission's central recommendation. Similarly, in 1994 the federal government conducted an extensive Science and Technology Review that brought together scientists, industrialists and the general public to debate the future direction of Canadian s&t policy.[4] Alas, federal government program review from 1994 to 1998 necessitated the cutting of s&t budgets across all science-based departments and agencies with the end result of the Science and Technology Review being only principles that departments were loosely committed to, but which required no major restructuring or increased expenditures.[5] NRC experienced a reduction in both expenditures on research ($505 million to $479 million) and staffing (3,307 FTEs to 3,097 FTEs) as a consequence of program review and other federal departments experienced even greater reductions.[6]

Once the federal Budget was balanced, the government began to re-invest in s&t. It moved to establish programs like the Canada Foundation for Innovation (CFI) and Genome Canada that compelled provincial governments to make substantial investments as well. The Prime Minister created an Advisory Council on Science and Technology (ACST) in 1996 to review Canada's performance in research and innovation, identify emerging issues of national concern, and advise on a forward-looking agenda. The October 2004 Speech from the Throne stated that the federal government had invested $13 billion in basic research and technology since 1997. However, the distribution of this new investment has strongly favored the university sector and had not been to the benefit of federal science-based departments and agencies and their policy and regulatory roles. The investment has largely benefited regional economies through universities, affiliated teaching hospitals and small and medium enterprises through programs such as the Canadian Institutes for Health Research, CFI and Technology Partnerships Canada. At the same time, the amounts going to the laboratories of Health Canada, Natural Resources Canada, Environment Canada and even the base budget of NRC have barely increased from their post mid-1990 program review levels. Between

1997 and 2003, Statistics Canada reports that the amount of R&D performed annually by the federal government has increased from $1.7 billion to $2.1 billion or 24%. In comparison, funding for research performed by the higher education sector has doubled from $3.9 billion to $7.8 billion and industry R&D spending increased by 42% from $8.7 billion to12.3 billion.[7]

Much of the learning and discussion that arose from the 1994 Federal Science and Technology Review fed into the development of a federal innovation strategy that was initially announced by the federal government in 2000. In so doing, the minister of finance at the time, Paul Martin, announced that Canada should seek to move from 15th to 5th in the world by 2010 in terms of gross domestic expenditure on R&D as a percentage of gross domestic product. This goal was confirmed in the 2001 Speech from the Throne and in January 2002 with the release of the government of Canada's Innovation Strategy – *Achieving Excellence: Investing in People, Knowledge and Opportunity.* The Innovation Strategy was estimated to have cost $14 million to develop and involved considerable consultation with stakeholders. As chapter 3 of this book shows, it did highlight a number of key challenges for Canada, most notably Canada's relatively poor performance in innovation and the need to double federal investments in R&D. At the same time, the report was optimistic about Canada's future economic prospects. Building on the legacy of S&T and innovation policy from the 1980s and 1990s, it also emphasized the centrality of the commercialization of knowledge in the process of wealth creation. For example, one of the goals of the Innovation Strategy was to create 10 new internationally recognized technology clusters, a policy which bolstered NRC's existing technology cluster development strategy in Atlantic Canada launched in 2000. NRC received subsequent budget allocations in 2002 and 2003 to expand its strategy for cluster development into other regions.

In 2004, emphasis on the commercialization of research was renewed with Prime Minister Martin's appointment of a National Science Advisor (NSA), Dr. Arthur Carty, to study how the commercialization environment could be improved so that Canada in the long term could be at the leading edge of commercializing intellectual property assets. Working closely with the ACST and bodies such as the new Canadian Science Academies, the NSA does not envision another centralized big government program to support commercialization but rather a series of well-coordinated and cohesive activities. However, the NSA has a budget of approximately $1 million, six staff and no mechanism for putting proposals or innovation policy issues before Cabinet, unlike its counterparts in the USA and the UK. Shortly after the creation of the office of the NSA, an interdepartmental working group produced a discussion paper titled "Commercializing Science and Technology" that introduces a new model for commercialization in Canada and makes a series of recommendations to improve commercialization.

This work built upon the reports developed and the consultation that took place during the creation of the Innovation Strategy and is the latest in a long line of organizing typologies on this subject. Issues that were identified as being important for future development include: effective collaboration and access to publicly funded research organizations; enhancing skills for commercialization; improving the environment for risk financing particularly later stage financing for successful Canadian small companies; fostering early use and adoption of new Canadian technology-based products and processes; facilitating links between Canadian and international markets; ensuring the regulatory environment supports commercialization; developing a more strategic, market-based approach to technology planning; and improvements to performance measures for policy development.[8]

The federal budget for 2004 allocated additional resources to the Granting Councils and topped up the annual fund for the indirect costs of research at universities. It also announced two pilot competitive funds for the commercialization of federally sponsored research at universities ($50 million over 5 years) and for the commercializing of research performed in federal research organizations ($25 million over 5 years). Only nrc's Industrial Research Assistance Program (irap) received an additional $5 million per year "to strengthen its support for the regional innovation and commercialization strategies." nrc was recognized for its contributions to Canada's technology, innovation and commercialization challenges but no funds were allocated directly to commercialization. The federal budget of 2004 reaffirmed the federal commercialization policy void that had been forming since the announcement of the Innovation Strategy.

As chapter 1 of this book has shown, Budget 2005 was relatively silent on commercialization, except for the opportunities arising from new investment in environmental technologies, in anticipation of a more fully developed commercialization strategy for Canada. In May 2005, the honourable David Emerson, minister of industry, announced the creation of yet another panel of leading Canadian experts to advise the government on how to ensure more new technologies and products make their way to the marketplace to benefit all Canadians. The government, through this panel, will identify new strategies to ensure Canada's performance improves in the years to come. It remains to be seen what commercialization strategies will emerge from this new panel of experts and whether the government will be able to move forward on the commercialization agenda.

The latest interdepartmental working group commercialization model establishes that the role of government in supporting commercialization is vital since government policies such as r&d tax credits can have a strong influence on private sector investments in human and physical capital, technological advancements, and market development. Within the commercialization model, firms are at the core with a base of science and technology as well as markets for testing and providing new ideas. The model has the free market and firms at the heart of the commercialization process and as a consequence supports theorists such as Koppel where it is assumed that the free market can allocate funds to innovations that make economic sense and divert funds away from those that do not.[9] Therefore, government R&D organizations play a supportive role to industry for commercialization of technology to the economic benefit of Canadians.

THE ROLE OF MEASUREMENT IN SHAPING PERFORMANCE

In the last decades, the role of performance measurement has influenced innovation policy in a growing way in the USA, Canada, the UK, Europe, and Australia. Performance measurement is continuously evolving as organizations come to grips with concepts such as accountability and the measurement of outcomes arising from investment in S&T. In addition, as in all evaluative research, the challenge of attribution must be dealt with. In other words, how much of a given observed change can be attributed to the government or a particular science organization or program as opposed to other contributing or causal factors.

The diverse nature of research, science and technology precludes the development of a prescriptive or universally applicable set of indicators for measuring S&T performance. Performance measures are ideally aligned with the mandates, strategic plans and objectives of science organizations. However, objectives can differ and as a consequence so do the performance measures. Most important for government S&T is that their role is quite unlike that of universities and industrial R&D performers. Unlike the basic knowledge growth focus of academia and the commercial innovation focus of industrial R&D, S&T in government research establishments is expected to support as well much broader government goals concerning public good and wealth creation.

NRC has set for itself a vision as a recognized leader in the development of an innovative, knowledge-based economy for Canada and realizes this through such strategies as licensing new technologies, creating new firms, and supporting small and medium enterprise innovation through IRAP.[10] As an example of how performance measurement and evaluation influences decision-making and policy at the level of a science organization, NRC has created a framework of 28 performance measures to monitor its performance toward achieving its goals and is implementing a system to ensure that performance measures are continually integrated into the planning and decision-making processes of NRC. In addition, NRC has conducted comprehensive evaluations that focus on relevance, success and effectiveness and use these results to shape future program delivery. For example, a socio-economic evaluation of IRAP determined the importance of the program to Canada's innovation priorities linking $4.2 billion in sales revenues and 32,600 jobs to IRAP assisted innovations. It also made several recommendations for improvements that were considered in the next round of strategic planning for IRAP.

At the federal level of innovation and commercialization performance, the Organisation for Economic Co-operation and Development (OECD) collects performance indicators across participating countries and produces a biennial scorecard that brings together the latest internationally comparable data on national science, technology and industry statistics which stress the creation and diffusion of knowledge, the importance of the information economy, the integration of economic activity, and factors relating to economic productivity.[11] These indicators have made their way into federal policy documents such as "Achieving Excellence" and the annual reports on federal science and technology performance from Industry Canada.[12] However, there is a recognized need to make improvements to the availability, timeliness and reliability of performance indicator data to support assessment of policy and decision-making on the part of government.

For the last twenty years, performance measurement and evaluation in the Canadian government has been an evolving force in policy making, planning and budgeting and, as with innovation policy, it has been shaped by political and government changes. Muller-Clemm and Barnes provide an in-depth, historical perspective on federal program evaluation in Canada from the 1930s until the mid-1990s.[13] In 1978, Treasury Board policy required the implementation of a program and expenditure management system to document program objectives, elements, causal linkages, and measurement indices. It also established a program evaluation branch to conduct evaluations of major government programs. In spite of these efforts to improve accountability and evaluation, the Lambert Commission in 1979 found that the policies at this time were not enforced and emphasized the need to improve federal program evaluation by recommending a cyclical five-year review of government programs.[14] In the 1980s, policies were issued to include performance information in the reporting process to Parliament through the Estimates documents and clearer guidance on performance measurement and evaluation was brought forward to improve evaluation products.[15] In 1994, a review policy was introduced by Treasury Board where the evaluation function was subsumed under review and audit for the purpose of strengthening value-added review at all levels of management.[16] Despite questioning the usefulness of the evaluation function during the 1980s and 1990s, the development of performance measurement and program evaluation during this time period constituted a significant innovation that was internationally recognized. As with innovation policy that focused on R&D investments or inputs and then on to commercialization outcomes, the policy regarding evaluation evolved during the 1990s from a focus on inputs, outputs and efficiency to one of outcomes and effectiveness.

In 2001, the Treasury Board Secretariat approved a new evaluation policy which separated the evaluation and internal audit functions and linked evaluation activities to results-based management. The new focus on results for Canadians was conveyed in a management framework that espoused modern management practices in the federal government and the importance of horizontal initiatives involving many departments working together to address complex problems.[17] In recent years, the new management agenda and the focus on results has resulted in the attempted embedding of the performance measurement and evaluation discipline into the lifecycle management of policies, programs and initiatives. These polices included: creating results-based management and accountability frameworks; the establishment of ongoing performance monitoring practices; developing and implementing program activity architectures which link departmental resources and activities to the end-outcomes; creating departmental Management Accountability Frameworks; conducting risk-based and strategically focused formative, mid-term and summative evaluations of programs; inputting expenditures, activities, outcomes, expected results and performance indicators into a Management Resources and Results Structure system; and providing information to the Expenditure Review Committee on questions of relevance, results and cost-effectiveness.

In summary, the federal government in the last decade has significantly moved forward on performance measurement and evaluation with the linking of plans, budgets and activities to results in an overall management accountability framework that is designed to improve performance, clarify responsibilities and control, and realize cost savings within government departments. For publicly funded R&D departments there are significant challenges to any performance management regime. These have been summarized by Cozzens[18] and include: the long time frames needed to show results from research activity; the ability to demonstrate the unique contributions to end outcomes from the various national and international, public and private institutional players involved; significant research events occurring unpredictably which causes the shifting of goals before the time to evaluate arrives; and the institutional challenges surrounding changing systems. The complexities of technology generation, transfer and commercialization processes make performance measurement and evaluation very taxing. These complexities are often not recognized or understood by those who are new to or unfamiliar with managing research organizations. Geisler has suggested that new models for assessing innovation performance, such as a stage-model, are required to have more effective methods to evaluate R&D along the entire continuum of innovation.[19] However, Rip[20] has shown that the major rationale for assessment has shifted and evolved from a desire to legitimize past actions and demonstrate accountability to a need to improve understanding and inform future actions. As a consequence, evaluation and performance measurement has broadened away from a narrow focus on quality, economy, efficiency and effectiveness, towards a more all-encompassing concern with management, performance improvement, and strategy development involving multi-lateral partnerships.

NRC'S INNOVATION DILEMMA: KEY INSIGHTS AND CHALLENGES

Science in the federal government is expected to contribute to the public good (through regulation, national standards or contributions to knowledge) and to the creation of wealth for the benefit of Canadians. These roles have not wavered significantly in past decades.

The challenge is how to manage and be accountable for results in both realms within a complex environment and in a period of financial restraint and significant uncertainty.

In this case study of recent strategic planning processes at NRC, the following key features have emerged:

- Canada's science-based organizations are operating at an information frontier where issues and target opportunities are in constant and rapid flux;
- The ability to form and mobilize coalitions to seize opportunities (referred to as "orchestrating") is a critical competency for successful performance;
- Government research organizations are learning to orchestrate but still lack the right organizational architecture
- Accountability concerns prevent radical change – but there are immediate changes in process that would better align government research organizations with the present and emerging environment.

The common thread running through each of the planning processes that underlie this case study was a framework that represents three elements of public value creation (see Figure 2.1). The insights and challenges discussed in the balance of the chapter are described in relation to political and community alignment, substance and operational capability.

Political and Community Alignment

The significance of political and community alignment, the first feature of our framework, cannot be understated. In a science-driven organization, selection of a target issue at the highest levels is paramount – it is the vision that triggers efforts to mobilize a confederation of programs, institutes, branches, and new initiatives. If it also represents an important problem or opportunity facing Canadian society, the unifying vision becomes a powerful statement of value to Canadians and policy makers. At present, the broader issues are not consciously identified and selected at a corporate level; rather

Figure 2.1
Alignment Within a Science Organization to Create Public Value

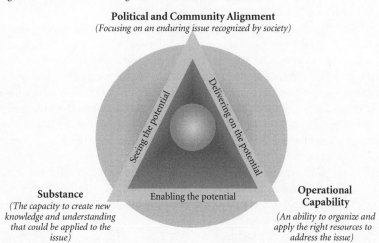

Political and Community Alignment
(Focusing on an enduring issue recognized by society)

Substance
(The capacity to create new knowledge and understanding that could be applied to the issue)

Enabling the potential

Operational Capability
(An ability to organize and apply the right resources to address the issue)

they are implied or indirectly influence the development of issues of interest to researchers. This ambiguity provides opportunity for vigorous debate at lower levels in the organization. While targeting and mobilizing effort would seem to make the best use of limited resources, the degree of uncertainty makes it difficult to focus. The challenge, as noted earlier, is that Canada's science-based organizations are operating at an information frontier where issues and target opportunities are in constant and rapid flux. This challenge has emerged from three factor conditions:

1) *An Information Frontier Environment Generates Many Possibilities* The present environment may be characterized as an information frontier – it is volatile and unpredictable. The present frontier has been fuelled and enabled by technology but it is not limited to technological advancement. It has been created by people who see opportunities or who want to solve problems as they see them. This means that technology and innovation are social constructs as much as they are leaps of genius by the inventors of the internet, telecommunications technologies, biotechnologies, and enabling technologies such as nanoscience and/or a growing list of converging technologies.

When all players, including consumers, capitalists, labour, not-for-profit sectors, political influencers and government are factored into this frontier, there emerges a heightened level of speculation, economic booms and busts, and high levels of confusion. Figuring out the most enduring issues, the right strategy and the proper objectives may prove nearly impossible. NRC has been evolving within this frontier environment. Strategic direction-setting (the process of seeking political and community alignment) strives to align organizational competencies with an advantageous position somewhere within a constantly evolving external environment.

2) *Political Priorities Can Cause Major Shifts* Beyond shortened time frames or windows of opportunity, science and technology organizations in the Canadian federal government sector are being shaped by the introduction of major initiatives such as the innovation agenda, the Kyoto Agreement, and sustainability. Expected outcomes and impacts may not be evident for years as innovation systems re-orient, re-design and work through project definition, execution and knowledge or technology transfer processes. Funding commitments and eligibility requirements supporting these intentions provide the impetus for change.

3) *Technology Trajectories Can Help Coalesce Multiple Priorities* Efforts to share risk, increase relevance, generate revenues (or recover costs) or influence economic development, have compelled government science organizations to form numerous partnerships. The nature and breadth of partnerships have become increasingly co-dependent, involving many sectors, as innovation and commercialization processes designed to foster economic growth are enabled within technology clusters located in host communities that bring together all the ingredients necessary for growth. One consequence of this phenomenon is to harmonize technology evolutionary paths or trajectories with regional commercial and political priorities.

Growth, volatility or complexity, provide opportunities for positioning of the organization. Opportunities are revealed within the interaction of competitive pressures felt by industry, a fluctuating economy and political priorities. The short windows of opportunity within this dynamic are at odds with the traditional pace of science and technology development. In seeking to make sense of this turbulent environment, science organizations are struggling with the challenge of on-going change in the following ways:

- *Differentiating Between Two Levels of Issues* – many potential target issues reside at the firm or regional level and often surface as a consequence of company or community involvement. However, there is another level of enduring issues that underlies many of the industry or regional issues and could easily be seen to be shared by an entire industry or industries or Canadian society. A focus on such issues is the rightful domain of a national science organization. Expression of these issues is to be found at the federal government and national industry association level.
- *Discerning Significant Targets* – within a decentralized science organization, filtering, assessing, and weighing issues is a critical central function. Once identified, cohesion becomes possible only when significant parts of the organization become oriented to addressing the target, including synthesis of the goals, objectives and alignment of the resources of all relevant parts of the organization. In Canada, there is a noticeable longer term and somewhat

predictable orientation to balancing economic prosperity with issues involving sustainability of resources, environment and health and wellness.

Substance

The second feature of our framework is the substance of the science, technology and knowledge. A national science organization has logically developed a deep knowledge base organized roughly around the disciplines of the physical sciences. Over time, NRC has remained current and indeed has evolved because of the extensive formal and informal science networks created by scientists to share common interests and to seek peer recognition and validation. This evolutionary process is being re-oriented by two significant decisions – extension of the core science process to embrace the transfer and commercialization elements of innovation and adoption of an innovation system perspective.

Extension of the Core Science Process to Incorporate Innovation The core science process has evolved over decades with a focus on discovery and making contributions to the world's base of understanding of fundamental science and engineering disciplines. The value of government science is realized in part when outputs are applied to issues or create opportunities to benefit Canadian society. With the adoption of a broader innovation mandate, transference of the outputs of science and engineering to the marketplace or to other channels of dissemination of know-how or knowledge has presented a significant challenge to science organizations seeking to contribute to practical outcomes. A broad range of mechanisms are now apparent at NRC, including incubator facilities to grow new companies to industrial assistance programming.

An Innovation System Perspective Science organizations have adopted the perspective that they are but a part of a larger process that contributes to the health of the economy by stimulating innovation. Value is created when there is a thread that connects: 1) the needs of the marketplace; 2) the ability to create products or processes that address market needs; and 3) the capabilities of a science and technology platform (see Figure 2.2). Communities tend to coalesce around particular issues or confounding problems that attract attention, compel action and provide a destination for scarce resources. This perspective has stimulated the pursuit of technology cluster initiatives, aggressive partnering strategies with other members of the research community and industrial collaborations.

When the three elements are working synergistically, public benefits are created by public organizations and profits are achievable by private enterprise. Continued growth is being driven by community recognition of the need to form stronger bridges or mechanisms that connect the three elements:

- To encourage the convergence of research and technology platforms to solve human problems (Platform to Market)

Figure 2.2
The Perspective Emerging in Government Science Organizations

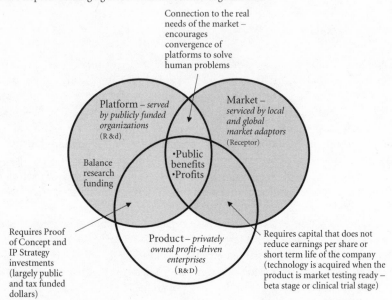

- To encourage transference of research outputs to the private sector (Platform to Product)
- To reduce the risk of introducing innovations to the market (Product to Market).

The adoption of this perspective is compelling many science-based organizations to work in the bridging space, a realm that involves relatively uncharted waters and which traditionally is the domain of policy.

Linking Needs and Knowledge When considering both the decision to extend the core science process and adoption of a systems perspective, effective performance suggests close relationships amongst many sectors – many of which fall outside the domain of traditional science (see Figure 3). The path to addressing either the needs of the consumer (to benefit the economy) or the needs of the citizen (to contribute to public good) is made possible only by working with intermediaries.

Science organizations strive to establish a purpose and pathways that create value for society through strategic planning, implementation and collaborative processes that have to involve these intermediaries. As noted earlier, the challenge here is to form and mobilize coalitions to seize opportunities (referred to as orchestrating) is a critical competency fo successful performance.

Science activity has been moving towards a more open process for some time now. The transference of technologies and the dissemination of knowledge

Figure 2.3
The Basic Relationships Underlying Science Organization Activity

commences with early involvement of the recipient in addressing the complexity of issues and emerging areas of science. This demands joint effort as creating solutions appears to be beyond the capabilities of any one group of researchers or any one organization. The targets and nature of research and technology activity continues to grow in complexity and scale. Economics and a tendency to focus around competencies have created an impetus for more open approaches[21] to the core innovation processes within many science organizations (see Figure 2.4). The primacy of open processes provides a foundation for a collaborative philosophy that is reinforced by other contextual elements facing science organizations.

Enabling openness or a more collaborative approach to innovation (including science) becomes more feasible with a collaborative spirit and blurred organizational and disciplinary boundaries. A nascent open culture (see Figure 2.5) is evident in pockets throughout NRC. Over time this culture will become more noticeable and thus exert pressures to change how things get done.

Addressing the challenge of collaboration to seize opportunities involves structural change to a more open approach and a cultural shift which takes time to develop. These changes are slow in coming primarily because of the present nature of science activity. The core researchers in any science organization are loyal primarily to their global peers – within their chosen discipline and outside of the organizations they work for. Peer recognition is built into the management frameworks and performance expectations of such organizations. The ultimate validation of the work of a scientist is to be found in citations of refereed journals, speaking invitations, and science awards.

Where there is conflict and there is potential for compromise, the path that holds the greatest potential for recognition will be followed. However, the emerging culture and systems perspective suggests that parts of the organization orient themselves to disciplines and others to clients. The organization

Figure 2.4
Open Innovation Processes Core to Science Organizations including NRC

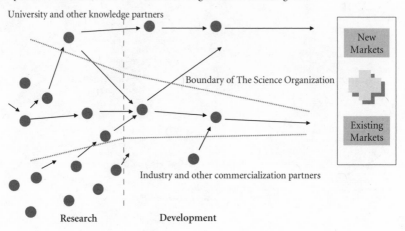

University and other knowledge partners

Boundary of The Science Organization

New Markets

Existing Markets

Industry and other commercialization partners

Research   Development

Figure 2.5
A Nascent Culture at NRC

Closed Innovation (Staying inside our boundaries)	**Open Innovation** (Working in and outside our boundaries)
• The smart people in our field work for us	• Not all the smart people work for us. We need to work with smart people inside and outside NRC.
• To profit from R&D, we must discover it, develop it and commercialize it ourselves	• External R&D can create significant value; internal R&D is needed to claim some portion of that value or to gain access to major multiparty initiatives
• If we discover it ourselves, we can get it to Canadian firms first	• We don't have to originate the research to make use of it for the benefit of Canada
• The research institution that gets an innovation into the market first will win	• Building a better transfer model is better than getting an idea to industry first
• If we create the most and the best ideas for an industry, we will win	• If we make best use of internal and external ideas, we will win
• We should control our IP, so that any one company doesn't profit from our ideas at the exclusion of others	• We should profit from others' use of our IP and we should buy others' IP whenever it advances our own aims and intentions

Migration to knowledge based economies

Adapted from Chesbrough, Henry; *The Logic of Open Innovation: Managing Intellectual Property*; California Management Review, vol. 45, No. 3, Spring 2003 as a whole is coming to orient itself to government policy and funding sources and to the broader innovation system (to best understand how they can play and how they can influence the system to achieve their goals). In time, this shift will create tension in the organization.

Operational Capability

The third element of our framework centers on operational capability. The unique traits of the frontier environment are organizational transparency, velocity, reduced transactional friction and the blurring of roles. The mindset increasingly needed in many science organizations is as follows:

- Seeing relationships as assets and collaboration as a means to effective participation – often including proactive involvement in value networks with a confluence of players (some of whom are considered competitors for scarce research funding);
- Seeing the organization as others experience it – often re-thinking basic processes to improve how to do business with NRC;
- The willingness and ability to be 'knowledgeably nimble' in a constantly shifting landscape and the resolve to respond rapidly;
- An efficient, streamlined enterprise operation that makes possible cross-enterprise cooperation.

The technology and emerging management practices are making an impact on how science organizations are coordinating to exert influence, disseminate knowledge and transfer technologies.

Operating Disciplines Government science organizations may be asked to play a variety of roles related to: national measurement standards, operation of national science facilities, a national member of non-government international science and engineering organizations, advancing knowledge, commercializing technologies and strengthening regional or national economies. Each adopted role suggests a different business model[22] (see Figure 2.6). Each operating model requires a fundamentally different discipline with quite different economic structures and performance expectations.

The traditional product (or technology) innovation process still predominates; the other two disciplines are to be found in much greater strength than in the past. The dilemma for management is how to design an organization that captures the benefits of these three operating disciplines.

The evolution of science organizations has been driven primarily by curiosity and personal motivation and secondarily by new funding. Over the past decade, science organizations have experimented extensively with the issue of transferring technology, resulting in closer, more collaborative relationships with industry. This relationship is beginning to shape the future.

Figure 2.6
Operating Disciplines Within an s&t organization

WITHIN A SCIENCE AND TECHNOLOGY ORGANIZATION – THREE DISCIPLINES		
	Customer relationship	*Product innovation*	*Infrastructure*
Economics	High financial and emotional cost of building and maintaining long term relationships makes it imperative to connect on multiple levels and in many different ways; economies of scope are key	Early breakthroughs and technological leadership attracts funding and significant knowledge partnerships and industry collaboration; speed is the key	High fixed costs make large volumes essential to achieve low unit costs; economies of scale are the key
Competition	Battle for scope; rapid consolidation; a few big players dominate	Battle for talent; low barriers to entry; many small teams thrive	Battle for scale; rapid consolidation; many potential outsourcing opportunities
Culture	Highly service oriented; customer comes first mentality	Researcher centred; coddling the creative stars	Cost focused; stress standardization, predictability, and efficiency
Representative Functions	Technology transfer, knowledge dissemination, policy networks	Science and technology research programs	Facilities, acommodation, it backbone, science activity support – conferences, libraries, publishing, etc.

As well, industry has been and continues to radically transform itself in response to major changes under the broad globalization umbrella. In short, industry has become more collaborative, constructing a more open architecture (see Figure 2.7).

In response, science organizations have been adapting to facilitate more intimate, connected relationships with industry and thus generate revenues to support growth. The most profound changes taking place in science organizations may be found in the extension and open nature of the core science process.

The shift to innovation in the public realm has given impetus to funding formulas encouraging collaboration, technology clustering, incubation strategies, and novel mechanisms to encourage spin-outs/spin-ins, and more aggressive management of intellectual property. Organizations are building this capability in part through revenue generated funds as core tax funding levels have been held steady for the past decade or have been reduced.

The extension of capabilities through partnership structures and their effects on the economics of science organizations[23] are being driven by:

Figure 2.7
The Shift in the Business Models of Industry

TRADITIONAL BUSINESS MODEL	EMERGING BUSINESS MODEL
• Competition-limited by location • Customers come from local market • Transactions • Assets • Focus on continuous improvement • Quality as a source of competitive advantage • Closed systems • Information hoarding • Subsidies • Stability • Business as an individual entity • End-product focus • Proprietary systems and processes • Value defined by: price and quality	• Competition from anywhere • World markets • Relationships • Knowledge • Focus on re-thinking the business • Knowledge as a source of competitive advantage • Open Systems • Information sharing • Incubation • Unpredictability • Integration between functions, businesses, and communities • Life-cycle management • Partnerships and Alliances • Value defined by: speed, convenience, personalization and price

1   PERSONAL MOTIVATION

The primary engine for change and progress in science organizations is to be found in the curiosity-driven scientific discovery process that is integral to all researchers. Through self-driven, on-going interactions throughout their technical communities of interest, scientists come to define their life long scientific pursuits – where they will make their contribution to the advancement of knowledge. In addition, with the extension of the core process to include commercialization, another strong motivator has taken hold. Satisfying the needs of industry, through marketplace interaction is becoming a competing and equally strong driver. Personal motivation is the organization's source of energy and its most effective means of connecting to the country's innovation systems.

2   ENFORCED COOPERATION

Stewardship of resources (accountability), politically-oriented initiatives and technology transfer activity compel scientists to cooperate. The structures and processes that enable cooperation allow the organization to align with societal issues, demonstrate relevance and ultimately, become an effective policy instrument.

Personal motivation will be compromised if alternative or secondary drivers lead to greater rewards – greater recognition, involvement in larger scale, multi-party initiatives, the opportunity to work on challenging pursuits or to partner with esteemed thought leaders. Within this frame, strategy emerges through the process adjustments, innovative initiatives, mechanisms, management and structural changes required to solve issues and problems at the interface of the organization and the innovation system and the marketplace. Directional or imposed strategy shifts the organization when it originates from funded political will or collaborative industry action. Emergent strategy is the most powerful driver of change in science organizations.

3 EVOLUTIONARY PATHWAY

A collaborative spirit and stronger partnerships are enabled by associative communities sharing common interests (a form arising from personal motivation), while accountability and major initiatives capable of making a significant impact are enabled by well defined structures, processes and management frameworks (a means of enforced cooperation). Throughout the present-day NRC, examples of both personal initiative and enforced cooperation are apparent[24] (see Figure 2.8).

Again, as noted earlier, the challenge here is that government research organizations are learning to orchestrate but still lack the right organizational architecture. While the proliferation of forms suggests that no single model has yet to take hold, it is apparent that *relational* forms of organization are becoming more prevalent. These forms are generally experimental and do not yet have much experience to draw upon when configuring appropriate governance or management frameworks.

Effective performance in a networked environment will require the development of greater competency in creating and orchestrating webs of industry and academic players – building talent, knowledge and opportunity marketplaces. Generalists with strong team building and leadership skills, an eye for collaborative opportunity and with sufficient foresight to create a linked innovative process provide the basic foundation. Building a supportive culture and infrastructure, recognizing webs as an organizing approach, integration into strategy and staff development will have to be pulled together to create this organizational capability.

These orchestrators[25] will help build the operational capability for effective networks through: recruiting participants into the commercialization process; creating incentives for participants; defining standards for communication; dynamically creating tailored business processes – involving multiple service providers – to meet market or policy based needs; assuming ultimate responsibility for the end product; developing and managing performance feedback loops to facilitate learning; and, cultivating a deep understanding of processes and practices to improve quality, speed, and cost-competitiveness of the network. As NRC continues to evolve towards increasing involvement in commercialization activities with Canadian firms, there will be a need to consider how to build this capability.

A further key challenge is that accountability concerns often prevent radical change but also that there are immediate changes in process that would

Figure 2.8
The Organization Forms at NRC

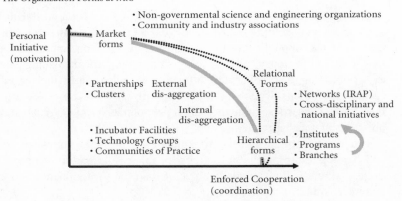

better align government research organizations with the present and emerging environment. The apparent changes in structure and process currently observable are characterized as strengthening coordination capabilities – ranging from flatter structures to the proliferation of task groups, work teams, committees, multi-party boards or management committees, etc. NRC has organized its institutes roughly around industries or broad fields of technology. As fields or disciplines converge and the pace of new opportunities accelerates, managing laterally and with partner organizations has become more critical to meeting expectations.

Hierarchical forms accommodate accountability through the assignment of responsibility to specific functions, reinforced by recruiting people with functional expertise to fill these positions. The dilemma is that the most effective agents of collaboration and co-ordinated effort are generalists with different competencies – roughly, team players capable of defining reasons to work together and bringing others to see the opportunity. These competencies are more apparent when reflecting upon the requirements of an orchestrator – an increasingly important role in the future.

The conundrum is that functional accountability (with attached resource budgets) inhibits cooperation across organizational lines yet represents our most reliable approach to accountability. There is work to be done in developing an accepted approach to team accountability – where the collective group assumes responsibility for results and control of resources, is capable of correcting poor performance without destructive finger pointing, and integrates front line training to ensure compliance with expectations.

While governance and accountability approaches will take some time to emerge, there are immediate adjustments possible that afford science organizations considerable flexibility and improve positioning in a networked context. The following are in various states of acceptance or practice.

1   ALIGNING PROJECTS

Aligning projects is an on-going challenge that has taken on greater urgency in an era of shifting priorities, scarce resources and greater concerns over the impact of public investment. The primary challenge appears to be how to deliver for today (revenue generation, serving clients, issuing patents, publishing, developing staff, attracting top talent, satisfying central agency expectations) while adapting for tomorrow's context. NRC seeks to meet the challenge of aligning the project portfolio with strategic goals and objectives in uncertain times.

Two significant adjustments are required – growing a project culture and creating a transparent and understandable road map for alignment. Project culture is fundamentally different than the predominant science culture in a number of ways (see Figure 2.9).

Alignment is controversial and goes to the heart of the organization. Creation of a road map must link strategic intentions of NRC with the objectives and investments represented by projects to construct the implicit strategy of the organization.

2   MANAGING PORTFOLIOS

As priorities shift, funding opportunities and the enduring issues of society evolve and competitive pressures reveal nascent technological needs for Canadian industry, science organizations have to establish the capacity to adjust portfolios or projects at the corporate level. Adjusting risk profiles, investment priorities, or shifting the balance between break through and continuous improvement research activity is fundamental to flexibility and responsiveness. Based upon the experiences of NRC, it would appear that these portfolios will settle into three categories:

 i. Regional cluster portfolios focused on a technology platform critical to local economic activity;
 ii. National portfolios aimed at the advancement of frontier science; and
 iii.National portfolios aimed at furthering the priorities of Canadian society.

In all cases, the projects involve contributors from many organizations.

3   SEPARATION OF PROGRAMS AND FACILITIES

Program design integrates expertise, specialized equipment and facilities with an underlying belief that they must be integrated. However, managing a research program with constituent projects is fundamentally different than managing a facility. As noted earlier, the operating disciplines are

Figure 2.9
The Clash of Cultures at NRC

NRC Science culture

- **Individualistic** – Motivated by personal achievement and recognition
- **Curiosity driven** – drive to contribute new knowledge versus contributing knowledge that fulfils market needs
- **Research excellence** – Aligned with NRC vision and value around research excellence
- **Peer orientation** – peer recognition drives career and project decisions; very often located outside of NRC
- **Competency/skill centric** – Seemingly make choices about the directions of institutes and how to run the organization based on current knowledge, skills and aptitudes
- **Opportunistic** – Appears that funding drives the pursuit of an opportunity and feeds perceptions of success within many institutes.

NRC planning culture

- Collaborative – Motivated by collective achievement
- Standards or accepted practices driven – drive to deliver services within accepted standards or practices
- Professionalism – aligned with central agency standards and best practices of managerial disciplines
- Client orientation – client recognition drives career progression; very often researchers without broad managerial experience
- Policy and management centric – Offer solutions for the directions of institutes and how to run the organization based upon policy directions, best practice and prevailing standards
- Flexible and Deterministic – Request, roadmap and end delivery date is prescribed for strategic planning; content is unknown and emerges

Horizontal management

Team oriented

Change oriented

Results oriented

Project management culture

Source: NRC Internal Assessment

fundamentally different – success in research is based on innovation and creativity while facility management strives for standardization and efficiency. The significance of the integration is that programs increasingly involve activity in several facilities and as a consequence require more complex frameworks for accountability.

4   ALLOCATING RESOURCES

A formal process of allocating resources to portfolios and specific projects in support of intentions completes the capacity to align groups of projects (programs) with strategic intentions. While done regionally or more accurately, within specific institutes, there is no formal mechanism at the NRC corporate level, although it is becoming more critical than ever if public value is to be enhanced.

5   MANAGING PERFORMANCE

Researchers will increasingly be operating semi-independently of their organizations within various combinations of experts, organizations, and project or program structures to pursue issues and opportunities. NRC, like any public organization, will have to demonstrate public value and thus is compelled to measure outcomes. Within a looser architecture, this will be increasingly critical to continued funding. Once an organizational equilibrium is reached, measurement at a more operational level is anticipated to supplement the present macro-level approach.

In general then, the broad constituency and multiple goals of a national science organization within fixed financial resources, suggests that there will have to be change in structure and management processes if intentions are to be realized. Linear "value chains" stretching from the laboratory and minds of original thinkers to companies integrating technologies into products and then to end consumers and ultimately to society are being challenged. In their place are emerging new network forms that can accommodate greater complexity and suggest the need for a central role to organize, invoke, and disband coalitions, seeking out high grade partners to join, while removing sub-par performers. This architecture seems well suited to the innovation system that supports the "discovery to application" continuum. The factors conducive to such an evolution are inescapable:

- Issues are constantly shifting in response to political or competitive pressures;
- Political initiatives are increasingly outside of the domain of any one department (innovation or sustainability are just two recent examples);
- Funding opportunity windows are short and funders induce multi-party, multi-sector responses;
- Federal government science-based departments are now formally seeking common issues, approaches and responses; and
- Cross disciplinary fields or technological sectors are emerging that can only be addressed by blended teams or coalitions.

Some simple principles are thus crucial:

- A collaborative approach is proving to be effective in disseminating knowledge and enabling commercialization;
- Opportunities to contribute, much like the galvanizing issues themselves, are fleeting and constantly shifting or changing;
- No one organization can do everything – issues are substantial and often complex, resources are essentially frozen, new funding encourages partnerships; and
- Partner organizations contribute most enthusiastically when they are able to influence the agenda.

Many of the changes are already taking place in pockets throughout NRC. Enlightened leadership and encouragement of these emergent approaches on many fronts will allow NRC and other federal government science organizations to become effective instruments of policy within the rules of the new economy. The revolution will take place within the ranks of leaders who are able to effect change, influence and mobilize communities and realize goals within a larger societal context. It is within these ranks that basic assumptions of planning, organizing, commanding, controlling and monitoring will be tested and re-designed for a post-frontier world.

CONCLUSIONS

The chapter has examined the challenges associated with NRC's evolution from a traditional science organization to one that adopts a systems perspective to address enduring issues and achieve results in an innovation era. The evolution has taken place in an environment where federal commercialization policy is uncertain, financial constraints are a reality, and performance management expectations for science organizations are high.

We have argued that performance management of science activity is greatly affected by the underlying logic and approach of the science organization in Canada, and that this logic and approach is undergoing fundamental change. Canada's innovation system is evolving towards greater connectivity in response to an increasingly uncertain and turbulent environment and ongoing technological convergence. A networked architecture is needed to connect the many players of that system to allow for flexible and effective contributions by science and technology to complex, evolving issues and economic opportunities.

The chapter has presented practical examples of the challenges that must be addressed by players in the Canadian innovation system if the promise of network agility is ever to be realized. Organizations need to connect largely self-directed individuals to its broad goals which, in turn, will operate within networked environments.

The issues are not exclusive to any one organization and one could safely argue that the present level of experimentation taking place in NRC bodes well for a robust and well considered approach to running our public institutions. Federal government science organizations will be greatly affected and likely very different, if we are successful in challenging key assumptions and in embracing the learning of fellow travellers in the frontier environment context focused on in this chapter. The outcome could provide a model for how nations with limited resources might contribute effectively to addressing enduring societal issues in part through effectively managed cooperative science.

NOTES

1 Industry Canada. *Achieving Excellence: Investing in People, Knowledge and Opportunity.* (Industry Canada, 2001).

2 Val Traversy, "Commercial Innovation: A Policy Stocktaking." *The Innovation Journal: The Public Sector Innovation Journal,* 9(2): 2004: 2-24.

3 Royal Commission on the Economic Union and Development Prospects for Canada. *Report* Vol 3. (Minister of Supply and Services Canada, 1985).

4 Canada, *Federal Science and Technology Review*. Regional Workshop Highlights reports. (Industry Canada, Science and Technology Review Secretariat, 1994).

5 John de la Mothe, "One small step in an uncertain direction: the science and technology review and public administration in Canada," *Canadian Public Administration*, 39[3]: 1996: 403-417.

6 Statistics Canada, *Federal Science Activities 2002–2003*. 88-204-XIE. 2003.

7 Statistics Canada, *Industrial Research and Development 2003 Intentions*. 88-202-XIE, 2003.

8 Government of Canada, *Commercializing Science and Technology*: Interdepartmental Discussion Paper. 2004.

9 Randal Morck and Bernard Yeung, *The Economic Determinants of Innovation*. ed. Someshwar Rao. no. 25. Industry Canada Research Publications Program. Occasional Paper. 2001. 1-89.

10 National Research Council of Canada, *Vision 2006: Science at Work for Canada*, 2002.

11 OECD, *Science, Technology and Industry Scoreboard 2003*. (OECD Economic Analysis and Statistics Division, 2003).

12 Industry Canada, *Science and Technology Advice: A Framework to Build On*. A Report on Federal Science and Technology – 2003. (Industry Canada, 2003).

13 Werner J. Muller-Clemm and Maria Paulette Barnes, "A Historical Perspective on Federal Program Evaluation in Canada," *The Canadian Journal of Program Evaluation*, 12(1): 1997: 47-70.

14 S.L. Sutherland, "The Evolution of Program Budget Ideas in Canada: Does Parliament Benefit from Estimates Reform?" *Canadian Public Administration*, 33, 2 (1990): 133-64.

15 Treasury Board Secretariat, *IMAA Handbook*, 1988.

16 Treasury Board Secretariat, *Manual for Review, Internal Audit and Evaluation*, 1994.

17 Treasury Board Secretariat, *Results for Canadians: A Management Framework for the Government of Canada*. 2000.

18 S. E. Cozzens, "Are New Accountability Rules Bad for Science?" *Issues in Science and Technology* (Summer): 1999: 59-66.

19 Eliezer Geisler, "The Metrics of Technology Evaluation: Where We Stand and Where We Should Go From Here." *International Journal of Technology Management*, 24, 4 (2002): 341-74.

20 A. Rip, "Societal Challenges for R&D Evaluation," in *Learning from Science and Technology Policy Evaluation*, ed. Shapira P and Kuhlmann S. (School of Public Policy, Georgia Institute of Technology, Atlanta and Fraunhofer Institute for Systems and Innovations Research, 2001).

21 Henry W. Chesbrough, "The Era of Open Innovation," *MIT Sloan Management Review*, 44, 3 (2003): 35-41.

22 Based loosely on the work of Michael Treacy and Fred Wiersema, "Customer Intimacy and Other Value Disciplines," *Harvard Business Review*, January-February (1993): 84-93.

23 D. Jonathan and James Wendler, "The New Economics of Organization," *The McKinsey Quarterly*, 1 (1998): 44-66.

24 Adapted from ibid.

25 Adapted from Remo Häcki and Julian Lighton, "The Future of the Networked Company," *The McKinsey Quarterly* 3 (2001): 36.

3 Canadian and UK Innovation Policies: A Comparative Analysis

MICHAEL ROSENBLATT
AND JEFFREY S. KINDER

In this chapter we compare innovation policies in Canada and the United Kingdom. Our intent is to focus on the "big" picture, comparing innovation policies at a macro level. We examine each country's innovation strategy at face value – that is, we leave it to others to evaluate the relevance or appropriateness of the specific strategic goals and approaches to the innovation environments found in Canada or the UK. Rather, we look at the goals of the policies in both countries and compare and contrast them. We assess whether the goals are clear, and whether there is a reasonable strategy to measure the results.

To focus our analysis we will limit ourselves to examining only the most recent innovation strategies of the federal governments in Canada and the UK. This includes *Canada's Innovation Strategy*,[1] released in February 2002, and, in the UK, the most recent innovation policy entitled *Science and Innovation Investment Framework, 2004–2014*,[2] released in July 2004. In the Canadian case, since it has been three years since the release of the policy, we will present preliminary results to determine progress. In the UK context, since only a year has passed, it is too early for results to be available.

We acknowledge that innovation policies are the result of many years' worth of effort, and build upon previous policies.[3] To complicate matters, in recent years, nations have located science and technology (S&T) priorities within their national innovation policies. Thus, although we will employ "innovation" as a shorthand term, we will examine the science, technology and innovation priorities as they appear in the countries' innovation policies.

Although our main focus is the policies, we also take a brief look at governance structures. We identify important political and senior bureaucratic actors and advisory bodies involved in the governance of innovation policy in each country and briefly describe their roles. Where applicable, we point out similarities and differences in these governance structures.

Innovation policies in Canada and the United Kingdom are broadly worth comparing because of the similarities between the countries, at both the political and economic levels, and in terms of performance of their respective s&t systems. Looking first at s&t indicators, in both Canada and the uk national r&d expenditures total about 1.9% of gdp, with Canada ranking 13th and the uk 14th in the world on this measure.[4] Both nations are major players in terms of scientific output with Canada producing 3.5% of the world's scientific publications (to rank 6th) and the uk producing 7.3% (to rank 3rd).[5] In both countries there is a significant pool of highly qualified people with each having about 5.8 researchers per thousand persons in the labour force in 2002.[6]

Both Canada and the uk have Westminster-style parliamentary systems. While Canada is a federal state and the uk a more unitary state (though with considerable devolved governance), in both countries it is the national government that plays a lead role in the area of innovation policy. In addition, both countries have market-based economies that are closely tied to a broader community.

Canada operates as part of a more or less integrated North American economy, with many of its technology industries inter-dependent with those in the United States. Although it is sometimes described as "punching above its weight class," with a relatively small scientific and research community, Canada often needs to look beyond its borders for new discoveries, technologies and personnel to solve scientific and technological problems. As globalization continues to draw international economies and scientific communities closer together, Canadian innovation policies must reflect these new realities.

In the uk, while the pull towards Europe is muted in a political and often nationalistic sense, there are still strong economic and innovation links with Europe. So while both Canada and the uk have domestic innovation agendas, they both need to be mindful of the broader environment in which they operate. Indeed, both are aware that a number of other countries, particularly the so-called "Asian tigers" and the Scandinavian "Viking tigers," have jumped ahead of them across a range of indicators of innovation performance.[7] In this context, both Canada and the uk have recently unveiled new innovation policies. While there are many similarities between the two countries, the potential differences in governance structures and innovation environments also make them interesting to study.

The chapter is structured into four sections. The first two sections describe respectively the most recent Canadian and uk innovation policies. This is followed by an examination of innovation policy structures. The overall strategies are then compared in the fourth section. Conclusions then follow.

THE CANADIAN INNOVATION STRATEGY

In February 2002 the Government of Canada set forward an innovation strategy outlined in two documents, the first entitled *Achieving Excellence: Investing in People, Knowledge and Opportunity,* and the second entitled *Knowledge Matters: Skills and Learning for Canadians.*[8] The fact that Canada's innovation strategy is split into separate documents could be a reflection of the desire to balance different facets of the broader Liberal agenda, namely: a "new economy" emphasis on improved economic performance through increased competitiveness and productivity with an "inclusion" emphasis on learning, immigration and measures designed to reduce poverty.[9] It probably also reflects the interests of various competing ministries (and Ministers).[10]

The strategy indicates three main priorities: knowledge performance; skills; and the innovation environment.[11] A fourth priority appears to be community-based innovation, although it does not appear to be as well integrated into the overall strategy.[12] The discussion of these priorities is found primarily in the *Achieving Excellence* document. The *Knowledge Matters* document sets out an agenda for learning and skills development, but its links to the innovation agenda are less direct, and as such we will focus on *Achieving Excellence.* We now consider each of the components of this strategy, and look at the goals and objectives and their measurability. Where possible, we also present preliminary results.

From the outset, there were concerns about what this document was intending to achieve. It has been argued that it is not a "strategy," because it is not visionary, nor adaptive. It has been argued that it is not necessarily an "agenda" because it does not have a plan or a set of benchmarks.[13] While we agree that there are shortcomings in this document, we think it is a step in the right direction of getting Canada on a better innovation footing.

Knowledge Performance Component

The knowledge performance challenge is to "create and use knowledge strategically to benefit Canadians: promote the creation, adoption, and commercialization of knowledge."[14] To meet this challenge, the government has set the following goals: vastly increase public and private investments in knowledge infrastructure to improve Canada's R&D performance; and ensure that a growing number of firms benefit from the commercial application of knowledge.[15]

The goals and strategies for this component appear to be clear, and relatively well defined. The government will concentrate on three areas: addressing key challenges for the university research environment; renewing the government's science and technology capacity; and providing incentives to small and medium sized enterprises to develop and adopt leading-edge innovations. While these three areas for improvement seem to make sense, it is not clear which actor within the government is responsible for the achievement of these goals. Many of them, such as the knowledge infrastructure would seem to touch on many different departments. Without strong coordination, it seems unlikely the government will be able to achieve its goals in the latter two areas.

The targets for the knowledge performance challenge are presented in the first column of Table 3.1. The measurement strategy for most of the goals is relatively clear. Interestingly, these measures are focused mainly on the inputs to the system, and appear to view innovation in a linear way,[16] where more inputs (spending) lead automatically to more outputs. Regardless of whether or not the specific results are achieved, it is important to note that a goal can still have value in setting direction and giving a clear signal of intent.

With respect to comparative targets, such as ranking in the top five countries in the world, there are problems with such an approach. While it is admirable to strive for improved performance vis à vis one's competitors, improvement in the rankings can be achieved through poor performance by other countries. Alternatively, if improvements in Canada's performance are matched by other countries, this gives the impression that the situation has not improved. In a dynamic context in which other countries are attempting simultaneously to improve their own performance, the use of a comparative ranking presents a moving target.

In terms of its GERD to GDP performance, Canada has improved its standing from 14th in 1999 to 13th in 2002.[17] While this is an improvement, there is a long way to go to reach the top five. From the outset of the innovation agenda, critics recognized that this goal was more of a call to action for industry, universities and communities, but were concerned that it could not be achieved using traditional policy instruments.[18]

For the target of doubling the government's investments in R&D, between 2001 (before the strategy) and 2003 (most recent figures available) spending had increased by $70 million to $2,114 million. In order to meet the target of doubling spending by 2010 to $4,088 million, if the expenditure increase was to be achieved evenly, spending would have to increase by about $200 million per year. While $70 million in additional spending is an improvement, it is not sufficient to meet the target. Unfortunately, several of the other measures for this component are not currently available.

Skills Challenge Component

The skills challenge of increasing the supply of highly qualified people who create and use knowledge has special meaning for a country with a relatively

Table 3.1
Addressing the Knowledge Performance Challenge, Targets, and Results

Strategy Target by 2010[19]	Measured by	Results Prior to Strategy	Recent Results
Rank among the top five countries in the world in terms of R&D performance	Comparing R&D spending relative to gross domestic product (GDP). Canada's relative standing will be determined by its ranking among OECD.[20]	1.8% of GDP, 14th in OECD	1.96% of GDP, 13th in OECD
At least double the Government of Canada's current investments in R&D	The federal government's contributions to Canada's gross domestic expenditures on research and development (GERD)[21]	$2,044,000,000 in 2001	$2,114,000,000 in 2003
Rank among world leaders in the share of private sector sales attributable to new innovations	Statistics Canada's Innovation Survey	In 1999, 80% of Canadian manufacturers introduced new and/or improved products or services over a three-year period 27% of Canadian firm sales could be attributed to these recent innovations, compared to Germany's 48%	Next survey scheduled for 2004, results not yet available
Raise venture capital investments per capita to prevailing U.S. levels	Statistics on Canadian venture capital investments are available from Macdonald & Associates Limited. U.S. data can be sourced from the National Venture Capital Association.	In 2001, Canadian venture capital investments totaled $3.7 billion, or $120 per person. This per capita amount was 58% of the corresponding U.S figure of $206 per person.	Not currently available

small population, like Canada. The government has two main goals in addressing the skills challenge: the first is to develop the most skilled and talented labour force in the world; and the second is to ensure that Canada receives the skilled immigrants it needs and helps them to achieve their full potential in the Canadian labour market and society.[22]

The targets for the skills challenge are presented in the first column of Table 3.2. While the targets are all at a relatively high level, they seem to be desirable to improve Canada's innovative performance. For many measures, there are attribution problems, as there are many different factors as to why Master's and PhD

Table 3.2
Addressing the Skills Challenge, Targets, and results

Strategy Target[23]	Measured by	Results Prior to Strategy	Recent Results
Through to 2010, increase the admission of Master's and PhD students at Canadian universities by an average of 5% per year	Statistics Canada's annual administrative data from the Enhanced Student Information System and the University Student Information System	In the 1998–99 school year, Full-time enrolment in graduate programs was 79,425, including the enrolment of 44,794 in master's degree programs and 23,809 in doctoral programs	From 1997/98 to 2000/01, the number of graduate students increased by 8,500, or 7%[24]
By 2002, implement the new immigration and refugee protection act and regulations	The government introduced the *Immigration and Refugee Protection Act* (Bill C-11)	Not implemented	The Act and regulations came into effect on June 28, 2002
By 2004 significantly improve Canada's performance in the recruitment of foreign talent, including foreign students, by means of both permanent immigrant and temporary foreign workers programs	Citizenship and Immigration Canada publications *Facts and Figures: Immigration Overview* and *Statistical Overview of the Temporary Resident* and *Refugee Claimant Population*	A total of 250,386 immigrants came to Canada in 2001 In 2000, 63,618 foreign students entered Canada, a 20% increase from 1999	A total of 221,340 immigrants came to Canada in 2003[25] 61,293 foreign students entered Canada in 2003
Over the next five years, increase the number of adults pursuing learning opportunities by 1 million	Statistics Canada's Adult Education and Training Survey (AETS)	In 1997, 3.97 million adults participated in job related training activities, for a participation rate of 24.3%	In 2002, 5.17 million adults participated in job related training, a training participation rate of 30.1%[26]

admissions and the number of adults pursuing learning opportunities increase or decrease. Similarly, the recruitment of foreign talent depends on many factors. It can be difficult to explain the specific causes of changes in these variables.

Based upon the most recent results available, the number of graduate students at both the Masters and PhD levels seems to be increasing. The number of adults participating in job related training has increased from fewer than 4 million in 1997 to just over 5 million in 2003. In spite of changes made to the *Immigration and Refugee Protection Act*, the total number of immigrants in 2003 was slightly lower than in 2001, and below target. Similarly, the number of foreign students in 2003 was also lower than the number in 2000, making it unclear whether this goal can be attained. Overall the preliminary results related to this priority are positive on the learning/education aspects and mixed on the immigration side.

Innovation Environment Component

The third component identified in the Canadian strategy is the creation of a better innovation environment. This involves building an environment of trust and confidence where the public interest is protected and market-place policies provide incentives to innovate.[27] The goals for this component are: to address potential public and business confidence challenges before they develop; ensure that Canada's stewardship regimes and marketplace framework policies are world class; improve incentives for innovation; and ensure that Canada is recognized as a leading innovative country.[28] The targets for this component are listed in the first column of Table 3.3.

In terms of corporate taxation, Canada appears to be meeting its targets. Based upon budget data, Canada's corporate taxation rates appear to be lower than the United States average. While this is an accomplishment, if Canada believes that competitive corporate taxation rates are important to innovation, it cannot be content to beat the US average, as any province is not competing against an average but rather the lowest tax rate in a competing state. For example, if a firm is deciding where to locate, and if Ontario has *below* the US *average* corporate tax rate but a *higher* tax rate than, say, Michigan, there is little competitive advantage to Ontario in beating the US average.

Another target called for a "substantial" improvement in Canada's ranking in international investment by 2005. Unfortunately, as Canada's ranking has slipped from 12th in 2001 to 16th in late 2004, it is not clear that this target will be reached. However, it is important to point out that Canada had improved performance in foreign direct investment in 2002, reaching 8th place in the world. Canada's FDI slipped in 2003 to 14th place, indicating volatility in these rankings.[35]

The strategy also lists a fourth challenge area: Community Based Innovation. The goals for this component are: that governments at all levels work together to stimulate the creation of more clusters of innovation at the community level; and federal, provincial and municipal governments cooperate and supplement their current efforts to unleash the full innovation potential of communities across Canada, guided by community-based assessments of local strengths, weaknesses and opportunities.[36] The targets for this component are listed in Table 3.4.

This priority represents an important area to build on because local innovation systems are a key source of economic growth and competitiveness, particularly in a country the size of Canada. Unfortunately, this component has a weaker measurement strategy than the other components. However, in terms of broadband access, it appears that Canada is doing very well, increasing the use of broadband Internet access from 20% in 2000 to 23.7% in 2001 among households, and from 48.4% in 2001 to 58.4% in 2002 among businesses.

Table 3.3
Addressing the Innovative Environment Challenge, Targets and Results

Strategy Target[29]	Measured by	Results Prior to Strategy	Recent Results
By 2004, fully implement the Council of Science and Technology Advisors' guidelines to ensure the effective use of science and technology in government decision making	Unclear	In 2000, the Government of Canada released *A Framework for Science and Technology Advice*	This framework was approved by Cabinet. Approaches to the use of science and technology advice vary across the government
By 2010, complete systematic expert reviews of Canada's most important stewardship regimes which would allow governments to revise any policies and/or regulations found to impede the economy's ability to innovate	Systematic, expert review of our stewardship regimes	N/A	N/A
Ensure Canada's business taxation regime continues to be competitive with those of other G7 countries	Department of Finance	In 2000, Canada's Corporate Income and Capital tax rate was 6.6% above US average rate[30]	In 2003, Canada's Corporate Tax rate (including capital taxes) was 0.6% below the US average rate[31]
			In 2004, Canada's average federal-provincial corporate tax rate was 2.3 percentage points lower than the average federal-state rate in the U.S.[32]
By 2005, substantially improve Canada's ranking in international investment intention surveys	FDI Confidence Index[33]	Canada ranked 12th in 2001	Canada ranked 16th in 2004[34]

While the other targets lack metrics, this does not negate the value of identifying local innovation as an important component of the overall strategy. However, it has been suggested that the strategy would be strengthened if it made fewer commitments to broader objectives and instead paid more attention to the interactions between institutions in the process – in other words, looking at innovation as a system.[39]

Table 3.4
Community Based Innovation

Strategy Target[37]	Measured by	Results Prior to Strategy	Recent Results
By 2010, develop at least ten internationally recognized technology clusters	There is no single definitive tool that defines, assesses and ranks clusters, and there is a limited capacity to look at emerging technology clusters from a data perspective	Canada has several clusters in various stages of maturity, including aerospace in Montréal and information and communications technologies in Ottawa, Toronto and Kitchener–Waterloo	Unknown
By 2010, significantly improve the innovation performance of communities across Canada	No comprehensive mapping of economic and innovation variables is currently available for monitoring progress at the local and regional levels	Unknown	Unknown
By 2005, ensure that high speed broadband access is widely available to Canadian communities	Statistics Canada Surveys	Statistics Canada reports that only one in five of the 40% of households with Internet access in 2000 had high-speed (broadband) access. In terms of business take-up, 48.4% of private sector firms connected to the Internet had high-speed access in 2001	Statistics Canada reports that 23.7% of the 48% of households with Internet Access had high-speed broadband access in 2001[38]. 58.4% of private sector firms connected to the Internet had high speed access in 2002

In sum, the Canadian innovation strategy lays out sensible goals and objectives. Most of the goals have reasonable measures attached to them. A shortcoming of the strategy is that there are not clear responsibilities assigned for the achievement of the goals, nor is it clear who is to provide an overarching coordination role. Preliminary results are mixed, with some notable improvements in areas such as taxation, Masters and PhD admissions, access to learning opportunities and broadband access but also some shortcomings in areas such as R&D spending and investment intention.

THE UK INNOVATION STRATEGY

The UK strategy is contained in the document entitled *Science & Innovation Investment Framework, 2004–2014*, published in July 2004. This document "sets out the Government's long term investment framework for British science, technology and innovation over the next decade."[40] The strategy builds on a fairly regular flow of reviews and white papers in recent years.[41] In this regard, the UK's latest strategy should be viewed in the context of a regular and ongoing process of examining science, technology and innovation policies with consistent, high-level attention to these issues.

The current strategy recognizes that in order for the UK economy to succeed in generating growth through productivity and employment, the UK must invest more strongly in its knowledge base, and translate this knowledge more effectively into business and public sector innovation.[42] Gordon Brown, chancellor of the exchequer, recently stated, "A Government that fails to invest in science is a Government failing to equip Britain for the new economy … in today's world a budget for investment in science is not only desirable – it is a necessity."[43] The UK's long term objective in this regard is to raise its GERD to GDP ratio from around 1.9% currently to 2.5% over the decade. But it is recognized that realizing this ambitious goal will require sustained action across a broad front.

In this context, the UK strategy sets out six goals which are described as "attributes of success" for the UK science, research and innovation system. These are:

- World class research at the UK's strongest centres of excellence;
- Greater responsiveness of the publicly-funded research base to the needs of the economy and public services;
- Increased business investment in R&D, and increased business engagement in drawing on the UK science base for ideas and talent;
- A strong supply of scientists, engineers and technologists;
- Sustainable and financially robust universities and public laboratories;
- Confidence and increased awareness across UK society in scientific research and its innovative applications.

As shown in the discussion below and accompanying tables, clear strategic targets and, in most cases, specific performance indicators are spelled out for each of these six goals. The strategy also commits the government to publish an annual stocktaking on progress against the goals and to conduct a more detailed assessment of progress every two years, to inform public spending reviews. Beyond merely providing the basis for audit and accountability however, the UK views this set of goals and indicators as the basis for an ongoing dialogue with stakeholders regarding the contributions of public and private funding and other actions towards achieving the nation's longer term science and innovation goals.[44]

Table 3.5
UK Goal: World Class Excellence

Strategy Target	Measured by
Maintain overall ranking as second to the U.S., and current lead against rest of OECD	Share of world citations, overall and in each of the nine broad science disciplines
Close gap with leading two nations where current UK performance is third or lower	
Maintain UK lead in impact and research productivity	• Citations/GDP • Citations/researcher • Citations/unit of research spend in higher education
Retain sufficient excellence to continue to attract internationally mobile R&D investment and highly skilled people	Benchmark UK top performing universities and public research centers against international peers
Ensure that leading UK centers are complemented by a broader network of strong institutions, departments and centers, to create a dynamic and competitive market for research funding and people	Benchmark research strength and impact of top 10 UK universities and departments against second tier of next 20 universities and departments

WORLD CLASS RESEARCH AT THE UK'S
STRONGEST CENTRES OF EXCELLENCE

The first goal of the UK strategy focuses on the capacity of its science base to conduct world class research across the full breadth of scientific disciplines, while increasingly targeting multi-disciplinary approaches. The UK has long enjoyed a lead position in research excellence and productivity and the strategy seeks to maintain this performance in the face of increasing competition from both industrialized countries and emerging economies.[45] Strategic targets include: maintaining the UK's overall ranking as second to the U.S. on research excellence, and current lead against the rest of the OECD countries; closing the gap with the leading nations where its current performance is third or lower; and maintaining its lead in research productivity. Progress will be measured through bibliometric measures such as publication and citation analyses.

New players are emerging in the global S&T enterprise, creating an international market for R&D talent and investment. Recognizing these trends, a second set of ambitions under this goal includes supporting world class centres of research excellence in universities to support growth in the UK's share of internationally mobile R&D investments and highly skilled people. Interestingly, the

Table 3.6
UK Goal: Greater Responsiveness

Strategy Target	Measured by
Research Councils' programs more strongly influenced by and delivered in partnership with end users of research	Engagement with business and public service R&D users in design, co-funding and delivery of programs
Overall improvement towards world-leading benchmarks in the performance of higher education institutions and public sector research establishments against these metrics (relative to total research activity)	• Quantity of patent applications and grants • Quantity and value of intellectual property licenses • Income from business for contract research • Research publications jointly authored with industry • Quantity and economic value of spin-out companies
Continued improvement in the level of business confidence in university knowledge transfer activities	(unclear)

strategy focuses on the health of "a small core of leading universities and other centres of excellence which perform a national role in making the UK a partner of choice."[46] Progress will be assessed through benchmarking exercises that build on the UK's already extensive university research assessment exercise.

Greater responsiveness of research base to needs of the economy and public services

Through the second goal, the UK strategy suggests that the major challenge for the UK science base in the coming decade is to translate S&T investments effectively into economic and public service impact. How exactly this will be achieved, however, is less clear. The strategy speaks of achieving "stronger synergies with other investment from a range of public and private sources, and increased engagement with business"[47] but it is short on specifics as to how such synergies and engagement will be pursued. As an initial step, the strategy seeks quantifiable improvements on indicators relating to patents, licensing of intellectual property, contract research, co-funding, etc. – i.e., measures that serve as proxies for responsiveness to economic and social needs.

Increased business sector investment in R&D and engagement with science base

The UK recognizes that delivering on its overall ambition for wealth creation and productivity growth through innovation will require significant and sustained private sector investment in, and engagement with, the science base in

Table 3.7
UK Goal: Increased Business Sector Investment and Engagement

Strategy Target	*Measured by*
Increase BERD/GDP from 1.25% towards goal of 1.7 % over the decade	Level of business investment in R&D as a share of GDP
Narrow the performance gap on business innovation *investment and activity* as measured by:	• Business R&D intensity by sector • Investment in innovation-directed activities, including R&D, as a percentage of business turnover • Patents granted per capita
Narrow the performance gap on business innovation *performance* as measured by:	• Share of firms introducing new product, service or process improvement • Average turnover in firms accounted for by new or significantly improved products and services • Share of firms that are 'innovation active'
Reach leading position in Europe and close gap with the US on:	Proportion of businesses that collaborate with HEIS and PSRES

order to effectively deploy personnel and translate research ideas into commercial innovations. Specifically, the UK seeks to increase business sector investment in R&D as a share of GDP from 1.25 percent to 1.7 percent over the decade. It also seeks to narrow the gap in R&D intensity and innovation performance between the UK and the leading European Union and U.S. competitors within each business sector, while allowing for the size distribution of companies in the UK. On the question of engagement, the strategy emphasizes the importance of linkages and collaboration between businesses and universities and government laboratories.

A more responsive supply of science, technology,
engineering and mathematics skills

The UK government recognizes the critical importance of human capital to the achievement of the nation's innovation ambitions. Given this understanding, the strategy seeks to ensure an increased and higher quality supply of science, technology, engineering and mathematics (STEM) skills across the education and training system and at every stage of the transition from school to the workforce. The government's overall aim is nothing less than a step change in the supply of scientists, engineers, and technologists, while at the same time monitoring demand to ensure that the skills delivered are the skills that employers need. Measures will include improving performance on standard exams, improving the recruitment and retention of teachers with

Table 3.8
UK Goal: Strong Supply of Scientists, Engineers and Technologists (SETS)

Strategy Target	Measured by
Improving the quality of science teachers and lecturers in every school, college and university	• Qualifications of the post 16 workforce • Reduced shortages of SET teachers • More institutions graded 'outstanding' or 'good' on quality of SET teaching and learning
Eliminate as far as possible the undershooting of the national Initial teacher Training targets by 2007/08	Recruitment into science teacher training
Improving the results of students studying science at GCSE level	Science GCSE results
Increasing the numbers choosing SET subjects in higher education	SET participation at A-level and other level three equivalents
Increasing the proportion of better qualified students pursuing R&D careers	• Post 16 learner success • Increased PhDs per capita
Increasing the proportion of minority ethnic and women participants in higher education	Increases at various levels, including among researchers, lecturers, professors and senior professors

strong STEM skills, increasing university participation and numbers of PhDs in STEM subjects, and ensuring women and ethnic minority groups are fully represented in these disciplines.

Sustainable and financially robust universities and public laboratories across the UK

The fifth goal of the UK's science and innovation strategy draws particular attention to the research funding mechanisms within the academic and government sectors. For funding university research, the UK employs a so-called Dual Support system that provides core, block grant funding for higher education institutions (HEIs) complemented by competitively awarded project funding for individual researchers, research teams and departments. In recent budgets, sponsored research spending has risen at an unsustainably faster rate than the core funding needed to sustain the increased volume of research activity.[48]

Therefore, the government has committed to working with the universities to improve financial sustainability through balancing direct and indirect funding, and working out various arrangements with other funders (e.g., government departments, industry and charitable foundations such as the

Table 3.9
UK Goal: Financial Sustainability

Strategy Target	Measured by
Ensure a financially sustainable level of activity across UK HEIS and PSREs, avoiding over-reliance on non-research incomes and under-investment in research infrastructure	Research costs versus revenues (public and private) across both sectors
Research Councils to provide close to full economic cost of university projects	Share of full economic costs paid by RCS for projects conducted at universities

Wellcome Trust) to do the same. A key element of this part of the strategy is the government's plan to eventually pay the full economic costs of university research supported by the Research Councils.

Within this goal, the strategy also explicitly recognizes that the UK's public sector research establishments (PSREs), including the Research Council Institutes and government laboratories, represent a world-class resource that face many of the same challenges as the universities in maintaining their research capacity.[49] A recent review found a common need for:

- improved capital investment, linked to better and forward-looking science-driven capital investment strategies;
- better recognition and recovery of the full economic cost of the research undertaken for others; and
- greater clarity of responsibilities within and between PSREs and their parent bodies.[50]

As with HEIs, the strategy seeks to ensure a financially sustainable level of activity across PSREs by early in the 2010 decade, avoiding over-reliance on non-research incomes and under-investment in research infrastructure. Progress will be measured by monitoring the distribution of research costs versus total revenues across these institutions.

Public engagement and confidence in science and research

In the sixth and final area, the government's goal is "for the UK public to be confident about the governance, regulation and use of science and technology, by both government and business, to be positively engaged with science activity and feel that its views are valued."[51] The strategy recognizes that relevant indicators in this area are poorly developed and the government commits to improve the evaluation of public engagement and confidence over the decade. Nonetheless, the strategy does specify a range of

Table 3.10
UK Goal: Public Engagement

Strategy Target	Measured by
Evidence of improvement in these indicators:	• independently measured trends in public attitudes towards key s&t issues • independently measured trends in public confidence in s&t policy • acknowledgement and responsiveness to public concerns by policy-makers and scientists • trends in media coverage of s&t issues

indicators against which the government will seek evidence of improvement, including trends in public attitudes towards key s&t issues.

In sum, the UK innovation strategy lays out an ambitious investment and performance framework organized around six broad goals for the science and innovation system. The framework identifies clear targets with, for the most part, quantitative performance indicators. As with the Canadian policy, however, the document does not clearly assign responsibilities for achievement of the various targets. Unfortunately, results are not yet available, at least in public form, although it is clear that the UK government is committed to producing regular assessments of progress.

GOVERNANCE STRUCTURES

The previous sections have described the strategies in place in Canada and the UK to enhance the contributions of science, technology and innovation to each nation's economic and social goals. These strategies will be compared in the next section. Prior to that, however, we wish to briefly examine the key governmental players (including advisory bodies) in each system that could be expected to play a role with respect to the strategies. The relative success or failure of these strategies will ultimately depend not only on what specific targets and indicators are outlined in the two documents but on the governance systems in place to ensure their implementation and ongoing evaluation. A comprehensive, comparative analysis of the innovation governance systems of Canada and the UK is not possible here. Rather, in this section we will briefly map the key players in each system.

At the political level, both countries have similar governance mechanisms through Parliament, Cabinet, and key ministers. Standing committees in both houses of both the Canadian and UK parliaments have oversight roles on science, technology and innovation policies. In the UK, these are supported by a Parliamentary Office of Science and Technology (POST) that provides independent, objective analyses and research on s&t-related issues. POST has established "a strong reputation for its balanced and carefully researched reports on a wide range of science and technology subjects."[52] In Canada, although the Library of Parliament provides some s&t research assistance, the level of support does not appear to be equivalent to that provided by the UK's POST.

Both the UK and Canada have decentralized systems such that no one minister is responsible for the whole strategy but rather ministers are responsible for the activities in support of their departmental mandates. In addition, both systems have identified key ministers who have a lead role for science, technology, and innovation policy. In the UK, this role is filled by the Secretary of State for Trade and Industry, supported by a Minister of Science. Implementation of the UK strategy benefits from high-level support from the Chancellor of the Exchequer. Indeed, one observer has pointed to the Treasury's "unprecedented interest in science in recent years with Chancellor Gordon Brown often referred to as the most important person in British science."[53] In Canada, the Minister of Industry has the mandate to lead the coordination of science, technology and innovation policies and strategies across the federal government in collaboration with his Cabinet colleagues.

Both countries have a chief scientific adviser although differences exist with respect to their purview and level of resources. In the UK, the Government's Chief Scientific Adviser (CSA) provides policy advice on s&t issues directly to the Prime Minister, the Cabinet, the Secretary of State for Trade and Industry, and the Minister for Science. As Head of the Office of Science and Technology, the UK's CSA has a large secretariat and budget at his disposal. In Canada, in 2003, the government created a new position of National Science Advisor to the Prime Minister to "provide advice on the full range of issues related to research and the impact of science considerations on public policy."[54] Some have suggested that the NSA's mandate is uncertain and that, to date, his office has not been adequately resourced.[55]

It would seem that a clear mandate and adequate resources are important pre-requisites for the successful implementation of a strategy. In Canada, the lack of a clear mandate and sufficient resources for the National Science Advisor would seem to present a challenge for the government in realizing its science, technology and innovation goals. This appears to be a key difference between Canada and the UK.

In both countries, high-level, external advisory bodies represent important components of the science and innovation governance systems. In the UK, the Council for Science and Technology (CST) advises the Prime Minister and the First Ministers of the Devolved Administrations on strategic cross-cutting issues related to research, science and society, education, science and government, and technology and innovation. In Canada, there are two relevant bodies: the Prime Minister's Advisory Council for Science and

Technology (PMACST) which advises on issues related to Canada's national system of innovation writ large, and the Council of Science and Technology Advisors (CSTA) which focuses its advice on the management of the federal government's internal S&T enterprise.

In addition, many countries make use of learned societies or national academies as part of their S&T governance systems, both to provide scientific assessments of key issues of public concern and to represent a nation's scientific community in international fora. In the UK, the Royal Society has long played these roles. When it becomes operational, the newly created Canadian Academies of Science will have similar functions. That the Canadian Academies have still not been launched, now more than three years after being highlighted in the strategy, is suggestive of a lack of priority placed on this aspect of Canada's innovation agenda, and is a clear difference from the situation in the UK.

We recognize that these governance systems were not "designed" and put in place in response to the implementation needs of the recently developed strategies. Rather, they have evolved incrementally over time, with various elements emerging in response to differing requirements. Nonetheless, one can expect that success in achieving a nation's science, technology and innovation goals requires a clear and effective assignment of roles and responsibilities across the governance system, as well as productive relationships among the key players. In this regard, attention to governance is important.[56] In summary, we observe similar governance structures in Canada and the UK, such as Parliamentary committees, key ministers, chief science advisors, and high-level advisory bodies. On the other hand, there appear to be differences between the two countries in the degree of supporting mechanisms, including human and financial resources, for these governance structures, which may impact on their relative success in implementing their respective strategies.

THE STRATEGIES COMPARED

We now turn to a comparison of the similarities and differences between the innovation strategies of Canada and the UK. The Canadian strategy rolls up many sub-components into three (or four) overarching challenges, while the UK strategy is organized around six broad goals. Although there is a difference in the way the strategies are structured, what is most interesting is the substantial overlap in both documents. While the language and terms are somewhat different, the main thrust of the policies is very similar. The overarching purpose of both policies is to create a roadmap towards improved innovative performance.

There is congruence between the specific goals in each strategy. For example, both countries recognize that knowledge is a key source of competitive advantage and one method both have identified to increase knowledge performance is through increases in overall expenditures on research and development. Interestingly, however, the specific targets for R&D performance are different not only in objective but in form. The UK is striving to achieve an *absolute* target of spending 2.5% of its economy on R&D. Canada, on the other hand, has adopted a *relative* target of ranking among the top five countries in R&D performance. This means that achieving Canada's goal is dependent on the performance of other countries.

In the Canadian context, there seems to be some confusion about how R&D performance is to be measured. In his reply to the January 2001 Speech from the Throne, then Prime Minister Chretien maintained that: "Canada must have one of the most innovative economies in the world. A key element in getting there is to ensure that our research and development effort per capita is amongst the top five countries in the world."[57] Regardless of whether the government uses the ratio of R&D spending to GDP or R&D spending per capita, achieving this goal represents a massive challenge for Canada.[58]

In fact, both countries recognize that achieving a more innovative economy will require major new investments in R&D by the private sector. But, again, there is an interesting difference. The UK sets an explicit target of raising private sector R&D spending to 1.7% of GDP, while the Canadian strategy shies away from setting hard targets for non-federal government actors, focusing instead on the provision of incentives to stimulate private sector innovation. Some critics might highlight that in both countries, there is too much attention placed on R&D spending and other input indicators, as opposed to output indicators, like patent activity.

While for the most part, the two countries have identified broadly similar goals, in each strategy there is an area of emphasis not found in the other. For the UK, this is its emphasis on the intersection of science and society and its goals regarding public engagement; for Canada, it is the emphasis on community-based innovation. In the UK strategy there is an explicit emphasis on ensuring public engagement and confidence in science and research. While its goals and measures in this area are less well developed than in other areas, the strategy clearly acknowledges the importance of responsiveness to public priorities and concerns. It should be noted that the Canadian strategy does address similar concerns where it discusses priorities with respect to stewardship regimes and ensuring government decision making is informed by S&T advice, but the "science and society" concern is more pronounced in the UK strategy.

On the other hand, the Canadian strategy more explicitly emphasizes the importance of communities in the innovation system. In this regard, the strategy seeks to address an apparent paradox of the modern era – namely, that in a globalized world economy dominated by international flows of knowledge, trade and investment the primary sources of competitive advantage tend to be localized.[59] The emphasis on communities may be a reflection of recent Canadian scholarship on systems of innovation, ranging from a North American innovation system[60] to *national* systems[61] and *regional* and *local* innovation systems.[62] While the UK strategy does include some discussion of communities, it can be said that its strategy is more informed by the *national* system of innovation concepts. This may also reflect the notion that Canada is often cast as a country of regions, whereas the UK still has many attributes of a unitary state, devolution to Scotland and Wales notwithstanding.

Another interesting difference between the strategies is that they do not use the same measurement strategy for similar goals. We have already highlighted the difference in how R&D investment performance is to be measured but the difference is pervasive. While differences are to be expected, in part because it is likely that each country would choose measures that are most relevant to its context and that are currently (or easily) collected, it is interesting that there is almost no overlap on the measures proposed. This leads us to the conclusion that while many of the goals are similar, they can be measured in different ways.

One final observation can be made from our review of the two innovation strategies. While both countries seem to recognize the importance of producing strategies with goals and measurable targets, they differ in their attention to ongoing evaluation of progress. In their strategy, the UK government commits to an annual stocktaking on progress, and a more detailed assessment every two years to inform reviews of public spending. The Canadian strategy lacks this commitment to ongoing review, and the authors had some difficulty locating performance information on some of its strategy goals.

CONCLUSIONS

We have looked at the innovation policies in Canada and the UK, and compared and contrasted them. We found that the main similarities of the strategies are that both lay out similar ambitious goals and objectives. Most of the goals in both strategies have reasonable measures attached to them, with some notable exceptions. Another similarity is that there are not clear responsibilities assigned for the achievement of the goals, nor is it clear who is to provide overall coordination.

The main differences between the strategies are found in the governance structures, particularly in the degree of supporting mechanisms and resources. It appeared that the UK had a better funded and clearer role for their chief scientific advisor. This may impact on their relative success in implementing their strategies.

Another difference in the strategies was that each used different targets and metrics to measure similar goals. This suggests that there are many ways to measure similar outcomes. Preliminary results of the Canadian strategy are mixed, with some notable improvements in areas such as taxation, Masters and PhD admissions, access to learning opportunities and broadband access but also some shortcomings in areas such as investment intention and R&D spending. In the UK case, initial results were not yet available.

In conclusion, it is clear that both Canada and the UK have embraced the view that knowledge and innovation will be the key drivers of economic growth and social well-being in the 21st century. Both have put forward ambitious innovation strategies that are intended to guide investments, decisions and actions over a ten year timeframe – these strategies provide a strong foundation for moving forward. In both countries, however, achieving success will require leadership, ongoing engagement, and sustained efforts across a broad front over many years.

NOTES

1 Published in two documents: Government of Canada, *Achieving Excellence: Investing in People, Knowledge, and Opportunity* (Government of Canada, 2002) [hereafter: *Achieving Excellence*] and Government of Canada, *Knowledge Matters: Skills and Learning for Canadians* (Government of Canada, 2002) [hereafter: *Knowledge Matters*].

2 HM Treasury, *Science & Innovation Investment Framework, 2004–2014* (London: HM Treasury, July 2004) [hereafter: UK *Framework*].

3 For a review of Canada's previous S&T and Innovation policies, see The Impact Group, "The Roles of the Federal Government in Performing Science and Technology: The Canadian Context and Major Forces," a report prepared for the Council of Science and Technology Advisors (Toronto: The Impact Group, March 1999). The current UK *Framework* builds on, for example, *Investing in Innovation: A Strategy for Science, Engineering, and Technology* (2002) and *Excellence and Opportunity: A Science and Innovation Policy for the 21st Century* (2000). For a review of earlier UK policies, see Kieron Flanagan and Michael Keenan, "Trends in UK science policy," in Paul Cunningham, ed., *Science and Technology in the United Kingdom* (Cartermill International, 1998, 2nd edition), 21-68.

4 OECD, *Main Science and Technology Indicators Database*, July 2005.

5 National Science Board, *Science and Engineering Indicators – 2004* (National Science Foundation, 2004).

6 Evidence, Ltd., "PSA target metrics for the UK research base," a report prepared for the UK Office of Science and Technology, October 2004.

7 OECD, *Main Science and Technology Indicators Database*, July 2005.

8 Introductory remarks for *Achieving Excellence* were written by Allan Rock, then Minister of Industry, and for *Knowledge Matters* by Jane Stewart, then Minister of Human Resources Development.

9 Geoffrey Hale, "Innovation and Inclusion: Budgetary Policy, the Skills Agenda, and the Politics of the New Economy," in G. Bruce Doern, ed., *How Ottawa Spends 2002–2003: The Security Aftermath and National Priorities* (Oxford University Press, 2002), 20-47.

10 For a more detailed exploration of the politics surrounding the strategy, see John de la Mothe, "Ottawa's Imaginary Innovation Strategy: Progress or Drift," in G. Bruce Doern, ed., *How Ottawa Spends 2003–2004: Regime Change and Policy Shift* (Oxford University Press, 2003), 172-86.

11 *Achieving Excellence*, 33.

12 The first mention of community-based innovation appears on page 72.

13 John de la Mothe, "Ottawa's Imaginery Innovation Strategy."

14 *Achieving Excellence*, 33.

15 Ibid, 84.

16 Tyler Chamberlin and John de la Mothe, "Innovation, Services, and the Canadian Transformation of the Canadian Industrial Structure," in G. Bruce Doern, ed., *How Ottawa Spends 2004–2005: Mandate Change in the Paul Martin Era* (McGill Queen's University Press, 2004), 89-108.

17 OECD, *Main Science and Technology Indicators Database*, July 2005.

18 John de la Mothe, "Ottawa's Imaginery Innovation Strategy."

19 *Achieving Excellence*, 84.

20 OECD, *Main Science and Technology Indicators Database*, July 2005.

21 Statistics Canada, *Estimates of Canadian research and development expenditures (GERD), Canada, 1992–2003 and, by province 1992–2001* (Ottawa, ON: Statistics Canada, Science, Innovation and Economic Information Division working paper, cat #88F0006XIE, no 003), January 2004.

22 *Achieving Excellence*, 86.

23 Ibid, 86.

24 Statistics Canada, *The Daily*, March 31, 2003, http://www.statcan.ca/Daily/English/030331/d030331b.htm.

25 Citizenship and Immigration Canada, *Facts and Figures 2003*, http://www.cic.gc.ca/english/pub/facts2003/overview/1.html.

26 Statistics Canada, *Working and Training: First Results of the 2003 Adult Education and Training Survey*, 34.

27 *Achieving Excellence*, 33.

28 Ibid, 87.

29 Ibid, 87.

30 Government of Canada, Finance Canada, *Budget 2001*.

31 Government of Canada, Finance Canada, "The Canadian Tax Advantage," *Tax Bulletin*, August 2003, accessed June 14, 2005, http://www.fin.gc.ca/toce/2003/cantaxadv_e.html.

32 Government of Canada, Finance Canada, *Budget 2005, Budget Plan,* http://www.fin.gc.ca/budget05/bp/bpc4de.htm.

33 In the text of *Achieving Excellence*, chart 19 lists investment intentions of major firms, but it would appear to be more relevant to use the investment confidence index, collated by the same company.

34 Global Business Policy Council, *FDI Confidence Index*, Vol. 7, October 2004, 44.

35 Ibid.

36 *Achieving Excellence*, 88.

37 Ibid.

38 Statistics Canada, *High Speed on the Information Highway: Broadband in Canada*, September 2003, 7.

39 David Wolfe, "Innovation Policy for the Knowledge-Based Economy: From the Red Book to the White Paper," in Bruce Doern, ed. *How Ottawa Spends*

2002–2003: The Security Aftermath and National Priorities (Oxford University Press, 2002), 137-56.

40 UK *Framework*, 1.

41 See list in HM Treasury, *Science andIinnovation:Working Towards a Ten-year Investment Framework* (London: HM Treasury, March 2004), 3.

42 David A. King, "The Scientific Impact of Nations," *Nature* 430 (15 July 2004), 311-16.

43 Gordon Brown, "Speech by the Chancellor of the Exchequer, Gordon Brown," March 16, 2004.

44 UK *Framework*, 5.

45 David A. King, , "The Scientific Impact of Nations."

46 UK *Framework*, 160.

47 Ibid, 162.

48 Caroline Martin, *Overview of UK Government S&T*, a Report prepared for the Council of Science and Technology Advisors (London: The Canadian High Commission, 2005).

49 Rebecca Boden, Deborah Cox, Maria Nedeva, and Katherine Barker, Scrutinising Science: The Changing UK Government of Science (Palgrave Macmillan, 2004).

50 UK *Framework*, 50.

51 Ibid, 165.

52 Paul Cunningham, "The Organization of UK Science and Technology," in Cunningham, *Science and Technology in the United Kingdom*, 69-126, 73.

53 Caroline Martin, *Overview of UK Government S&T*, 3.

54 Government of Canada, "New Structures in the Prime Minister's Office and Privy Council Office," Office of the Prime Minister news release, December 2003.

55 Debbie Lawes, "National Science Advisor seeks broader mandate to move science agenda forward," *Research Money*, 19, 1, January 24, 2005.

56 Rebecca Boden et al., "Scrutinizing Science."

57 The Hon. Jean Chrétien, "Address by the Prime Minister in Reply to the Speech from the Throne," House of Commons, Ottawa, January 31, 2001 (emphasis added).

58 David Wolfe, "Innovation Policy for the Knowledge-Based Economy: From the Red Book to the White Paper."

59 *Achieving Excellence*, 72; see also David Wolfe and Matthew Lucas, eds., *Global Networks and Local Linkages: The Paradox of Cluster Development in an Open Economy* (McGill-Queen's University Press, 2005).

60 See, for example, Charles Davis, "Competitiveness, Sustainability, and the North American Regional System of Innovation," in Robert Anderson et al, eds., *Innovation Systems in a Global Context: the North American Experience* (McGill-Queen's University Press, 1998), 23-57.

61 See for example, John de la Mothe and Gilles Paquet, "National Innovation Systems and Instituted Processes," in Zoltan Acs, ed., *Regional Innovation, Knowledge and the Global Economy* (New York: Pinter, 2000), 27-36; Jorge Niosi, *Canada's National System of Innovation* (McGill-Queen's University Press, 2000).

62 Wolfe and Lucas, *Global Networks and Local Linkages*. See, for example, John de la Mothe and Gilles Paquet, *Local and Regional Systems of Innovation* (Boston: Kluwer Academic Publishers, 1998).

4 The Federal Sustainable Development Strategy Process: Why Incrementalism is Not Enough

FRANÇOIS BREGHA[1]

Along with many others, the Canadian government formally endorsed the concept of sustainable development (SD) in the wake of the 1987 landmark report of the World Commission on Environment and Development (the "Brundtland Commission"). According to the Brundtland Commission, sustainable development is "development that meets the needs of the present without compromising the ability of future generations to meet their own needs."[2] In the almost two decades since, the federal government has created several new organizations, made changes to its decision-making processes and invested large sums of money to promote sustainable development, both domestically and internationally. Its single most important initiative was to amend the Auditor General Act in 1995 (i) to require each of 24 federal departments to prepare a sustainable development strategy every three years and report on it annually, and (ii) create a commissioner of the environment and sustainable development within the Office of the Auditor General to monitor the progress being made under the strategies.

This initiative has been the cornerstone of the federal approach to SD and it is on its implementation that this chapter focuses. The amendment to the Auditor General Act is noteworthy in two major respects:

1 The federal government's decentralized approach to SD planning is unique internationally. Most countries that plan for sustainable development have developed national or government-wide strategies to guide their SD efforts.[3] While such national strategies may include sectoral plans, these exist under a common policy framework of national goals and priorities. The Canadian approach provides no such central

coordination but instead is based on the premise that all government departments must be actively involved to promote sd successfully.

2 The creation of an independent Commissioner to monitor and report publicly on progress was also an innovation.[4] It recognizes that sd planning is a long-term process that is likely to be achieved incrementally. It sets up therefore a dynamic of continuous improvement under which departments prepare their strategies and are audited on their implementation. While the cesd does not have the power to change departmental strategies, it can highlight exemplary practices and, conversely, embarrass poorly-performing departments by noting implementation gaps.

After a decade of experience, important design and implementation flaws have become apparent which place this process at a critical juncture. Unless these flaws are remedied, the process risks fading into irrelevance, putting into question the government's ability to promote sustainable development.

TURNING THE TALK INTO ACTION

Having mandated the regular preparation of sdss in legislation, the federal government drafted *A Guide to Green Government* in 1995 to help departments identify their sustainable development objectives and set out a common process for the development of the strategies (Box 1). As a demonstration of the government's commitment, the *Guide* was signed by all cabinet ministers including the prime minister, an unusual feature even for a government-wide policy statement. In their preface to the Guide, ministers write that "we are turning talk into action ... We are providing the necessary guidance for making sustainable development a reality."[5]

A Guide to Green Government outlines five key sd objectives, which are intended to serve as a common starting point for departmental strategies, and to serve as a foundation from which additional and more concrete commitments can be established. These objectives are:

1 Sustaining natural resources – sustainable jobs, communities and industries;
2 Protecting the health of Canadians and of ecosystems;
3 Meeting international obligations;
4 Promoting equity; and
5 Improving quality of life and well-being

All departments defined as a "category 1 department" under the Financial Administration Act are required to submit a sustainable development strategy to Parliament every three years.[6] Thus far, departments have prepared three rounds of strategies, which were published in 1997, 2001, and 2004.

BOX 1. RECOMMENDED ELEMENTS OF DEPARTMENTAL SUSTAINABLE
DEVELOPMENT STRATEGIES

Departmental Profile
- Identification of what the department does and how it does it

Issue Scan
- Assessment of the department's activities in terms of their impact on sustainable development

Consultations
- The perspective of clients, partners and other stakeholders on departmental priorities for sustainable development and how to achieve them

Goals, Objectives and Targets
- Identification of the department's goals and objectives for sustainable development, including benchmarks it will use for measuring performance

Action Plan
- How the department will translate its sustainable development targets into measurable results, including specific policy, program, legislative, regulatory and operational changes

Measurement, Analysis and Reporting of Performance
- What mechanisms the department is establishing to monitor and improve performance

Source: A Guide to Green Government

The fourth round is due in December 2006. The Commissioner, during that time, has issued nine annual reports, as well as two additional reports that set out expectations of what the strategies should contain.[7] At first, the Commissioner's reports focused largely on departmental compliance with the Act's requirements and on the adequacy of internal processes to manage sustainable development activities. More recently, the Commissioner has also begun to address issues of program relevance and effectiveness, in other words, what degrees of success departments are having in promoting sD.

The departmental commitments, typically presented as a hierarchy of goals, objectives, targets and actions, constitute the bulk of each strategy. These commitments describe how each department intends to reduce the environmental impacts of internal operations, as well as promote sustainable development more broadly through its policies and programs. Knowing that the Commissioner would comment publicly on their strategies, departments have felt compelled to demonstrate their commitment to sD by making a lot of promises. Collectively, departments made over 2900 commitments in 1997, over 2600 in 2001, and over 2200 in 2004. While this number may at first appear impressive, it is misleading as it includes existing activities repackaged under an sD label, many of questionable significance, and some whose results are not measurable. More importantly, this extraordinary number – about one hundred commitments per department per iteration – speaks to a scattering of effort that has blurred the focus of many strategies and made them more difficult to manage.[8] It also speaks to the fact that

---

BOX 2. ROLES OF THE COMMISSIONER

The Commissioner of the Environment and Sustainable plays three main roles:

- *Auditing for results*: the Commissioner's performance audits look at whether activities designed to respond to federal environment and sustainable development policies are implemented effectively and delivering results.

- *Monitoring sustainable development strategies*: The Commissioner assesses the quality of the strategies, and monitors and reports on the progress of departments and agencies in meeting selected commitments made in their strategies.

- *Managing the petitions process*: The Commissioner administers a petitions process under which Canadians can seek timely answers from federal ministers on specific environmental and sustainable development issues that involve federal jurisdiction.

---

many departments view their SDS at least as much as a communications opportunity to outline what they are doing to their various stakeholders as a planning tool to set priorities.

Nevertheless, the strategies have had a number of positive impacts. They have greatly raised awareness of SD issues within departments and across government. They have legitimized SD concepts and raised them to an accepted part of the policy discourse. Departments have also increased their capacities to analyze the environmental dimensions of their programs. The strategies have also led departments to think about how to promote SD and forced them to articulate action plans to address specific issues.

However, with some exceptions, the strategies remain poorly integrated with departmental business plans and focus heavily on "business-as-usual" programming. They are largely introspective in nature, focusing most of their attention to greening departmental operations, raising staff awareness and building internal capacity through background studies and research. They also show a predisposition to "soft" policy instruments (e.g., exhortation, voluntary initiatives) as opposed to "hard" instruments (e.g., regulations, taxes). While such soft instruments clearly have a role, they are insufficient in and of themselves to achieve the SD visions departments have articulated, let alone to achieve them quickly. Many of the commitments departments have made are inconsequential (e.g., develop a commuter options strategy for departmental staff; measuring greenhouse gas reductions in aboriginal communities; considering SD principles and practices in developing contracts with external organisations) and it is unclear how achieving them would make a material contribution to the five SD objectives listed in the Guide to Green Government.

After ten years and three SDS iterations, it is becoming increasingly evident that the expected continuous improvement dynamic between the CESD and departments is not working as expected. The strategies are heavily oriented to the status quo, vary greatly in quality, and do not address most of the root causes contributing to the unsustainable lifestyle of Canadians, such as high resource consumption, land degradation, toxic pollution, loss of biodiversity, etc. With the exception of greening their operations, departments have had difficulty coordinating action on shared issues (see below). The government has not used the sds process to develop important sd initiatives related to issues such as climate change, technological innovation, urban infrastructure, marine conservation or agriculture, implying that the process remains marginalized and poorly integrated with the government's priority setting and policy-making agenda. In other words, the sdss have not become the instruments of social, environmental and economic change they were initially envisaged to be. The two Commissioners,[9] for their part, have not achieved the leverage their position was intended to play. Their repeated reporting on recurring deficiencies implies that some departments are ignoring their advice and getting away with it, or are incapable of acting on it.

This record forces one to ask why the sds process has not lived up to expectations. Is it only because the process is poorly applied, even though it is fundamentally sound? Or is the process itself deficient? The evidence so far implies that both reasons apply.

THE CHALLENGES TO INCREMENTAL CHANGE

sd challenges deep-seated societal values and attitudes (e.g., that Canada is a largely empty country with plentiful natural resources; that the costs of environmental degradation are low and acceptable; that the pursuit of undifferentiated economic growth should be one of the prime goals of public policy). The successful promotion of sd requires not only changes to these values but also changes to our institutions, policies and decision-making processes. Institutional change, however, is never easy. "Even when people are convinced, changing institutions, cultures and policies is extremely difficult in a world where these things have been built up over long periods of time."[10] Over its first decade, the sds process had to confront several challenges, including lack of central leadership, insufficient incentives, competing policy priorities, weak exogenous pressures and inadequate management practices.

Lack of central leadership

Having provided the initial impulse behind the sds process, Ministers, including the Prime Minister, appeared to place it on automatic pilot and have offered no sustained leadership through its implementation. In testimony before the Senate, Environment Minister Stéphane Dion noted that "I have been a Minister of Intergovernmental Affairs for eight years and I do not remember one situation where the environment was a part of the discussion, unless it was a meeting of the Ministers of the Environment."[11] Most departments were in effect left to their own devices with only symbolic public encouragement from Ministers. This state of affairs turned the SDS process into an essentially bureaucratic one, largely divorced from political priority-setting.

In the federal government, several central agencies are responsible for horizontal coordination (*viz.*, the Privy Council Office, Treasury Board, the Department of Finance, the Department of Justice). None is playing a strong role in SD governance. By and large, they do not have the expertise required to do so nor have they been given an explicit mandate to coordinate departmental efforts.[12] In the absence of leadership from the centre, the SDS process has become an institutional orphan. No one is accountable for the process as a whole: not the individual departments who are only responsible for producing their own strategies; and not the central agencies who do not accept this role and not the Commissioner whose role it is to audit but not to manage the process. When the government failed to respond to the Commissioner's suggestion in 2004 that it conduct a review of the first decade of SDS experience to learn what had worked and what needed fixing, its silence not only spoke to a growing disinterest over the mechanism but highlighted a fundamental flaw in the design of the process.

The central agencies' indifference to the SDS process has allowed confusion to thrive about what departments were supposed to do. Over the past decade, departments have heard both (i) that they should focus on integrating environmental considerations into decision-making and take a broad approach to SD that includes social factors; (ii) that SD requires transformative change and that it can be achieved incrementally; (iii) that they should take a longer-term view and that they should produce auditable results every year. Such inconsistent messaging has created uncertainty and discouraged initiative.

In addition, the central agencies' general passivity has reduced the availability of certain tools to promote SD. Because Finance Canada does not innovate in the area of economic instruments for environmental protection, for example, line departments do not have access to these instruments and one of the most important approaches to implementing more sustainable forms of development is thus under-utilised.[13] In a different vein, the Privy Council has inconsistently enforced a 1990 Cabinet Directive (re-issued in 1999) mandating all departments to prepare strategic environmental assessments of Cabinet proposals where relevant. Because such assessments are a key analytical tool in the promotion of sustainable development, the lack of consequences for failing to apply this tool has reduced the progress departments could have been expected to make otherwise.[14]

To remedy some of these deficiencies, the Standing Senate Committee on Energy, the Environment and Natural Resources recommended in June 2005 that the government develop a federal SDS and that a Sustainable Development Secretariat be established within PCO to ensure compliance with the strategy.[15]

Insufficient incentives

Governments need to create internal incentives to promote institutional change. Not only are there few positive incentives in the federal government to promote SD but, in many cases, there is a lack of consequences for failing to meet SD-related commitments.[16] Through bad luck, the first round of SDSS coincided with the mid-90s government-wide Program Review, through which many departments lost up to a third of their program funds. These cuts, not surprisingly, made it very difficult to fund new initiatives. In 1996, the year before the first departmental sustainable development strategies were due, the Deputy Minister Task Force on Managing Horizontal Issues noted that "for much of the last decade, the leadership in government has been focused on reductions, rationalizations, and vertical restructuring. As a result, departments have become increasingly focused inwards."[17] This was an inimical policy context in which to think expansively about new public policy concepts such as SD.

In another vein, Ministers have had little incentive to take a personal interest in their department's SDS because these have focused so largely on operational issues. With no new money and the government preoccupied with other issues, SDSS have provided little opportunity to reflect the personal priorities of various ministers.

Competing priorities

The introduction of the SD process has suffered from bad timing for other reasons. During the 1990s, sustainable development was effectively squeezed out of the dominant decision making arena as Canadian policy makers were preoccupied with other, more immediate issues, such as reducing the deficit,[18] and the ongoing debates over division of powers between the provinces and the federal government. More recently, the pre-occupation with security for a time pushed all other issues to the backburner. As Pal notes,[19] the political system as a whole can only handle a limited number of ideas at any one time: in the absence of sustained policy leadership from the centre, more pressing issues have crowded out departmental SD planning.

Weak exogenous pressures

Democratic governments respond to public pressure. In the early 1990s, when public concern over environmental issues was very high, the federal and provincial governments competed with each other to launch several major environmental initiatives. Since then, other concerns have pre-occupied the public, and governments accordingly have devoted less attention to environmental issues. While Canadian environmental groups have mounted several successful campaigns during that time, they have understandably not focused on machinery of government issues such as the SDS process. Contrary to certain European countries, Canada has also proven to be infertile ground for the emergence of a Green Party.[20] As a result of all these factors, the government has had no political price to pay for its slow progress in implementing sustainable development strategies.

Inadequate management practices

The CESD has variously criticized federal departments for their inadequate management of SD implementation. These criticisms centered on: the absence of clear roles, responsibilities and accountabilities for strategy implementation; inadequate management and control practices; low reliability of performance information; lack of compliance with certain government-wide obligations, including reporting guidelines; and inadequate procedures to ensure that corrective action is taken when performance is not meeting expectations.[21]

These inadequate practices help to explain why, in 2001, departments on average were meeting only 35 percent of their commitments and only a quarter complied fully with Treasury Board's guidelines on performance reporting.[22]

There have been noteworthy exceptions to this pattern. Some departments have taken steps to integrate SD into their own governance structures by creating "SD champions" at senior levels, aligning their business plan with their SDS, articulating measurable results, auditing progress against performance indicators, and integrating SDS goals with their minister's agenda. They have made meaningful commitments, started to re-orient their policies and programs and report substantively on their performance. Such departments, however, remain the minority.

AUDITING IS NOT ENOUGH

The SDS process is relatively young and it is not surprising that it should have experienced some teething problems given its ambitious scope. Departments have addressed some of these as evidenced in the slowly-increasing quality of their SD strategies. However, it is not clear that the resolution of the problems listed above would be sufficient to create the "framework in which environmental and economic signals point the same way"[23] that Ministers were thinking about when they signed the *Guide to Green Government*. Other systemic barriers also account for the lack of progress Canada has made over the last decade. The main ones are policy inertia, the absence of objectives, the Commissioner's insufficient powers, inadequate government coordination of horizontal issues and the process's own inflexibility.

Overall policy inertia

Although each department develops its own SDS, it does so within an enve-lope of government-wide strategic choices that limit the scope of its action plan. If environmental protection and conservation are low on the govern-ment agenda, if the government favours voluntary approaches to more intru-sive regulatory instruments, if it is reluctant to use fiscal instruments to correct market imperfections, if it reduces departmental budgets to fight the deficit, these government-wide orientations colour both the policy options and resources available to all departments. The government's overall policy stance therefore constrains the scope for implementation available to indi-vidual departments in pursuing SD initiatives.

Absence of national SD objectives

The government has not articulated a government-wide vision for SD or na-tional SD objectives to guide departmental strategies. There are no indicators to determine whether Canada is more sustainable today than it was ten years ago. This is a weak foundation on which to make policy and allocate financial resources. In the absence of national SD objectives, some departments have defined their own, based on their individual mandates. Not surprisingly, these do not add up to an agenda that would transform the way Canadians live or consume natural resources.

Developing national SD objectives in a large, regionally diverse, federal state such as Canada would not be easy. Even a small unitary state such as Sweden took a decade to define 15 environmental quality objectives (along with 71 more specific targets). It has found that the major benefit of these objectives has been to focus the attention of all levels of government, in-dustry and non-governmental organizations on the highest priorities, leading to greater efficiency and coherence in environmental protection efforts in the country. These objectives have also created a transparent and stable policy framework for all governmental programs (i.e., sectoral departments cannot pursue policies that would undermine the achieve-ment of the objectives) and helped guide environmental efforts at all levels of society.[24]

The CESD has repeatedly called on the federal government to articulate "a compelling, explicit vision of a sustainable Canada and a government-wide strategy to realize the vision."[25] Such a vision would not only help to clarify priorities but also the role of individual departments in meeting them. While Environment Canada has recently begun to develop national environmental objectives, there are only a first step towards SD objectives and it is still too early to tell whether these will provide government-wide direction.

Commissioner's powers

As stated earlier, the federal sd model is designed to be self-correcting and relies on the positive feedback mechanism of the cesd to encourage departments to improve their performance. The last decade has shown the inherent limitations of this model.

In the early 1990s, when the position of a Commissioner was first mooted, a debate ensued as to what roles such a Commissioner should play. Should it be primarily an audit (i.e., compliance) role? Should it be an ombudsman? Should it include an advocacy function?[26] The government rejected the advice of the House of Commons Standing Committee on the Environment and Sustainable Development[27] to create an independent parliamentary commissioner, as Ontario had recently done under its Environmental Bill of Rights, in favour of locating the Commissioner within the Office of the Auditor General, a decision that had profound implications for the cesd's powers. According to the Act, the Commissioner's main role is "to provide sustainable development monitoring and reporting on the progress of ... departments towards sustainable development."[28] Notwithstanding her broad-sounding title, the Commissioner is primarily an auditor who checks both departmental progress against their sdss and performance in incorporating environmental considerations in government programs. She also administers a public petitions process, giving her position aspects of all three models above.

Perhaps the biggest difference between an auditor and a commissioner is that an auditor must remain neutral on policy matters while a commissioner can champion certain values. An auditor can review the performance of government programs for their "four Es" (efficiency, effectiveness, economy and environment) but cannot comment on policy matters. In other words, an auditor must focus on the question "is the government doing things right?" while a commissioner can also ask "is government doing the right thing?" This is a major limitation where one seeks to introduce a far-reaching new value in decision-making, such as sustainable development. An auditor is far more constrained than a commissioner as an advocate for policy changes.[29]

To their credit, both Commissioners who have occupied the position have interpreted their role broadly to include both coaching departments and being a champion for the process. They have published good practice guides to help departments develop and manage their strategies, and they have set out as well clear expectations in advance of the individual rounds of strategies to help departments focus on them. The cesd, however, is uncomfortable playing a larger promotion role for the sds process which, given her mandate, she rightly sees as an inappropriate transfer of management responsibility to the auditor. Under the federal sd governance model, the primary responsibility for the promotion of sd falls to individual government departments, not the Commissioner, and not the central agencies.

The Commissioner's influence arises principally from her power to embarrass poor performers by reporting publicly on their inaction. Over the years, criticisms from the Auditor General have led the government to put in place increasingly elaborate procedures to manage its programs better and account for public moneys. Departments or programs that are singled out for criticism can cause serious embarrassment to the government and impose heavy political costs (e.g., the fall-out resulting from the audit of the sponsorship program).

The expectation that CESD audits would similarly incite departments to superior SD performance in order to avoid public embarrassment has proved unfounded. Contrary to financial or value-for-money accounting, SDSS rank low in the public's and civil servants' mind and there is little political price to be paid for producing a poor SDS or failing to implement it fully. Neither the SDSS themselves nor the Commissioner's reports receive much press coverage and the SDS process occurs largely in the shadows of the machinery of government. The lack of meaningful consequences for inaction is a major weakness in the federal SD governance model as it encourages inertia and militates against the institutional and policy changes that SD demands.

Inadequate coordination

SD transcends the responsibilities of single departments and requires departments to coordinate their management of cross-cutting issues. Under the government's decentralized approach, however, each department is responsible for making progress on sustainable development within its own mandate. The legal requirement that each department table its own SDS reinforces the "stovepipe" approach to decision-making and makes horizontal coordination more rather than less difficult as individual Ministers are made accountable for their own action plans and not the coherence or comprehensiveness of the government's approach as a whole. In the absence of strong central leadership, efforts at coordination have been largely unsuccessful. The CESD has noted that, while a number of departments may be responsible for different aspects of an issue, in many cases, none is responsible for the whole.[30]

The government's decentralized approach also imposes high transaction costs to any horizontal coordination efforts because these need to accommodate the large number of departments involved, however peripheral some of these might be to the issue at hand. These transaction costs are not negligible and are responsible in part for the slow progress the government has made on SD.

It is instructive to contrast the approach the government follows to develop new policies or programs with the approach it applies to preparing departmental SDSS. In the former case, departments are required to consult all affected departments and take their concerns into account before seeking Cabinet approval. Indeed, PCO will not place a departmental proposal on the Cabinet agenda until it is satisfied that these consultations have occurred.

There is no similar process for the preparation of departmental SDSs although informal interdepartmental exchanges do take place. The expectation is that SDSs will be developed within the existing policy framework, will require few if any new resources and therefore will not challenge the status quo.

From the beginning, EC has played the role of SD champion within the federal family. It developed the 1990 Green Plan, widely praised internationally at the time as one of the first government attempts to put SD into practice; it coordinated the preparation of the *Guide to Green Government*; it created and chaired the Inter-departmental Network on Sustainable Development and chaired the deputy-minister level Sustainable Development Coordinating Committee and co-chaired its successor the Environment and Sustainable Development Coordinating Committee. It invested considerable effort in coordinating the development of a federal SDS without being able to achieve inter-departmental consensus on the purpose of such a strategy. It also promoted the development of a new analytical tool, the "SD lens" to integrate social, economic and environmental considerations in policy analysis, but eventually had to abandon these efforts in the face of methodological difficulties and insufficient interdepartmental support.

EC's leadership role was justified when the government's original SD efforts were largely environmental, but appears less appropriate now that these efforts seek explicitly to incorporate economic and social issues. As an environmental agency primarily responsible for only one of SD's three main dimensions, EC is not well-placed to play such a corporate role. Moreover, it has traditionally been a weak institution in the federal policy-making process[31] and does not have the legitimacy to lead horizontal efforts that central agencies possess. EC's inability to "bring money to the table" has also discouraged other departments from assuming new roles or undertaking new programs and has as a result weakened the effectiveness of its coordinating efforts further.

EC now appears to have stepped back from its self-appointed interdepartmental leadership role on SDSs in favour of promoting its new Competitiveness and Environmental Sustainability Framework. Ironically, the development of this framework has benefited from management processes that have been lacking in the case of the SDS process: a Cabinet committee and a Deputy Minister Policy Committee on Environment and Sustainability (that replaces the Environment and Sustainable Development Coordinating Committee) have been created to oversee the Framework's development. This framework has the PCO's explicit support and could become a de facto federal SDS. At the time of writing, its implications for the SDS process, however, remain unclear: will departmental SDSs become the tool to implement the framework's various initiatives or will the Framework simply be superimposed on the existing institutional landscape, crowding it further?

After ten years, it is evident that neither the Commissioner nor Environment Canada have been able to fill the leadership vacuum left by central agencies. The Commissioner's role as an auditor cannot substitute for management by the centre. In and of itself, the auditing function is too weak a driver to lead to meaningful continuous improvement if departments are unwilling or unable to make greater efforts to promote SD. For its part, Environment Canada does not have the legitimacy or the capacity to force interdepartmental coordination beyond the lowest common denominator.

Lack of flexibility

All listed federal departments have to table their sustainable development strategy at least every three years, regardless of elections, when the government announces its priorities in the Speech from the Throne or their own internal policy cycle. This requirement has made it difficult to integrate the SDS process with either the government's overall policy-setting agenda (which is politically driven and whose timetable is therefore unpredictable) or the departments' mandatory annual planning. In some departments, this disjunction has been reinforced by giving the responsibility for the preparation of the SDS to a different group than corporate planners. Because the SDSs are not directly tied to departmental or political priority-setting processes, they have had a marginal influence on resource allocation, one of the reasons for their small impact to date.

In summary, the federal approach to SD has not met its original objectives for a number of reasons:

- It was premised on a mistaken analogy that SD auditing could drive improvements in performance over time just as financial and value-for-money auditing historically have;
- It was incomplete because it did not include specific national objectives which could have provided guidance to departments;
- It did not require departments to review systematically their existing policies and programs to ensure that they supported sustainable development;
- Its execution ran into problems such as inadequate incentives, competing priorities and the absence of sustained leadership.

The experience of the last ten years has led to growing frustration on the part of everyone concerned:

- Many believe that Canada is not addressing important SD problems as effectively as it must;
- Departments are incurring preparation and reporting costs to develop strategies many believe add little value to the management of their programs;
- The Commissioner is providing advice that Parliament and some departments are not listening to.

MOVING FORWARD

The way forward is unclear as none of the three obvious options – improving implementation of the process, strengthening it by amending the Auditor General Act or scrapping the process altogether – appears viable for the reasons given below.

Option 1: Improving the process
There is no shortage of ideas on how to improve the existing process. These include:

- Strengthening horizontal coordination through various measures such as (i) more explicit terms of reference for the Deputy-Minister-level Policy Committee on Environment and Sustainability; (ii) the preparation of a federal sustainable development strategy to provide a policy umbrella for departmental strategies;[32] (iii) a more active and better funded Interdepartmental Network on Sustainable Development Strategies (INSDS); (iv) developing a new *Guide to Green Government* to update government-wide guidance on the SDS process. This Guide is now 10 years old and its influence has waned as the people who were directly involved in its development have moved on. A new Guide should focus on operational issues and could address matters such as performance measurement.
- Emphasize the CESD's coaching role more. The CESD could devote greater effort to providing operational guidance to SD planning, implementation and monitoring.
- Integrate the SDS more closely into departments' planning processes.
- Strengthen accountability mechanisms by, for example, making deputy ministers more directly accountable for meaningful progress on their departmental SDS through their performance contracts.

This option, however, does not address some of the systemic problems such as lack of leadership and the absence of a national SD vision to drive the process. To a large extent, it represents what has been tried already and begs the question of why this approach would work better now than it has to date: there is no public chorus asking for improvements to the process and the government continues to be pre-occupied by more immediate concerns. In and of itself, it is likely to yield only modest improvement.

Option 2: Making the process more prescriptive
A second option would involve strengthening the current process, by being more prescriptive either through guidelines or by amending the Auditor General Act. A more prescriptive approach could involve the preparation of a federal sustainable development strategy to which departments would have to

conform in their own strategies. Alternatively, the government could invoke Section 24 (5) of the Act which authorizes the governor-in-council "on the recommendation of the Minister of the Environment, [to] make regulations prescribing the form in which sustainable development strategies are to be prepared and the information required to be contained in them." This authority is quite broad and the government could use it to address some of the substantive deficiencies that the CESD has noted in the strategies tabled to date.

It is unclear, however, that a more *dirigiste* approach would be effective:

- Other recent attempts to impose government-wide management improvement frameworks have had limited success.[33]
- A regulation is unlikely to resolve many of the implementation deficiencies discussed in this chapter which flow from poor management practices in certain departments. In any event, the regulation would have to be passed by the governor in council and it is highly unlikely that the Minister of the Environment would succeed in persuading his colleagues to take this course of action.

Option 3: Replacing the process
As a third option, the government could repeal the process altogether on the premise that it is already effectively promoting sustainable development through other means. In this regard, the government could, among other things, point to (i) the creation of new institutions for policy research (e.g., International Institute for Sustainable Development), innovation (Sustainable Development Technology Canada) and for stakeholder consultation and consensus-building (e.g., the National Round Table on the Environment and the Economy); (ii) the inclusion of SD in the legal mandates of some departments and agencies (e.g., Natural Resources Canada, Industry Canada, Canadian Environmental Assessment Agency); (iii) the development of new tools to integrate environmental factors into policy decisions (e.g., strategic environmental assessment), measure progress (e.g., SD indicators) and increase resource efficiency (e.g., pollution prevention planning provisions under the Canadian Environmental Protection Act); and (iv) significant new investments in science to address global and domestic environmental issues.[34]

It is highly unlikely, however, that the government would be prepared to incur the political cost of repealing the SDS provisions in the Auditor General Act as it would highlight the process's poor implementation and open itself to accusations that it was silencing a critic (the CESD) and no longer supported sustainable development. The government, therefore, faces a conundrum. It does not appear prepared to improve the implementation of the process except at the margin but neither can it abandon it altogether because it might find the political cost unacceptable. Unless resolved, this conundrum could condemn the process to growing irrelevance.

A fourth option?

Without repealing it, the government, however, could focus the SDS process more narrowly by articulating a few clear priorities. The SD definition in the *Auditor General Act* is very broad[35] and as a result provides no operational guidance on what decision-makers should do differently. Defining SD to include "the integration of social, economic and environmental concerns" encompasses most of what the government already does and turns the concept into an empty vessel devoid of meaning.[36] It would be more appropriate to define SD narrowly, at least for the immediate future, as addressing the environmental implications of economic decisions. This, arguably, is where the priority lies as the main challenges to SD in the developed world result from the environmental consequences of untrammelled economic development, and not from ill-considered social policies. What the government needs to do is not a wholesale re-examination of everything it does to ensure it conforms to the broad concept of sustainable development but to act in a number of specific areas, such as energy policy (including climate change), transportation and consumption.

If SD is fundamentally about reconciling environmental and economic imperatives, it requires implementing a transformative agenda focusing on achieving significant gains in energy and material efficiency. This agenda will require moving beyond largely-separate environmental protection and industrial eco-efficiency policies to integrated policies that foster the sustainable consumption and production of products. This focus gives economic and environment departments a large role to play in promoting SD but less obviously so to social departments.[37]

One advantage of this approach is that it might reduce the number of departments having to prepare an SDS. Currently, 25 departments are considered "category 1" departments under the Act and have to develop strategies. Four more do so voluntarily. This number will grow as a result of government reorganization (*viz.*, the split of both Human Resources Development Canada and the Department of Foreign Affairs and International Trade into separate departments and the addition of new agencies). While the relevance of SD to resource-based or economic departments is obvious (*viz.*, the environmental costs of energy consumption, urban sprawl, some industrial processes, land clearing, wastes generation, etc.) it is less so to social departments, many of which continue to struggle with the concept.

This approach would offer the benefit of focusing government efforts on the SD issues of greatest immediate importance. The current all-inclusive "one size fits all" approach imposes planning requirements on departments that do not see, or fully benefit from, its value as well as transaction costs on government as a whole. SD is only peripherally relevant to the mandate of some departments and the application of the SDS process to fewer departments would simplify horizontal coordination. Focusing the SDS process on departments with clear SD roles would also likely give this initiative greater legitimacy.

At the same time, the government could rely on a more rigorous application of certain tools, such as strategic environmental assessment, economic instruments, and environmental goals and indicators in order to achieve its policy objectives. These instruments would still require a significant political and bureaucratic commitment to become effective. Setting binding and meaningful environmental targets, for example, represents a difficult challenge (*viz.*, the time and effort it has taken the government to develop its climate change plan to reach Canada's Kyoto commitments) but several European countries (e.g., Sweden, The Netherlands, Great Britain) have developed such targets. Alternatively, some jurisdictions have established "Progress Boards" to report annually on their progress against a wide range of environmental, social and economic indicators.[38] Canada also lags behind several OECD countries in the use of economic instruments to protect the environment.

CONCLUSIONS

The SDS process is now at a critical juncture. Either the next generation of strategies due in December 2006 addresses the major deficiencies noted in this chapter or the whole exercise risks becoming increasingly ritualistic. In spite of their names, SDSs have not become the strategic documents they were intended to be. Rather than setting the government's SD direction, they have in many ways become communications vehicles for initiatives developed elsewhere or for other reasons. Timid, under-funded, and without an overarching vision, these strategies have become shopping lists of actions that do not greatly challenge the status quo. It is now clear, if it was not earlier, that a combined plan-implement-audit process is not enough to support a transformative agenda.

As stated above, the government has not limited its SD activities to the SDS process. Nevertheless, the design and implementation weaknesses in this process limit the effectiveness of its overall efforts and detract from the presentation of an aggregated, coherent, government-wide perspective on SD. The government therefore needs to rethink the process and either strengthen it or replace it. The benefits to undertaking a review include the possibility of:

- A more effective process that will better promote Canada's SD objectives;
- A process better tailored to departmental policy needs;
- A more efficient process that will lower the costs of preparing, and reporting on, an SDS;
- A more constructive dialogue between departments and the CESD.

NOTES

1 I gratefully acknowledge comments from John Chibuk, Ann Dale, Bruce Doern, Bob Masterson, Neil Maxwell, Cynthia MacRae, David McRobert, and John Moffet on an earlier draft of this chapter.

2 World Commission on Environment and Development, *Our Common Future* (Oxford University Press, 1987), 8.

3 Darren Swanson, Lazlo Pinter, François Bregha, Axel Volkery, and Klaus Jacob, *National Strategies for Sustainable Development: Challenges, Approaches and Innovations in Strategic and Co-ordinated Action* (International Institute for Sustainable Development, 2004).

4 At that time, only New Zealand and Ontario has established similar parliamentary commissioners.

5 Government of Canada, *A Guide to Green Government* (Government of Canada, 1995). Preface.

6 25 departments are now required to submit strategies. 4 others do so voluntarily.

7 *Moving up the Learning Curve* (1999); *Making a Difference* (2001).

8 Commissioner of the Environment and Sustainable Development, *Report*, 2002, chapter 5, Sustainable Development Strategies. This problem is not unique to Canada and has also been found in Europe. See James Meadowcroft, "Strategic Engagement with Sustainable Development: Progress at the Central Government Level (unpublished paper, Carleton University, 2005).

9 The two commissioners to date have been Brian Emmett and Johanne Gélinas.

10 D. Pierce and E. Barbier, *Blueprint for a Sustainable Economy* (Earthscan Publications, 2000), 250.

11 Quoted in Standing Senate Committee on Energy, the Environment and Natural Resources, Sustainable Development, *It's Time to Walk the Talk* (Second Interim Report, June 2005), 6.

12 Except for specific matters that fall clearly within their traditional roles. For example, the Treasury Board Secretariat contributes to reporting and management systems on a government-wide basis and PCO is responsible for ensuring that Memoranda to Cabinet include a strategic environmental assessment, where required.

13 The OECD has repeatedly criticized Canada for not relying to a greater extent on economic instruments. In 2004, the OECD noted that "increasing the use of economic instruments is a *matter of urgency*" (emphasis in the original). See OECD, *Environmental Performance Reviews, Canada*, (OECD, 2005), 125.

14 Commissioner of the Environment and Sustainable Development. *Assessing the Environmental Impact of Policies, Plans and Programs.* (Commissioner of the Environment and Sustainable Development, 2004).

15 See note 11.

16 See Commissioner of the Environment and Sustainable Development, *Report*. The Commissioner's Perspective, 2004, 7. The governance problem posed by inadequate incentives or consequences is of course not unique to SD.

17 *Report of the Deputy Minister Task Force on Managing Horizontal Policy Issues* (Privy Council Office, 1996), 28.

18 Taking into account the full sphere of sustainable development considerations, one could suggest that the rebalancing of the federal budget, and the paying down of the federal debt are themselves important contributions towards sustainable

development and will allow future generations an increased scope of choice in determining their own priorities for the use of public funds.

19 Leslie Pal, *Beyond Policy Analysis – Public issue management in Turbulent Times* (International Thompson Publishing, 1997), 80.

20 Many European countries use systems of proportional representation to elect their legislators, which makes it easier for candidates from small parties to be elected than Canada's "first past the post" system.

21 Commissioner of the Environment and Sustainable Development, *Report.* 2004.

22 Commissioner of the Environment and Sustainable Development, *Report,* 2001, chapter 3, 6-7.

23 Government of Canada, *A Guide to Green Government*, Preface.

24 For more info see www.miljomal.nu and www.naturvardsverket.se.

25 Commissioner of the Environment and Sustainable Development, *Report*, The Commissioner's Perspective, 2004, p 10. For an example of what such a vision could look like, see David Boyd, *Sustainability within a Generation: A New Vision for Canada* (David Suzuki Foundation, 2004) www.davidsuzuki.org.

26 See François Bregha and Philippe Clément, "A renewed framework for government accountability in the area of sustainable development: Potential role for a Canadian parliamentary auditor/commissioner for the environment (National Round Table on the Environment and the Economy Working Paper, 1994).

27 See Glen Toner and Carey Frey, "Governance for Sustainable Development: Next Stage Institutional and Policy Innovation," in Bruce Doern (ed.) *How Ottawa Spends 2004–200: Mandate Change in the Paul Martin Era* (McGill-Queen's University Press, 2004),198-221.

28 Auditor General Act, Section 21.1.

29 Toner and Frey note that a strong advocacy function "is not possible within the womb of the OAG, which has a strong, legitimate, and longstanding proscription against commenting on policy." See Glen Toner and Carey Frey, "Governance for Sustainable Development: Next Stage Institutional and Policy Innovation," p. 213.

30 Commissioner of the Environment and Sustainable Development, *Report.* 2000. In the context of another horizontal issue, biotechnology, M. Sharaput notes that "while many ministries … have a hand in the bag, few wish to be caught holding it." (See M. Sharaput, "Biotechnology Policy in Canada," in Bruce Doern, ed. *How Ottawa Spends 2002–2003: The Security Aftermath and National Priorities* (Oxford University Press, 2003), 168.

31 Bruce Doern and Thomas Conway, *The Greening of Canada: Federal Institutions and Decisions* (University of Toronto Press, 1994).

32 In this regard, the government made a commitment at the 2002 World Summit on Sustainable Development to have a national SDS in place by 2005.

33 In a provocative article ("Distinguishing the real from the surreal in management reform," January 2005, unpublished), two former deputy-ministers, Ian Clark and Harry Swain, argue against creating government-wide "utopian management frameworks," such as sustainable development, which in their view create "surreal requirements" that

departments find very difficult to meet. See also Gilles Paquet's discussion of polycentric governance in *The New Geo-governance: A Baroque Approach* (University of Ottawa Press, 2005).

34 During the 1990s, the Government of Canada outpaced all but three other OECD member states (OECD: *Science, Technology and Industry Scorecard*, 2001), by increasing its expenditure on research and development in support of environmental protection by more than 10% annually. As a result, while OECD nations' environmental protection R&D expenditures average 2.5% of total government budget outlays for R&D, Canada is second only to the Netherlands, both directing greater than 4% of the total R&D towards environmental protection R&D.

35 "a continually evolving concept based on the integration of social, economic and environmental concerns, and which may be achieved by, among other things:
    (a) the integration of the environment and the economy;
    (b) protecting the health of Canadians;
    (c) protecting ecosystems;
    (d) meeting international obligations;
    (e) promoting equity;
    (f) an integrated approach to planning and making decisions that takes into account the environmental and natural resource costs of different economic options and the economic costs of different environmental and natural resource options;
    (g) preventing pollution; and
    (h) respect for nature and the needs of future generations."

36 This problem has also arisen in the European Union. See James Meadowcroft, "Strategic Engagement with Sustainable Development: Progress at the Central Government Level (unpublished paper, Carleton University, 2005).

37 See John Moffet, Stephanie Meyer, and Julie Pezzack, "Collaborative Public Policy for Sustainable Production: A Broad Agenda and a Modest Example," in Glen Toner (ed.). *Sustainable Production: Building Canadian Capacity.* (UBC Press, in press).

38 Oregon was the first jurisdiction to do so. Created by the Legislature in 1989, the Oregon Progress Board is an independent state planning and oversight agency responsible for monitoring the state's 20-year strategic vision, Oregon Shines. The 12-member panel, chaired by the governor, is made up of citizen leaders and reflects the state's social, ethnic and political diversity. See http://egov.oregon.gov/DAS/OPB.

PART TWO

Sectoral or Area ISE Policy Issues and Institutions

5 The Natural Sciences and Engineering Research Council as a Granting and Competitiveness-Innovation Body

DÉBORA C. LOPREITE

As this book shows overall, all of the three main research granting councils have undergone change both in response to government policy and to the underlying changes in the nature of research and research capacity in their respective realms both in Canada and internationally. But the first of the granting councils to undergo major transformational change was the Natural Sciences and Engineering Research Council (NSERC). The Medical Research Council (MRC) and its transformation into the Canadian Institutes of Health Research (CIHR) occurred in the latter part of the 1990s and the SSHRC's overt transformation, as Chapter 6 shows, is occurring now.

This chapter explores NSERC and its longer trajectory of change from the late 1980s and early 1990s to the present, particularly under the impetus of policies regarding the "so called" knowledge-based economy (KBE) and related notions of competitiveness and later under the federal innovation strategy from 2002 on and under the Martin era effort to forge a commercialization focus in S&T policy. It also examines NSERC in terms of the actual dynamics of the KBE and competitiveness-innovation as they affected markets, which increasingly made new demands on universities, and hence on NSERC's support for research, for the development of highly qualified persons, and also with respect to how it delivered its research funding.

As a result, new more explicitly expressed institutional objectives emerged for NSERC centred on two primary areas. The first is skills development and the building of the changing science competencies thought to be important to national economic success and to research in the natural and engineering sciences. The second is to promote networks and partnerships between university research programs and the private sector with the expectation of enabling knowledge transfer and the commercialization of new technologies, products and processes.

Three main themes or arguments are developed regarding NSERC's evolving role. The first is that while NSERC's granting function remains at the core of what it does, it is clear from its own discourse and activities that its competitiveness-innovation roles are ever increasing both in terms of resources and its own sense of itself. A second argument is that NSERC's relative success in recent years in garnering more resources for its overall role means that it is, in effect, creating its own future demand for yet further resource needs. As well, growing demands are also emerging on NSERC from the other increased investments in related aspects of federal S&T such as CFI investments and the Canada Research Chairs program. But as these demands increase, there is no guarantee that budgetary resources will in fact be forthcoming from the Martin Liberals to meet these demands. The third key theme is that the Martin Liberals want to see NSERC play a more overt commercialization role and to persuade universities about the value and legitimacy of such a role for universities and also to become demonstrably more of an overt national body rather than just a federal body by enhancing its regional presence.

The chapter is organized into five sections. The first section provides a brief look at NSERC's origins and mandate. This is followed by an outline of the main policies developed by NSERC from the late 1980s and early 1990s on, particularly the formation of Highly Qualified Personnel (HQP) programs and the promotion of public-private partnership programs. The third section then looks more closely at public-private partnerships per se. The fourth section examines some of NSERC's performance achievements and challenges under its competitiveness-cum-KBE policy paradigms and with the onset of a more explicit federal innovation strategy in 2002, and also vis-à-vis continuing and strong traditional concerns for independent peer- reviewed research. This is followed by a brief look at Martin era government policy impacts on NSERC. Conclusions then follow.

ORIGINS AND MANDATE AS A GRANTING COUNCIL

NSERC's programs and operations are directed at stimulating R&D, encouraging linkages between research performers, and disseminating the results of research to potential users. The legal mandate of NSERC is "to promote and assist research in the natural sciences and engineering other than the health sciences, and advise the Minister in respect of such matters relating to such research as the Minister may refer to the Council for its consideration."[1] To that end and according to the Act, the Council spends money appropriated by Parliament for operations and then publishes technical, scholarly and scientific information related to NSERC work.

The main objective of the Council's programs is to promote and support both research and the formation of highly qualified personnel for the Canadian system of science and technology. The sub-objectives intended to achieve these results are: i) to support a diversified base of high quality research in the natural sciences and engineering; ii) to assist in the development of highly qualified personnel; iii) to promote and support targeted research in selected fields of national importance; and iv) to encourage closer links between the university community and other sectors of the economy. The last of these sub-purposes, but others as well, mean that NSERC has a more overt mandate regarding economic and commercial matters than do the other two major granting councils.

In the context of supporting Canada's need to deal with the imperatives of the new economy and international competitiveness, NSERC has defined three areas of investment: people, discovery and innovation. The goal is "… to build a strong Canadian economy and to improve the quality of life of all Canadians."[2] To do this, NSERC provides scholarships and research grants through peer-reviewed competition and assists in building partnerships among universities, colleges, governments and the private sector. Its mission is "to provide the largest possible number of Canadians with leading-edge knowledge and skills to help Canada flourish in the 21st Century."[3]

The institutional origins of NSERC go back to 1978. In that year NSERC was spun off from the National Research Council (NRC) providing a more politically detached environment for its various national research priorities and granting functions. Prior to that, while it was a part of NRC, NSERC was tarred with some of the overall criticisms of NRC at the time, which centred on the fact that NRC was insufficiently focussed on its core industrial R&D mandate.[4] Within the first few years and with the objective of preventing a possible shortage of qualified personnel, NSERC created three key programs: Undergraduate Student Research Awards (USRA), University Research Fellowships (URF), and Industrial Research Fellowships (IRF). In addition, NSERC continued the programs created by NRC but focused on an integrated research agenda. Historically NSERC has also attempted to address integration between industry and universities, increasing the budget in this realm since 1993.

NSERC supports two kinds of activities. First, it provides support for basic university research through discovery grants and project research through partnerships among universities, governments and the private sector. Second NSERC promotes the advanced training of highly qualified people.

NSERC reports directly to Parliament through the Minister of Industry. It is not a part of Industry Canada as a department but its President and senior employees are well plugged into the debates and currents of thought going on in Industry Canada which has the lead coordinating role for federal S&T,

innovation, and commercialization policies. A Board of Directors governs NSERC and membership on the Board is by appointment granted by the Governor-in-Council. Membership is derived from industry and universities as well as from other private and not-for-profit sectors. Members serve part-time, and receive no remuneration for their participation. The President serves full-time and functions as the Chair of the Board and the Chief Executive Officer of the Council. The Council is advised on policy and programming matters by several committees.

The following permanent council committees were created to give advice in specific policies and programs: The Program Evaluation and Audit Committee, the Committee on the Research Base, the Committee on Scholarships and Fellowships, the Committee on Targeted Research and the Committee on International Relations Advice.

From the end of World War I up to 1978, NRC provided support for university-based research. Then in 1978 NRC's office of Grants and Scholarships programs became NSERC. NSERC's inception coincided with the growth and intensification of R&D activity during the 1960s, which in turn coincided with the expansion of the university system in Canada.

In the 1970s NSERC introduced strategic grants and other initiatives such as the industrial postdoctoral fellowships and the first university-industry grants that preceded the current university-industry programs. In the early 1980s, NSERC introduced the university-research fellowships in order to reduce the skills shortage of highly trained personnel available to fill positions in the Canadian universities. In NSERC words: "developing and strengthening the research base, facilitating the interface between the university and the user community, and helping address the question of the supply of highly trained personnel are, and have been, the basic thrusts of NSERC programs."[5]

As expressed in 1990 NSERC had three main responsibilities:

- To secure a healthy research base and, as a corollary, to secure a sound balance between the research base and the more targeted programs of research;
- To secure an adequate supply of highly qualified personnel who have been well educated in basic science and trained with "state-of-the-art facilities";
- To play an active role in facilitating collaboration between R&D performing sectors in Canada, and in providing mechanisms that will improve the transfer of knowledge and technology.

Regarding the formation of HQP programs, NSERC's strategy was oriented to two different groups: new applicants and top performers. NSERC has stressed that "the right balance must be maintained between the funding for the top performers, the starting researchers, and the large group of good to excellent researchers that constitute the foundation of our university research system."[6]

Another relevant issue was to build "an equipment budget that will not automatically be the first target of annual budgetary vicissitudes as has often been the case in the past. Our aim is to have an equipment budget that will be about 10 percent of out total program budget: this should assure an approximate success rate of 33 to 35 percent for requests for equipment support."[7]

Due to the increasing cost of equipment NSERC applied a "negotiated" approach to equipment funding and infrastructure support. Consequently, NSERC encouraged private funding support to develop appropriate equipment for R&D. As well, NSERC introduced collaborative research initiatives (CRI), which strengthened and emphasised a multidisciplinary R&D approach. In NSERC words, "Team projects, multidisciplinary projects and 'multi-funded' projects will increasingly emerge as dynamic avenues for research."[8]

The main objectives of NSERC for the 1990s were based upon the progressive increment of the federal government budgets. From 1990 to 2003–04 the budget has increased 21%, from $518,552 in 1990 to $629,166 in 2003–2004.[9] In essence a political environment favourable to R&D, a central policy goal to stimulate innovation through investments in research, and implementation of several institutional changes to reformulate the regulatory framework of research activity has lead to an increase in appropriations to NSERC.

NSERC AND A RESEARCH-LED STRATEGY FOR COMPETITIVE ADVANTAGE

In 1988–89 NSERC developed a new strategy for R&D based on Canadian needs for competitive advantage in a knowledge-based economy (KBE). As part of that strategy, NSERC emphasized the need for more integration between Canadian universities and the private sector. NSERC's priorities then and into the early 1990s related partly to three new core technologies that had the potential to transform all industrial sectors: biotechnology, microelectronics and new materials. These were also gaining increased emphasis in the federal government's competitiveness strategies of the early 1990s, when the discourse of competitiveness was used rather than the later focus on innovation in the mid and late 1990s.[10] The development of these new technologies affected a mix of research across the R&D spectrum but also across all the traditional disciplines of the natural sciences and engineering. In many ways, they were helping to breakdown some of the boundaries that traditionally separated or distinguished core scientific disciplines.

In this context, the Canadian challenge was to strengthen and maintain its competitiveness in its older economy "resource" industries (for example forest and agro-food products), to develop the new technology-intensive industries (for example telecommunications), and, in the process to establish also a more ecologically benevolent industrial base under the emerging paradigm of sustainable development. One of the main problems for Canada was the lack of adequate numbers of highly trained and specialized personnel with knowledge and expertise in these fast-forming fields. In this regard, NSERC stressed that such personnel. "Must have the expertise needed to invent or enhance technologies and when outside purchase is necessary be capable of identifying and adapting the needed product, process or system."[11]

At this time period NSERC noted that the position of Canada was being challenged in the international market by then newly industrialized countries such as Korea and Singapore which "can out-compete us in the manufacture of electrical household goods and clothing. Chile under-prices us in copper and India can undersell us in basic steel products. Brazil grows trees faster than we can, and produces forest products more cheaply."[12] Looking at other industrialized nations that moved ahead in the development and application of new resource-related technologies, Canada still needed more basic research in biotechnology and new materials. For example, Finland and West Germany, through research in biotechnology and new materials created new product substitutes, which threaten sections of whole resource industries. Consequently, the NSERC diagnosis was that

Our capacity to renew the resource sector and to create new industrial opportunities through innovation depends on Canada having a strong and well structured base in science and technology. It is clear that accelerated technological development will be an important vector of our economic well being, but we cannot forget that a narrow approach towards industrial and technological growth has in the past exacted far-reaching environment costs. Phenomena such as acid rain, global warming, ground water pollution and waste disposal are disturbing fallouts of an attitude to industrial development which externalized all impacts that are not strictly economic.[13]

As a result, a proper balance between scientific and engineering research directed towards industrial technology applications and basic research on the environment was at the top of the NSERC priorities to strengthen the Canadian R&D system. In NSERC's view, "Canada will meet its objective of decreasing environmental deterioration, using clean technologies and achieving international industrial competitiveness as well."[14]

In this early 1990s context, NSERC sought to strengthen the Canadian R&D system by paying attention to three main economic and political-institutional aspects: spending and investment; a new institutional and policy environment; and a new role for the university system.

i) Spending and Investment in Canada's Research System.

The NSERC diagnosis by 1990 was that "... international comparisons reveal that Canadian spending on research and development is one of the lowest of major industrialized nations. In terms of gross expenditures on research and development (GERD) as a percent of the gross domestic product (GDP) the OECD statistics for 1987 showed that Canada, at 1.38%, stood far below other countries, such as the United States (2.83%) and Japan (2.78%). In terms of research scientists and engineers the United States, at 6.5 researchers per 1000 labour force and Japan, at 7.9 were far above Canada at 4.2 per 1000."[15]

Indeed Canadian expenditures on research and development declined until 1984, and had virtually no growth in real dollar expenditures until 1990. The general conclusion of NSERC was "Clearly, Canada must endeavour to increase its industrial R&D investment substantially, and rapidly if it wishes to make significant contributions to, and benefit effectively from, advancement of knowledge and technological development."[16]

NSERC, like the other granting councils, suffered significant budget cuts under the mid-1990s Program Review but overall in the period from 1990 to 2003–2004 total expenditures increased in NSERC's three main categories of R&D: people, discovery and innovation. The creation and strengthening of the Centres of Networks of Excellence also benefited from increased federal expenditures. In 1994–95, from a total expenditure of $492,608 millions, NSERC had allocated 56.3% in discovery, 18% in people, 14.1% in innovation, and 6.4% in the Centres of Networks of Excellence. By 2003–04 NSERC allocated 27.3% of its total budget in people and 47.7% in discovery revealing the organizations efforts with the formation of HQP. Budget expenditures however showed increments in all categories of R&D from 1994–95 to 2003–04.[17]

ii) Institutional Changes and Policy Initiatives.

Several federal institutional changes and policy initiatives were also a part of NSERC's operating environment during this period. The Mulroney Conservative Government tried to create a new policy-regulatory framework to develop a cohesive science and technology policy and to invest more in research and development. On the structural side it was highlighted by the creation of the Parliamentary Standing Committee on Research, Science and Technology, the establishment of the National Advisory Board for Science and Technology (NABST) which reported to the Prime Minister, and a new department structure for science and technology. The latter involved merging the Ministry of State for Science and Technology with the former Department of Regional Industrial Expansion to form a new Department of Industry, Science, and Technology (which later became the present Industry Canada). During the same period, the federal government began a strategy for science and technology called InnovAction. "The objective of this policy is to focus federal science and technology activities in five specific areas: industrial innovation and technology diffusion, strategic technologies, management of federal resources, human resources in science and technology, and the promotion of a science-oriented culture."[18] In addition, the federal government and the provinces created the Council of Science and Technology Ministers with the official mandate to monitor the implementation of this program at the federal, provincial and territorial level. According to NSERC reports, the political agendas of the provinces also showed the growing importance of science and technology although there are significant differences in the amount of R&D that each funds. Many provinces had then started efforts to encourage research, especially in areas that are perceived as a priority by the provinces. Quebec's strategy for technological development, Ontario's Centres of Excellence program, Alberta's Heritage Fund, and British Columbia's Fund for Excellence in Education were examples of these efforts at the provincial level. The development of convergence between federal and provincial programs was also considered an important feature of national research and development policy in the context of the funding of university research.

iii) The Relevance of the Canadian University Research System.

NSERC's emerging view at this time was that research was increasingly based on the development of team approaches involving the natural sciences (for instance in areas such as resource management and research and technology management). In addition, research funding in the future must have responsive mechanisms for the support of interdisciplinary research. Consequently, research collaboration became a priority in order to allow for technology transfer from the university system to the industrial sector. NSERC emphasized that "the challenge of the university in the present period of economic transformation is twofold: to remain the guardian of the traditional charge by supporting researchers' attempts to attain peaks of excellence at the international level; but as well to take on a new and dynamic role encouraging increased interactions for both the creation and the transfer of knowledge."[19]

NSERC stressed also that the business sector was increasingly moving from targeted research towards basic science. It noted, "Research linkages with universities have multiplied. Industry interest in developing new mechanisms of cooperation is exemplified by the establishment of the Corporate-Higher Education Forum, by publications and activities of the Canadian Manufacturers Association, and by the emergence of new industrial associations founded on common technological interest."[20]

The involvement of governments is also another important factor in making efforts to increase linkages between universities and the private sector. For instance, the emerging federal matching funds policy was designed to stimulate collaboration and accelerate the transfer of knowledge and technology. Collaboration was developed through the government laboratories (which have a long history in Canada). NSERC stressed the importance of the proximity between researchers and the government, such as "in the mutual access to facilities, enhanced opportunities for student apprenticeships, and increased awareness of each other's research programs ... [These] are all valuable aspects of government laboratory-university interaction."[21]

NSERC also continued in this overall context to note the need for highly qualified personnel in R&D. It noted that a "variety of studies indicate that the emerging technologies are bringing about a change in the occupational labour force in industrialized nations. Two major changes are evident – a relative increase in jobs requiring higher skills, and a growth in professional, technical, and higher management occupations. In particular, private sector demand is growing for personnel with expertise in the new technologies – scientists and engineers, computer specialists, and managers of R&D, engineering, and production."[22] In particular, science intensive sectors such as electronics, biotechnology, telecommunications and information technology require an adequate supply of research personnel. They project that the demand for a specialized work force will increase during the next 10 years, particularly in universities where the demand for doctoral graduates continues to increase.

This rise in demand affects all three research-active sectors – private industry, university and government laboratories – all of which compete for a relatively small number of skilled personnel. In NSERC words, "there is a reason for concern about the supply of these highly skilled workers. First, demographic trends show us that around the industrialized world, population numbers, in the 18-24 age group (those usually entering university system) have been decreasing for the last fifteen years. Analysts predict this steady decline will continue until the mid 1990's. Second, the time-lag necessary to produce a postgraduate researcher is twenty-five years when counted from entry into the education system, and seven years at best, when counted from entry into an undergraduate science or engineering program."[23]

Clearly, there was a great need for Canada to support skills development in areas of R&D. As such, NSERC's HQP was created to provide financial support to students in different areas of R&D. This support is provided to students at different levels of educational achievement (e.g., undergraduate and graduate). The scholarship and grant program is divided in three major categories: research base, scholarships and international programs, and targeted research.

Grants under the *research base* category are intended to award individual-researchers or groups located in Canadian Universities. Types of grants are: i) *Operating grants*: to develop and maintain high quality research in the natural sciences in Canadian universities by funding individual researchers and/or research groups; ii) *Collaborative Research Initiatives*: supporting special programs of regional, national or international relevance to develop workshops and conferences and to support equipment; iii) *Equipment Grants*: to support the acquisition of research equipment;[24] iv) *General Research Grants*: every year university presidents receive funding proportional to the NSERC research grants awarded to the institution during the past year. Besides, NSERC supports other general activities such as, scientific publication grants and the most prestigious NSERC award, the EWR Steacie Memorial Fellowship.

Under the *scholarships and international programs* category there are a wide variety of awards offered to undergraduate and graduate students, postdoctoral fellows and scientists and engineers for advanced study and research. These scholarships are held both by Canadian universities and by industry. In addition, Canadian citizens studying abroad can also qualify for these awards.

The category of *targeted research* involves research in strategic or selected fields of national relevance. They include targeting research partnerships that promote high quality research of relevance to both industry and federal government departments. These programs are university-industry programs financed jointly by NSERC and private sector partners. Among these programs there are the cooperative R&D grants for research carried out by university researchers in cooperation with industry and/or the federal government. The targeted programs can be a source of controversy among universities, researchers and public partners given the potential tension between academic research, on the one hand, and the intellectual property rights derived from that type of cooperative research on the other.

A second development of relevance to targeted research is the quest for innovative ways to conduct research in order to satisfy the requirements of a new more competitive economy. In this regard, the public-private partnerships have become key to fostering technology transfer, providing funding in a context of later fiscal austerity and for human resources training. With the emergence of the knowledge-based economy and overall competitiveness strategies NSERC greatly increased its efforts in this period toward building collaboration between the university system and the private sector.

NSERC AND PUBLIC-PRIVATE PARTNERSHIPS

In NSERC's view "Canada's universities supply a steady stream of innovative ideas, while industries specialize in exploiting that expertise to create exciting new commercial opportunities. These partnerships have led to productivity improvements and have created a pool of cutting-edge researchers. They have also created knowledge based industries and jobs that ensure future scientists and engineers will find career opportunities in Canada."[25] Examples of partnerships included microelectronics research in which, according to NSERC "they show the power and the potential of university-industry synergy – and the path to the future."[26]

NSERC thus sponsors several programs that foster collaboration. They include i) Industrial Research Fellowships which allow companies to hire a highly qualified researcher for up to two years to advance R&D in an area of strategic importance; ii) *Industrial Postgraduate Scholarships* which offer a cost-effective way to enhance a company research capabilities; iii) *Undergraduate Student Research Awards in Industry* which allow a company to develop a working relationship with a university's most promising young researchers – before they graduate; iv) *Collaborative Research and Development Grants* which expand research capacity by giving companies access to the state-of-the-art knowledge and experience found in Canadian university research labs; v) *Technology Partnership Program Grants* which support very applied research at the commercialization end of the R&D spectrum, with extensive industry collaboration; vi) *Research Partnership Agreements* which offer the advantage of three way cost sharing to capitalize on the complementary R&D capacity of industry government and university research labs; vii) *Research Networks* which advance a company or university research agenda by bringing together a diverse group of researchers to collaborate on a common theme; viii) *Strategic Projects* which help make the costs of high-quality, pre-competitive research more manageable by supporting university research in partnership with industry; ix) *Industrial Research Chairs* which allow a company to work with a distinguished researcher and research team on a major research initiative in an area important to the company; x) *The New Faculty Support Program* which allows companies to share the cost of setting up a promising researcher in a university faculty position that is relevant to their business."[27]

Another well-known program used by NSERC specifically to foster partnerships among industry, universities and government is the Networks of Centres of Excellence (NCE) program. Numerous NCEs were formed and supported in many diverse areas, including: arthritis; bacterial and genetic diseases; computer-aided learning; forestry and environment; geomatics; health information; structural innovations in civil engineering; mathematics; mechanical wood-pulps; microelectronic devices; photonics; protein engineering; robotics; and telecommunications.[28] NSERC, the Canadian Institutes for Health Research, the Social Sciences and Humanities Research Council, and Industry Canada administer the NCE program.

In addition, in 1991 there were three cooperative research and development activities through which NSERC university-industry programs fund research and development in Canadian Universities. This included Collaborative Research and Development (CRD) Grants, Industrially Oriented Research (IOR) Grants, and Shared Equipment and Facilities (SEF). The CRD grants include "well-defined" research projects that ensure cooperation of universities and the private sector. And all the material and personnel resources required to achieve the specific objectives are carried out according to its particular time frame. NSERC asks, "The proposal requires evidence of detailed planning and sound budget justification. Both the university researcher and the collaborating company must periodically report to NSERC on progress. They also require a close working relationship between the partners, and the partners usually have a formal research agreement that sets out the disposition of intellectual property arising from the project. These projects require a cash contribution from the company. Also, the industrial partner may be willing to contribute directly to the project with in-kind contributions, such as by: providing, services or special facilities, assigning personnel to work under the principal-investigator, or donating materials and equipment."[29]

The *Industrially Oriented Research Grants* support less specifically focused projects than the collaborative research and development grants. These grants are of interest to industrial partner who primarily wants to: a) enhance the research and learning environment of the university; b) support generic research and train research personnel in its area of interest; or c) lay the foundation for a closer interaction with a university researcher. NSERC's provisions note "applicants for industrially oriented research grants are not required to demonstrate short-term industrial benefit and impact. The company's substantial cash contribution is considered by NSERC to be evidence of industrial relevance. The company must usually contribute half the project cost. The company is encouraged to make in-kind contributions, but NSERC will not take these into account in determining its contribution."[30]

The *Shared Equipment and Facilities Grant* helps universities to acquire specialized equipment or facilities that they will share with the industrial partner. These grants make available facilities that neither partner could afford. NSERC develops special recommendations for the shared use of equipment between universities and industries. "The equipment remains the property of the university, and the company negotiates guaranteed access for its personnel. The program goal is to assist the university and the company to do industrially relevant research, alone or together. However, the university and the company do not need to make a firm commitment to conduct collaborative research. If the company does not want to use the equipment or its own research, the company could better channel its contribution to equipment purchase through an industrially oriented research grant proposal. The industrial contribution is usually cash forward the cost."[31]

A further relevant issue that emerged from the development of the public-private partnership programs is intellectual property rights. According to the rules implemented by NSERC, the university owns any rights to the intellectual property arising from NSERC grants. It also requires that the university must recognize the rights of access to an industrial partner proportionally to the company contribution.[32] It follows that there is no comprehensive regulatory framework for the recognition of property rights. Rather property rights must be negotiated between the university and the company before starting a collaborative research project. This applies particularly if a company feels it would have a legitimate claim to joint ownership because of its contribution to the resulting discoveries. NSERC provides general advice to the researchers and universities: "When applying for grants, applicants must describe any agreements being negotiated or in place on the protection and disposition of intellectual property, exploitation of research results and publications. In some cases, NSERC may award a grant on the condition that the university and the company reach an agreement on the disposition of intellectual property rights. If the company is very concerned about divulging scientific detail in the proposal, if the company would exclusively own the research results, or if publication delays would be excessively long, the applicants are advised that they should consider a university research contract instead of an NSERC grant."[33] NSERC has also introduced mechanisms for conflict of interest resolution, review processes (peer review) and confidentiality of proprietary information.

NSERC PERFORMANCE AND
THE 2002 INNOVATION AGENDA

In 2002 NSERC published a performance report on its evolving work. It defined the new challenges and priorities in the context of the Chrétien government's paper on innovation "Achieving Excellence – Investing in People, Knowledge and Opportunity." The paper was built on "the Prime Minister's commitment to move Canada into the world's top five countries in R&D per capita, and to make Canada one of the most innovative countries of the world."[34] For its part NSERC argued "the Government of Canada introduced its innovation strategy, placing research at the forefront of our government agenda. Key to this national innovation strategy is our progress in science and technology and it is for this reason that one of the targets of the strategy is to make Canada one of the top five ranking countries in research and development (R&D) performance by 2010."[35] NSERC stressed that the new century creates a lot of opportunities for prosperity and improvement in the high quality of life of Canadians. For that reason, the NSERC council "must be more dynamic, flexible, innovative and forward-looking."[36] Among the most successful NSERC activities identified by NSERC was its search for partnerships to connect university researchers with Canadian industries.

NSERC highlighted two main performance achievements as part of the most important objectives of the organization. One is the implementation of an extensive peer-review system to fund "the best professors and students, and the best research programs and projects. NSERC involvement guarantees objective and fair review of applications for support."[37] Another focal point of NSERC is the partnerships to develop new strategies in basic and oriented research. Clients and partners are the universities, companies and government department and agencies. NSERC stressed that in the case of the universities more than 9,200 university professors and more than 15,500 university students and post doctoral fellows are supported by NSERC. Also they support research associates and university technicians. Regarding companies,

NSERC says that during the years of the implementation of the major changes in the R&D system since the late 1980s and early 1990s, a strong growth has taken place in the number of companies that have contributed to NSERC collaborative university research industry research programs. More than 1,500 firms have participated since the beginning of the university-industry research programs. Finally, government departments and agencies at the federal and local level have collaborated with NSERC.[38]

However, to make Canada one of the most innovative countries in the world, NSERC's own evaluation of performance affirms that increasing private investments in knowledge infrastructure has to be the priority of the R&D system. It asserted that these investments must include: "a) support (for) the indirect costs of university research, b) leverage the commercialization potential of publicly funded academic research and c) provide internationally competitive research opportunities in Canada."[39] The goal must be to develop the most skilled and talented labour force in the world, and the targets include "increasing the admission of Master's and PhD students at Canadian universities by an average of 5 percent per year until 2010, and significantly improving Canada's performance in the recruitment of foreign talent, including foreign students."[40]

To reach these objectives NSERC's view was that several steps had to be taken, including: a) the provision of financial incentives to students registered in Master and Doctoral level programs; b) support for, and facilitation of, a coordinated international student recruitment strategy led by Canadian universities and implement changes to immigration policies and procedures to facilitate the retention of international students; c) the establishment of a system which combines formal academic training with extensive applied research experience in a work setting."[41] NSERC is thus committed in these newer ways to the training of highly qualified people (HQP) to increase the volume of R&D. Three main initiatives are a part of this HQP strategy. First, scholarships and awards are to be offered to undergraduate and graduate students.[42] Second, NSERC is looking at other sources of HQP such as: immigration, retraining people already in the workforce and repatriating Canadians now abroad. Third, changes are being urged to yield academic programs, which reduce the amount of time for graduating while keeping the quality of academic education.

Measuring Performance

NSERC measures its performance by evaluating its programs of research and training support, their impact, cost effectiveness and continuing relevance. NSERC performance expectations include:

- Maintaining a high-quality research capability across all areas of the natural sciences and engineering;

- Facilitating access and use of new knowledge from around the world,
- Creating a knowledge base for developing policies and regulations, and making decisions, for government and industry;
- Creating and putting to productive use knowledge in support of new products, processes, services, policies, standards and regulations in the private and public sectors;
- Meeting the needs of industry and the public sector for highly qualified personnel;
- Creating a stronger economy based more on knowledge, due to more technology transfer via highly trained employees in the public and private sectors, university-business partnerships and through the creation of new businesses by trained individuals."[43]

The performance indicators of NSERC are divided in the three categories of their purposes and main programs: (1) people, (2) discovery and 3) innovation. Also, NSERC addresses performance issues in its administration activity, including quality of service initiatives. Thus, performance issues are measured against efficiency and quality service for both Council staff and the research community.

With respect to *people* NSERC's evaluation emphasizes the demand for highly qualified personnel in the natural sciences and engineering job market. NSERC stresses positive features such as: the "very low unemployment rate for Canadians in the natural sciences and engineering, less than one-half the rate for the general population; the employment growth for natural science and engineering occupations is strong and is the highest of all occupation groups; and the fact that the unemployment levels fall and earnings increase as university graduates in the NSE earn higher degrees. Regarding HQP, NSERC has invested $235 million or 42% of total expenditures in 2001–02 to train science and engineering graduates. This training support is provided in two ways: 1) directly through national competitions to selected individuals; and 2) through indirect support provided by an NSERC-funded professor from his or her NSERC grants.

a) *Undergraduate Students*: NSERC provides four-month jobs for undergraduate students in the natural sciences and engineering through our Undergraduate Student Research Awards (USRA) program; b) *Masters and Doctoral Students*: NSERC provides scholarship support for Canadians to pursue a masters or doctoral degree in the natural sciences and engineering; c) *Postdoctoral Fellows*: NSERC directly funds postdoctoral fellows (PDFs) for up to two years to continue their research training; d) *Industrial Research Fellows*: Another route for doctoral graduates to gain additional research experience is through NSERC Industrial Research Fellowships (IRF) program. This relatively small program invests approximately $3 million per year to help place 175 Canadian Ph.D.s annually in industrial laboratories.

Regarding 'people,' NSERC allocates expenditures in three ways: 1) HQP, that is scholarships for students in the different levels. From 1994/5 to 2003/4 expenditures were increased about 40%, 2) promoting/rewarding research excellence through programs such as Canadian Research Chairs and Women's Programs, an increase from $8.7 million to $63.1 million, 3) Industrial-Government Interaction initiatives increased from $3.1 million in 1994/5 to $25.8 million in 2003/4 revealing an exceptional increment of about 731%. The total expenditure on people has increased from $88.7 million in 1994/5 to $172 million in 2003/4.[44]

Regarding the investment in *discovery and innovation* NSERC argues that "When measured as a percentage of GDP, Canada conducts roughly the same amount of university research as most of its G7 competitors."[45] Some related statistics are cited by NSERC in its performance report as follows: 1) University professors conducted 33% of all Canadian research, as measured by expenditures, in 2001; 2) Of the $6.8 billion of direct and indirect investment in Canadian university research in 2001, 43% was allocated to the natural sciences and engineering; 3) Over the past five years the federal government share of funding has remained relatively stable; 4) Canadian university researchers perform 4% of the $115 billion in university research in the OECD. Discovery Programs include discovery grants, collaborative research initiatives, Research Tools and Instruments, Subatomic Physics Envelope, and International Programs. By 2003/4 total expenditures in Discovery Programs reached $300 million. Finally, Innovation Programs include Strategic Projects, Research Networks, University-Industry Project, Technology Partnerships Program, Research Agreements, University-Government Projects and NSERC Innovation Platforms. The total expenditure for these innovation programs in 2003/4 reached the amount of $92,917.[46]

The results of the current and prior year investments are described below under eleven indicators: 1) *Publications*: in a scientific or engineering journal; 2) *Collaboration Partnerships*: Canadian researchers in the NSE are collaborating with international partners and benefiting from the globalization of R&D; 3) *Editorial Board Memberships*: as an indicator of "excellence"; 4) *Patents*: a good measure of this activity is the number of U.S. patents being issued to Canadian universities; 5) *Awards and Prizes*: NSERC has collected data on 191 international awards and prizes over the past ten years. 6) *Licenses*: Commercial use of the licensed technology results in loyalty income to the university and typically the researcher, 7) *Leveraging*: The total contribution from NSERC partners over the 1990s was $739 million. The ratio of partner contributions to NSERC funding has increased from a low of 1.27 in 1992–93 to 1.84 in 2003/4, 8) *Industrial Survey Results* and 9) *Companies linked to NSERC-Funded Research*.

These evaluations of performance suggest that NSERC's first program category, people are at the "heart" of NSERC activities. The increments in budget allocations over the years reflect a major effort regarding the formation of highly qualified personnel, a policy that became a national priority due to the negative demographic trends and the shortage of HQP under a new international KBE and competitiveness paradigm. The NSERC evaluations also show the increasing impact of the federal government in fostering a competitive economy attached to discovery and innovation.

NSERC's evaluations and its documents overall also show the permanent efforts of the organization to secure a proper balance between basic research and research projects oriented towards national priorities. This does produce tensions between the orientation of NSERC peer review process and the demands of the university system. An attempt to solve this contradiction can be seen in two related ways. On the one hand, it has resulted in the NSERC compromise to limit one third of budget allocations for targeted research. On the other hand, NSERC has also sought to encourage potential private partners to support long life projects by arguing that basic research can be the needed prior step for the applied research directly oriented to industry activities.

RECENT DEVELOPMENTS
IN THE MARTIN GOVERNMENT ERA

While this chapter examines the longer overall trajectory of NSERC's evolution, more recent developments, though harder to judge, are of interest in telling us more about how it is interpreting the final part of the Chrétien government's agenda and the emergence of a Martin Liberal government's agenda.

First, in the context of the 2002 Chrétien government's innovation strategy, NSERC conducted its own consultation strategy in the spring of 2002 with more than 300 stakeholders, including students, university and college professors and administrators, industry leaders and federal and provincial public agencies. Following these and other consultations, NSERC announced its five year Investing in People-An Action Plan. These plans built on past programs but also were clearly geared to dealing with more specific challenges that emerged from the consultations (and from the larger federal innovation agenda). Smaller initiatives were promised to deal with: 1) increasing the pipeline of young people interested in science and engineering, through science promotion activities and increasing the number of undergraduate student research awards; 2) ensuring that Canada develops a skilled and talented labour force to satisfy the anticipated demand for HQP (in part by increasing the value of NSERC postgraduate scholarships but also by studies to determine why research fellows often do not return to Canada); 3) ensuring that Canadian research is world-class and internationally competitive (through measures such as improving its work in the intellectual property management program); and 4) minimizing the time a researcher (or student) spends in applying for funding and peer review funding proposals.[47]

After further consultations in the context of the arrival of the Martin Government, other several smaller scale NSERC initiatives and so-called "pilot projects" were being devised and implemented.[48] These small-scale projects were seen as a way of working within current resources but also as ways of showing that NSERC as a federal agency was starting to act as "national agency." Among these projects were pilot programs for: 1) research capacity in Canada's smaller universities (which often was a synonym for regional universities); 2) helping community colleges in innovation; and 3) improving science and math education. The creation of two new NSERC regional offices in Moncton and Winnipeg were also announced. In addition consultation was underway on a framework for dealing with and managing Big Science to be carried out through the new Martin-era creation of the Office of the National Science Advisor.[49]

Also of some interest in these changes was a move by NSERC to change "its label." By this it meant that its name would legally be the same (the Natural Sciences and Engineering Research Council of Canada) but it would now be labelled and marketed as "Science and Engineering Research Canada." This allowed NSERC to drop the words "natural" and "council," two words which had apparently been causing some confusion when dealing with the public.[50] By 2005 when the Industry Minister introduced NSERC's latest departmental plans and priorities to Parliament, he referred to the granting council by both its older name and its new label.

These 2005 plans were premised by David Emerson, the new Industry Minister, on the view that NSERC (and other agencies) had to "ensure that the research and development efforts of the universities and government find their way into the market place."[51] In these Budget plans NSERC had transformed, at least for purposes of communication, its older "people, discovery, and innovation" programs into "tomorrow's innovators" (people), "brain gain" (discovery), and "realizing the benefits" (innovation).[52]

The remainder of the document pointed out the considerable success of NSERC (and related federal S&T-innovation programs) but then flagged issues that were both matters of remaining weakness, and challenge, many of which were the result of the NSERC success in creating, in effect, its own demand which now had to been met with a further new supply of funds and programs. The "realizing benefits" language was inserted to express what in effect is the commercialization gap, which the Martin government broadly has been trying to express. Thus the NSERC now had to solve what the report referred to as the "culture gap." The report thus stressed "one of NSERC's goals is to broaden acceptance by universities and faculty of the importance and legitimacy of the commercialization of university research results in Canada, given the low level of industrial R&D for economic, cultural and historic reasons."[53] Other gaps were also identified such as the research transfer gap, the receptor capacity gap (in industry) and the skills gap (in areas such as business management).

With respect to the opportunities and challenges, the report again noted changing university demographics but in this case it was the extraordinary growth in the number of first time applicants (in effect a product of past policies, now creating new demands). It also stressed the direct and indirect impacts of CFI funding which created new equipment and facilities at universities but which now needed to have the HQP and grants to make facilities actually operational.

CONCLUSIONS

This chapter has explored NSERC and its longer trajectory of change from the late 1980s and early 1990s to the present, particularly under the impetus of policies regarding the "so called" knowledge-based economy (KBE) and related notions of competitiveness and later under the federal innovation strategy from 2002 on. It has also looked at the current Martin era effort to forge a commercialization focus in S&T policy. It has also examined NSERC in terms of the actual dynamics of the KBE and competitiveness-innovation as they affected markets, which increasingly made new demands on universities and hence on NSERC's support for research, for highly qualified persons, and also with respect to how it delivered its research funding.

Three main arguments have been advanced regarding NSERC's evolving role since 1978. The first is that while NSERC's granting function remains at the core of what it does, it is clear from an analysis of its own discourse and activities that its competitiveness-innovation roles are ever increasing both in terms of resources and its own sense of itself as an institution. This is visible in two different but related ways. First, despite the constant NSERC's assessment of under funding, the organization has increased budgetary allocations from the early 1990s to the present. Budgetary growth however, was mainly attached to the need to encourage targeted research of national importance based upon the greater use of private-public partnerships. Second, a renewed emphasis on "marketing" through the diffusion of NSERC's activities was carried out since the 1990s. For example the creation of a special Direction of Communications in 1997 responded not only to the need of searching for new partners to invest in the R&D Canadian system but also to communicate to tax payers on the evolution of budgetary allocations.

Second, the chapter has shown that NSERC has been relatively successful in recent years in garnering more resources for its overall role but that this means that it is, in effect, creating its own future demand for yet further resource needs. As well, growing demands are also emerging on NSERC from the other increased investments in related aspects of federal S&T such as CFI investments and the Canada Research Chairs program. But as these demands increase, there is no guarantee that budgetary resources will in fact be forthcoming from the Martin Liberals to meet these demands. In addition, some voices, like the Auditor General, have been raised questioning the lack of enough accountability of new foundations such as CFI. This creates new demands for Martin's government in order to answer how foundations like CFI fix into the more institutionalized set of R&D agencies such as NSERC.

The third key theme is that the Martin Liberals want to see NSERC play a more overt commercialization role and to play a more aggressive role in persuading universities about the value and legitimacy of such a role for universities and also to become demonstrably more of an overt national body rather than just a federal body by ensuring that it has greater regional presence and involvement.

NOTES

1 Natural Science and Engineering Research Council Act, 1976–77, c. 24.

2 NSERC, *Ten Years to 2000: A Strategic Document* (Ottawa, 1999), 2.

3 Ibid., 2.

4 See Bruce Doern and Richard Levesque, *The National Research Council in the Innovation Policy Era* (University of Toronto Press, 2002), chapter 2.

5 NSERC, *Ten Years to 2000*, 16.

6 Ibid., 19.

7 Ibid., 20.

8 Ibid., 20.

9 Source: NSERC statistics information available at www.nserc.ca.

10 Bruce Doern, "Looking for the Core: Industry Canada and Program Review," in Gene Swimmer, ed. *How Ottawa Spends 1996–97: Life Under the Knife* (Carleton University Press, 1996), 73-98.

11 NSERC, *10 Years to 2000*, 22.

12 Ibid., 22.

13 Ibid., 22.

14 Ibid., 23.

15 NSERC Annual Report 1990–91.

16 Ibid., 9.

17 NSERC statistical information available at www.nserc.ca.

18 Ibid., 24.

19 Ibid., 12.

20 Ibid., 12.

21 Ibid., 12.

22 Ibid., 14.

23 NSERC has suggested the possible causes of HQP shortage. It argues: "Many personal, societal and market factors influence students in the decision to undertake extended studies in the sciences or engineering. A low participation rate is due to many competing factors including a large supply of well-paid jobs, disillusion with higher education systems, a lack of interest in research, a lack of awareness of challenging

research opportunities, the perception that few job opportunities exist for those having masters and doctoral degrees, and the desire to obtain experience in industry before returning to postgraduate studies." Ibid.,14.

24 In this case, NSERC funds the acquisition of small equipment items for researchers. In recent years, however, the Canada Foundation for Innovation (CFI) has started a wide range of programs to stimulate innovative research attached to the acquisition of big equipment and large infrastructure. In this case, CFI gives funding to universities rather than directly to researchers.

25 NSERC, *The Synergy Awards: Defining Successful University-industry Partnerships for R&D* (NSERC, 1999), 2.

26 Ibid., 2.

27 Ibid., 4.

28 Ibid., 5.

29 Ibid., 27.

30 Ibid., 28.

31 Ibid., 28.

32 NSERC expects that "scientifically interesting results arising from research funded under the university-industry programs will eventually be published in the open scientific literature. In industrially oriented research and shared equipment and facilities projects, which involve primarily generic research, ownership of intellectual property should not be an issue. In collaborative research and development projects, however, to project intellectual property and to allow it to take full advantage of the project results, the university must use caution in disseminating scientific or technological findings. The company may wish to negotiate prior screening rights with the university or ask for reasonable delays in presenting or publishing the results. These delays generally range from 30 to 90 days, and usually should not exceed six months." Ibid., 31.

33 Ibid., 32.

34 NSERC, *Department Performance Report* (NSERC, 2002), 1.

35 Ibid., 2.

36 Ibid., 2.

37 "NSERC Scholarships and Fellowships programs are judged on the student's academic qualifications, as well as his or her potential for research achievement, and an assessment of his or her leadership qualities. NSERC recognizes that success in graduate studies, and in a subsequent research career, is dependent on more than academic excellence; an enquiring mind, adaptability, and the ability to work well in a team are also essential. In addition, many other students receive NSERC support indirectly, through research grants awarded to their faculty supervisors." Ibid., 4.

38 As an example of the integration between NSERC and government agencies, the partners in 2001–2002 were: Agriculture and Agri-Food Canada, Canada Mortgage and Housing Corporation, Canadian Heritage, Canadian Institutes of Health Research, Canadian Space Agency, Cape Breton Development Corporation, Environment Canada, Fisheries and Oceans Canada, Health Canada, Indian and Northern Affairs Canada, National Defence, National Research Council Canada, Natural Resources

Canada, Public Works and Government Services Canada and Social Sciences and Humanities Research Council of Canada. As part of the partnerships in the provincial level NSERC collaborated with Alberta Energy, Alberta Environment, Alberta Innovation and Science, Alberta Oil Sands Technology and Research Authority, Alberta Research Council, Alberta Transportation, Forest Renewal BC, Manitoba Conservation, Fonds FCAR (Quebec), Ministry of Environment (Quebec) and Ministry of Transportation (Quebec) and Ontario Ministry of Agriculture." Ibid., 5.

39 Ibid., 13.

40 Ibid., 14.

41 Ibid., 14.

42 Canadians universities annually award about 2,000 PhD's, 5,000 Master's, and 27,000 Bachelor's Degrees in engineering, mathematics and science.

43 Ibid., 15.

44 NSERC statistical information available at www.nserc.ca.

45 Ibid., 20.

46 NSERC statistical information available at www.nserc.ca.

47 NSERC, *Investing in People-An Action Plan* (NSERC, 2003), 3-8.

48 See NSERC, *New Government for Canada, New Vision for NSERC* (NSER) 2-5, and NSERC, *Update on NSERC's Vision Initiatives* (NSERC, 2004).

49 See Office of the National Science Advisor, *A Framework for the Evaluation, Funding And Oversight of Canadian Major Science Investments: Draft Discussion Paper,* January 31, 2005.

50 NSERC, "*New Government for Canada, New Vision for NSERC,*" 2.

51 Treasury Board of Canada Secretariat, *Report on Plans and Priorities 2005–2006: Natural Sciences and Engineering Research Council of Canada* (Treasury Board of Canada Secretariat, 2005), 1.

52 Ibid., 3.

53 Ibid., 5.

6 The Social Sciences and Humanities Research Council: From a Granting to a Knowledge Council?[1]

RUSSELL LAPOINTE

The Social Sciences and Humanities Research Council of Canada (SSHRC)[2] is well into a process of change to transform itself from a "granting council" to a "knowledge council." This transformation will have significant impacts on the social sciences and humanities research community in Canada. Research in the social sciences and humanities has already changed markedly over the years since 1977 when the SSHRC emerged as granting body from the former Canada Council. Technological innovations, issues such as research ethics, and the development of different methodologies and disciplines demonstrate this. However, it is important to understand if the transformation of the SSHRC into a knowledge council is an evolutionary change or a revolutionary change in research in the social sciences and the humanities. Do the changes simply confirm what the SSHRC had already gradually become or do they involve a major further change? Does change mean that social scientists and researchers in these two fields become the servant to yet more political and social masters and end up pleasing none of them very well?

The Council justifies the movement to a *knowledge* council, a council that better disseminates and relates knowledge to society, by pointing out that how research is conducted has evolved with changes in technology, with heightened concerns for ethical issues and by demands by both the public and government that there be greater accountability for the public money that funds research. The Council sees the movement to a knowledge council as being an opportunity to enhance and demonstrate the importance of research in the social sciences and humanities to wider publics, users, and beneficiaries.

This chapter analyzes the changes to the Council as it moves from a granting council to a knowledge council. It also looks at how the research community has changed and also at the values that do not change in that community. The first area here is identifying the evolution of the researcher. This involves the demographic aspects of who is doing the research, how the research is being done and why the researcher is doing the research. The concern with the last point is not simply the altruistic motivation of researchers, which unmistakably influences researchers' reasons for examining a topic or problem. It also includes the career motivations of researchers, particularly academic researchers. The second area identifies the involvement of the state in funding research into the social sciences and the humanities. The purpose here is not only to identify levels of support from both the federal and provincial governments but identify why they are supporting research. This will be done with a concentration on the federal government's involvement through the SSHRC.

Three main arguments are developed in the chapter. The first is to agree that there are indeed changes in the research process that justify the broad direction of change being pushed by the SSHRC but that there are significant contradictions and tension points in the new SSHRC. The second argument advanced is that the SSHRC was already becoming a knowledge council, defined in its own terms, well before the change in name implied in the current granting body to knowledge body exercise. The third argument is that these changes conform to the larger pressures and world views that the federal government has of all the granting councils and of science and government in general but that this view contains the considerable danger of requiring researchers to be the servants of too many masters in such a way as to satisfying few or none of them very well or as well as they could.

The analysis proceeds in four sections. First, the SSHRC's rationale for change is set out. Second, the Council's core funding programs are profiled. Third, the chapter examines the transformation process and where the impetus for change came from. This is followed by a brief look at the consultation process and some of the reactions from researchers and universities to the proposed transformation. Conclusions then follow.

THE COUNCIL'S RATIONALE

The SSHRC evolved out of the Canada Council which was the federal government's first organization to fund social science and humanities research in a general way. The SSHRC was officially created on June 29, 1977 by an act of Parliament and began functioning on April 1, 1978. It was and still is empowered to "promote and assist research and scholarship in the social sciences and the humanities."[3] The SSHRC was created at the same time as two other granting councils: the Medical Research Council (MRC) and the Natural Sciences and Engineering Research Council (NSERC). The MRC evolved into the Canadian Institutes of Health Research (CIHR) in 1999–2000. Although all the granting councils have had a number of ministers responsible for them during their lifetimes, currently Industry Canada is responsible for SSHRC and NSERC and Health Canada is responsible for CIHR.[4] In both cases, they report through the minister to Parliament and are not a part of the two departments per se.

The SSHRC continued the major function performed by the Canada Council of being a grant awarding organization for the social sciences and humanities but its actions were now based on a specific mandate with four goals outlined in the 1976 Act. They are to:

- support such independent research as in the judgement of scholars will best advance knowledge;
- assist in and advise on maintaining and developing the national capacity for research;
- encourage research on themes considered by the Council to be of national importance; and
- facilitate the communication and exchange of research results.[5]

These four goals have evolved into five core principles in the SSHRC mandate.[6] These are, first, that the SSHRC will only fund research that is of excellent quality and meets international standards that are determined by a peer review process which is balanced by factors such as: region, linguistic, gender, discipline and the size of the university. The second core principle is that the process of selection for grants will be a competitive process that is free from governmental and bureaucratic influence. The third core principle is that funding will not be limited to particular fields, but rather will be open to all fields of research and will be committed to sharing all knowledge and ideas. The fourth principle is that the SSHRC is committed to consistently renewing Canada's research capacity. The fifth core principle is that Council is committed to the accurate reporting and stewardship of public funds.

The Council stressed throughout the 2004–05 consultation process that it would protect these core principles while adding two new principles. After proceeding through a highly participatory consultation process, although a process not without its critics (see more below) the Council added two new principles.[7] These two new core principles are *interactive engagement* and *maximum knowledge impact*.

Interactive engagement is the principle which the Council envisions as supporting linkages between and among researchers through partnerships that: are interdisciplinary, span academic and non-academic institutions, connect small and larger research institutions, connect the regions and connect Canadian researchers with international researchers. The problem the Council believes this principle addresses is the barriers such as location, region, language and cultures that Canadian researchers face in attempting to connect or even having knowledge of other researchers that are examining similar topics or fields. As the Council states "(t)he net result for the Canadian human sciences community is that it is hard for people to know each other well, to trust each other to work together over time and distance."[8] The Council would like to solve this problem by developing research networking clusters similar to those developed in the natural and bio-sciences communities (anchored by NSERC and CIHR). They want to move the social sciences and humanities research community to develop research clustering networks because they believe this "would dramatically increase [the research community's] intensity, flexibility and to address wickedly complex issues ..."[9] The Council wants to follow the footsteps laid by the work at NSERC and particularly the work done at the older Networks of Centres of Excellence (NCE) program and by the Canada Foundation for Innovation (CFI).

The second principle, maximum knowledge impact, is one which compels the Council to work "with a wide range of interested parties to build a greater understanding of research and its applicability-and thus for maximizing the impact of knowledge-in government, business and elsewhere, in both the short term and long term."[10] The Council believes that within the present system where research outcomes are being disseminated through peer reviewed journals, scholarly conferences, books, teaching and the mass media is good but is not done very quickly or efficiently. In particular, the dissemination of knowledge to the general public is not being done effectively. The Council believes the present system involves a paradox where the social science and humanities community is producing research and knowledge but it is not being seen by citizens and taxpayers. They want to create a connection between the research community and the public that involves not only the dissemination of information from the researcher to the public but also a connection by the public back to the researcher. As the Council stated: "If Canadians are to see, understand and value what these disciplines do, what they contribute, then researchers, when they define their research questions, must listen to the concerns of fellow citizens. Researchers must also use new and different ways to share what they learn. This is 'two-way street' is a central requirement for enabling thoughtful public discussion, enhancing appreciation of cultural richness, and maintaining a democratic civil society."[11]

The Council wants to influence this "knowledge-cycle" more directly. It wants to move from not just funding research but also finding ways to ensure that the knowledge that comes out of funded research gets into the hands of private and public decision makers and the general public. They want to move from the present state of the "knowledge-cycle" being driven by chance encounters and happenstance to one where it is based upon "permanent interfaces."[12] These interfaces would co-ordinate the production, mediation and use of knowledge. Two tools that the Council points to as methods of moving knowledge through the cycle faster are the development of lay journals for mass public consumption and programs like the Community-University Research Alliances (CURA).[13] Both of these options may succeed in achieving this goal but they also may have implications with regards to the academic researcher's career aspirations and goals. Also, many researchers will have to be taught how to communicate their research with mass audiences, something the Council acknowledges.

What is also being addressed by these two principles are the issues of accountability and the rise of multidisciplinary work. Researchers are being asked through the principles of interactive engagement and maximum knowledge impact to demonstrate accountability for the funding they receive. Although the notion of the researcher being accountable to the SSHRC for funding is not new what is new is the concept of some form of accountability to the public. While this may not be strictly a positive or negative outcome what it does do is pose challenges. For example, this may be difficult for researchers in some disciplines to do that are not exactly suited to exchanges with the mass media. Some topics and disciplines do not lend themselves well to forms of media that want quick and concise answers to problems that the mass media are concerned with. This is not to say it is not impossible but there will need to be a concerted effort on the part of the Council and researchers in order for this to happen.

The movement to multidisciplinary research through research clustering and the building of networks does seem to reflect the changing dynamics in the social sciences and humanities research community. Historical disciplines like economics, political science and history have evolved in some ways to use the techniques and methods of other disciplines. Also, new fields of research have developed that are combining many disciplines to create general disciplines like public policy and business administration. Disciplines are being created that are including social sciences and humanities with the natural sciences such as resource and management programs.

However, with the changes that the SSHRC is proposing, multidisciplinary work must be given more credibility with regards to acceptance within the academic structure. For example, in many disciplines multidisciplinary journals are not highly regarded and when an interdisciplinary researcher tries to publish in the strict discipline journals it may be rejected solely because it is does not conform to the discipline and not whether it is high quality research. This can have an affect on career advancement for the academic researcher because the ability to achieve tenure may be based upon being published in these types of journals, and thus their research may proceed away from multidisciplinary to more disciplinary related work. This may especially be an issue for new academic researchers.

It is very important to note that the Council has stressed repeatedly that adding these two new principles will not affect the other principles.[14] Thus, to understand the implementation of these two new principles it is important to understand how the original core principals are expressed in the programs that have made up the Council's funding activity during the last few years.

THE SSHRC'S CORE FUNDING PROGRAMS

There are currently five basic grant and scholarship programs that have allowed SSHRC to fulfil its core principles. These programs have evolved since the creation of the Council but the changes to the programs have not significantly altered from their original form. The five programs can be categorised as: 1) basic research; 2) research training; 3) strategic or thematic research; 4) research communication support; and 5) institutional support.

The first program, which the Council describes as *investigator-framed research* deals with providing traditional research support through Standard Research Grants (SRG) and the Major Collaborative Research Initiatives Program (MCRI).[15] SRGs have consistently been the largest program that the SSHRC administers with decisions on grants being made by discipline-centred committees and anonymous (to the applicant) peer review reports. This peer reviewed grant is a prestigious form of recognition for any faculty member to receive and can help one to achieve career advancement. The MCRI has similar traits to the Negotiated Grants Program, an original SSHRC program. Both these deal with larger scale research projects that involve a number of researchers dealing with a large topic that is multidisciplinary in its approach and that involved study over a period of years.[16] In the first year SSHRC funded only two projects: *Historical Atlas of Canada* and the *New Directions in Ocean Law, Policy and Management*.[17] From 1993 to 2003 the number of MCRI research projects funded was 98 with a high of seven being approved in 1999 and low of one being approved in 1996.[18]

The second major program concentrates on funding the *training of new researchers and scholars*. These programs consist of grants and scholarships to students at the master, doctoral and post-doctoral levels.[19] This program, along with the SRG has been a program that is held most dearly by the research community. Doctoral fellowships and postdoctoral fellowships dominate funding in this area although there also exists a number of smaller awards.[20]

The third major program concentrates on *strategic and thematic research*. The strategic or thematic research funding programs are different from the two programs above in that these programs provide funding for research into a particular area of concern that is determined by the Council but with the Council in turn being influenced by its discussions with government officials and also with researchers who may be lobbying them. A research area is given this level of concentration over a given amount of time. Where the first two programs above have a history in the Canada Council that preceded SSHRC, the thematic research program was developed with the launching of SSHRC.

The federal government on June 1, 1978 announced that they would be providing research funding "to further research in areas of national interest."[21] Thematic research programs were developed in all the granting Councils, with almost all funding going to MCI and NSERC at the beginning. Although SSHRC provided some of its funding ($2 million dollars) to help speed up the publication of the *Dictionary of Canadian Biography* they choose to look at the Ageing of the Canadian Population as its first thematic research area.[22]

Throughout the existence of SSHRC there has been criticism by parts of the academic community about thematic research. But other parts also lobby for key themes or get government officials to plant the seed as to why a given topic or issue deserves attention. The criticism has been, as J. R. Miller pointed out, that the Council's decision to move to thematic research meant that the Council was bending to the desires of the federal government.[23] The belief is that thematic research and the funding that is tied to it will ultimately influence how and what type of research will be funded in a larger sense as well. Despite this criticism the Council persisted with thematic research and during its second year period funded five more themes: The Human Context of Science and Technology; The Family and Socialisation of Children; Language and Literacy in Canada; Relations among Canadian Communities; and Women in the Labour Force.[24] This became an important program to the Council as they started to use it as a way of connecting what they did with the non-academic community broadly defined.

The number of strategic or thematic research programs has since grown over the years particularly since the late 1990s. From 1998 to 2004 SSHRC has provided 40 grants in specific areas. One of the most successful programs has been CURA grants which was a pilot project started in 1999 and has had three competitions funding a total of 52 projects. For example, one focused on the challenges of globalization at the local level and what can be done at the local level to deal with these challenges.[25] The most recent strategic and thematic areas of research that SSHRC is concentrating on are Aboriginal Research, Environment and Sustainability, Culture, Citizenship and Identities (including Official Languages), Image, Text Sound and Technology; and Northern Research.

Two other specific funding programs, although not situated in the strategic research grants program but which are parts of the targeted research and training initiatives are the Initiative on the New Economy (INE) and a newly established programme on the Social Economy. Funding for the latter came from a larger policy initiative on this area announced by the Martin Liberals. The INE was created in 2001–02 through a $100 million dollar and five-year initiative "aimed at helping Canadians understand and take advantage of the forces transforming Canada's (and the world's) economy."[26] This program has turned into a significant part of the overall research budget. INE moved from 3.2 percent of the overall budget (minus the indirect costs part of SSHRC's overall budget) in 2001–02 to 8.2 percent in 2003–04. When you compare that to the overall budget for strategic grants whose budget fell from 15.9 in 2001–02 to 9.0 percent in 2003–04 it becomes easy to see the importance that INE has had.[27] The new Social Economy initiative will be funded for five years at $3 million annually.[28]

Communications is the fourth major program area that the Council administers. The Council is concerned about how research is disseminated and used. As the Council stated in 1978–79 and believes today, "research is not done in a vacuum."[29] In these early days research communication was centred upon how research was primarily being used by other scholars. Funding then was primarily centred on supporting learned journals, helping to publish scholarly manuscripts, funding scholarly conferences, and supporting the Learned Societies.[30] The Council also funded the publication of scholarly manuscripts with block grants through the Social Sciences Federation of Canada and the Canadian Federation of the Humanities.[31] Communication is still seen as an important program for SSHRC because it is also the method in which it justifies itself to the non-academic community. This justification is important as the Council endeavours to continue to receive and request more public funding. Communications has become an integral part of the transformation process of SSHRC to a knowledge council as seen in the new principle of "maximum knowledge impact." The changes in the political discourse in the 1980s and 1990s, which will be elaborated on further below, concerning value for tax dollars and government accountability in general put pressure on institutions like the SSHRC to demonstrate their value and importance. Changes in technologies with the development of the Internet also greatly increases the ability of researchers to communicate with each other electronically and has opened up new opportunities and challenges for SSHRC in this area.

The fifth program area is concerned with the funding of *research institutions*. While post secondary education is a provincial matter and the building of universities are a provincial government decision the SSHRC provides institutions with funding to cover costs with regards to building research infrastructure.[32] SSHRC has had a history of helping aid libraries and research centres with initial funding to develop research infrastructure, such as collections and data centres. Specifically, the SSHRC has a program designed to help small universities in creating and strengthening their research capacity.[33]

Two large government wide programs have also had an effect on the Council. These are the Networks of Centres of Excellence (NCE) and the Canada Research Chairs program (CRC). The NCE was started in the early 1990s and then was permanently established in 1997 as part of the federal governments Innovation Strategy. The mandate for NCE involved Industry Canada and all three federal granting agencies developing a multidisciplinary and multisectorial approach to creating partnerships between universities, industry, the government and non-profit sectors.[34] This program is a peer reviewed program that attempts to create networks of knowledge and to increase the impact of research on Canadian society. It is also crucially dependent upon the ability of researchers and universities to find partners in industry. The NCE program received a significant boost in funding in 1999 when its budget was increased by $30 million dollars to $77 million dollars.[35] NCE expenditures from the SSHRC fluctuated from 5.8 percent of its budget in 1998–99 to 8.9 percent in 2000–01 then to 5.3 percent in 2003–04.[36] Although the expenditures for the NCE program have fluctuated this program plays an important role in the SSHRC's transformation because in many ways its goals and mandate are similar to that of the transformation to a knowledge council and the new principles.

SSHRC also administers and hosts the Chairs Secretariat for the CRC program but is not involved in the awarding of the Chairs. The CRC was established in 2000 with $900 million to establish 2000 research chairs.[37] The political context for the program partly expressed concerns about a Canadian "brain drain," especially to the United States. The Chretien Liberals established the CRC to help universities to recruit and retain highly skilled individuals and to advance research in specific areas. At present, the program is funding 1,507 chairs, with the natural sciences and engineering fields having 44 percent of the chairs, health 32 percent, and the social sciences and humanities 22 percent.[38]

All these programs have played a specific role in SSHRC's evolution as the organization enters its transformation stage to becoming a knowledge council. They have influenced the social science and humanities research community as well as the SSHRC as a granting council. The evolution to these programs are evident through evolving changes in how both social science and humanities research are funded but also in the changes to how research has been conducted. Changes here range from technological advances to the development of ethical norms and standards when researching.

THE IMPETUS FOR CHANGE
AND THE TRANSFORMATION PROCESS

It seems likely that the process of transforming SSHRC will have many phases but thus far there have been only two phases. The first phase was the completed consultation phase and second will be the implementation phase which the Council has indicated will occur in the next five years.[39]

The process of changing from a granting council to a knowledge council has been a SSHRC-led initiative. It did not particularly emerge out of a groundswell demand for change from researchers (but see more below). While the Council points to the changes within the research community as providing an impetus to changes there were also triggering developments that led the Council to propose the transformation.[40] In short, the impetus to this change came from the Council itself. As the Council stated in its requests for input in the consultation process:

What we are aiming for is a new council-one that remains in charge of delivering grants awarded through peer review, but one that also directly supports and facilitates the sharing, synthesis and impact of research knowledge. In short, we are aiming for a knowledge agency. We need to work out concretely what it means to the human sciences to contribute to a knowledge society. Everyone has to take stock, both those who produce knowledge and those who rely on it to do their work effectively.[41]

The Council points to a number of reasons for the council to change. Four reasons and/or pressures seem to be predominant. First, there are the changes within the research community which include: demographic changes; an increased movement towards multidisciplinary research; and how research is being done in general. Second, the new focus on research by the federal government that started in the late 1990s has been pivotal. A third factor is a new era of accountability within government expressed through the demonstration of value from public money and results-based management. And finally, there is the rising demand for research in the social sciences and the humanities.

The research community within the social sciences and humanities is a large one. The SSHRC has consistently had the largest number of people (full time faculty and graduate students) to support and a broader range of disciplines that fall under their mandate than the other two granting councils. Nonetheless, it has been receiving lower amounts of funding than the other granting councils from the government. The SSHRC's clients come from 90 universities and are over half of the full time faculty and graduate students.[42] The Council points out that there are a number of demographic changes taking place within theses two groups. Full time faculty are getting older and being replaced by younger faculty members. The SSHRC points to the increase of 62 percent in new scholar applications for SRC grants between 1999–2003 compared to only 11 percent increase in regular scholars over this time.[43] The Council estimates that over the next ten years one third of full time professors will retire.[44] This means that new researchers will have to be trained to replace them. There is a concern that new researchers are not being hired in the tenure track positions or being funded adequately enough.[45] With a new generation of researchers the Council recognizes there will be demands and challenges that will be different than their predecessors and they have to be met.

While this evidence is not representative of a strict cause and effect linkage, it does point out that the research community is in a transition phase with regards to average age and the experience of researchers. With this taking place new challenges with regards to what the future researchers will want from SSHRC will change. Younger researchers are more concerned about career advancement and have on average more external responsibilities, for example raising young families, than their older established colleagues. They also compete in an increasingly competitive labour market. The competitive nature of tenure and career advancement is still based on the old adage of "publish or perish" and publishing for most researchers means publishing in specific journals. Thus, the desire to make sure one moves forward in their careers has to mesh with the desire that the Council has in making sure the knowledge that is created from their research has an impact in society.[46]

The Council has also pointed to changes in other areas that are focused on how research is being done.[47] The Council points to the two specific areas that are both connected but yet somewhat separate. As already described, the Council points to the rise of multidisciplinary research with the development of teams of researchers as examples of the changing culture of the research community away from strictly individual and disciplinary based research.[48] They believe that the reason behind this is because more research is being driven by trying to find solutions to problems and related applied research motivations. As the Council explained because of the need to get at the "multiple dimensions" of research questions there needs to be a multidisciplinary approach that could possibly create a process where "existing disciplines change and new ones may appear."[49] The Council views the ongoing process of collaboration growing within the research community happening not only across disciplines within social sciences but specifically within areas that create collaboration with areas of hard science, such as health and engineering. The introduction of the new core value of interactive engagement (or Connection[50]) is focused on these issues.

Besides the interconnection among disciplines the Council indicates there increasingly is more research being done by those outside the academic community and that this is therefore changing the research community. More research is being done at institutions such as governmental departments, non-governmental research organizations and not-for-profit organizations.[51] SSHRC has also increased funding of research organizations without university affiliation from one percent of all SSHRC grantees in 1997–98 to eight percent in 2002–03.[52]

Other significant change is due to technology. IT and Internet technology has influenced not only the ability to do research quicker, but also allows one to publish research in many forms. The ability to access information and data nationally and internationally has allowed researchers to do more with that information as well as share research with other researchers without the barriers of time and place that existed in the past. A counter to this is that while technology has made it easier to produce research it has also increased the demand and expectations on young and new scholars to have produced a significant amount of research upon entering the workforce and also when actually in the workforce. Overall, the research demand is coming not only from employers but also from governments who fund research and want answers to problems.

The second significant change that the Council points to is that there is a new focus on research from the federal government and specifically the increased levels of funding. As discussed in chapters 1 and 2 of this book, after years of retrenchment in the mid-1990s the federal government significantly increased the investment into already existing and new research initiatives. These programs and initiatives demonstrated a definite change of focus or a refocus with the federal government. This change was also accompanied with an increased emphasis on the issues of accountability and demonstrating the value of social science and humanities research.

Accountability is the third change within the research community. These new programs evolved out of a change in overall government policy generated by practices such as the Core Review process. What was increasingly being asked of researchers was to demonstrate how their research is going to impact society. From the inception of government funding of research in Canada there has been a level of governmental involvement in attempting to get certain kinds of research done. As well, governments are looking to ensure that the research that is funded produces tangible results that will demonstrate the usefulness of research. Specifically, the Council has stated that the federal government expects "the three university granting councils ... to demonstrate how research they fund under their mandates contributes to national scientific priorities and to intensify their co-operation with federal partners."[53] This theme is very much part of both new principles.

The final change that the Council points to is the rise in the demand for research in the areas of social sciences and the humanities. The Council points to changes in society brought about by globalization, science and technological changes and how events such as 9/11 have provided challenges to society that are "socio-cultural" in nature.[54] While this is arguably a realistic point these challenges to society and the need for research from a social sciences and humanities perspective have consistently been there. It is hard to argue that all of a sudden social science and humanities research is important and needed. There always has been a need.

The Council points to two other specific influencing events and processes: the creation of the CIHR from MRC and the 2002 Killam Lecture given by Dr. Martha Piper, the President of the University of British Columbia.[55] The CIHR was an obvious model because it had already completed its own earlier transformation from the Medical Research Council, and thus, in effect had switched from being a granting council to a knowledge council centred on, or augmented by, its several new institutes for health research and also by major increases in funding.

In her lecture Dr. Piper argued for the need to enhance the development of civil society by arguing that there needs to be dialogue between citizens and that the social sciences and the humanities research community must be involved in helping create this dialogue. She argued that the research community should find ways to allow knowledge to be transferred more easily thus improving such dialogues. Piper felt that the Council had to be renewed in four specific ways.[56] First, she stated that the Council should have at minimum "1 percent of all public expenditures on 'civil society' programs."[57] Second, the Council should be restructured to create networks of scholars across the country that will focus on specific issues of concern for Canada. Third, the Council wanted to make research matter more by transferring this knowledge to both private and public decision makers. Fourth, Piper suggested that the Council change its name to better reflect the outcomes of research rather than academic disciplines. The final three points were something that the Council could change whereas the first was beyond its control. Dr. Piper's voice was one of considerable influence, since she has also been one of a small handful of university presidents who had previously lobbied the federal government to get the Canada Foundation for Innovation (CFI) established in 1997. Although what Dr. Piper stated in her lecture is a unique vision it is not that new. The themes of knowledge impact, creating networks and focusing on outcomes are evident in the five-year plan of SSHRC from 1996–2001. Moving forward from this point it seems that the Council saw this as a chance to implement some of the ideas that they were expressing earlier.

THE CONSULTATION PROCESS

The changes that the Council has approved and are moving forward on have been developed not only internally within the SSHRC but also through a national consultation process. The Council partnered with the Association Francophone Pour le Savoir, the Association of Universities and Colleges of Canada, the Canadian Association for Graduate Studies, and the Canadian Federation for Humanities and Social Sciences in developing the consultation process.[58] The participation within the process was extremely high, indeed arguably one of the largest consultation processes on the social sciences and humanities ever in Canada's history. In all 81 universities, 71 scholarly associations, 20 colleges and institutions, 38 voluntary sector organizations, 30 think tanks and philanthropic foundations and 29 government departments and agencies participated in the process.[59] In addition, universities and colleges held their own individual internal consultation process to develop their submissions.[60]

The Council asked the research community to provide reflection and comment on the addition of the new principles of interactive engagement and maximum knowledge impact. They also sought views on how new knowledge council might work in five areas: a) the basic goals and values of a knowledge council; b) new programs and approaches; c) improving current programs and increasing linkages; d) knowledge flows outside universities and; e) next steps.[61]

The consultation process produced for the Council support their proposal to transform to a knowledge council but it was not without some caution expressed from the research community, particularly the academic research community.[62] What was most stressed was that although the new principles have importance the Council must not abandon what it did as a granting council and it must protect or enhance the original core programs. In the University of Toronto submission to the consultation process it stressed that: "the finest, most significant work in the social sciences and humanities is done at the basic, foundational level. It is the core work that frames and supports the best in practical or applied work. Whatever else SSHRC does it must not lose focus on this fact."[63] The belief in, and the defence of, the core program were universal. The submissions even stressed and looked for confirmations that only new money would be committed to the engagement of these new additional principles. At the Simon Fraser University consultation process this was a significant issue. They were concerned with the problem that if the Council goes through with the transformation process but there is no additional funding budgeted by the government for it, this would adversely effect the core programs.[64] The Council reiterated to SFU and others "that *new structures* would only be created with *new money*, and in no way cut into the budget of existing programmes."[65]

Another shared idea that is connected to the protection of the core programs is the belief that pure or discovery research should be given as much support as applied. Many institutions read the transformation documents as overly emphasizing applied research and not giving much credence to pure research. For example, McGill University recommended that the Council must provide a balance and be flexible for both pure and applied research because many researchers do not have the skills to produce "policy digestible material" and since decisions made by governmental departments are essentially political there may be little need for results of applied research.[66]

The nature of the university submissions stressed similar ideas about the two new core principles but each submission was unique with regards to the needs of each institution. Smaller universities and geographically isolated ones made submissions that focussed on creating "an equal playing field" where the researchers at small and prominently undergraduate universities are recognized by the Council even if they do not have the tools that the larger universities do.[67] Thus, they call for the recognition of undergraduate students as having a part in the research process. They also point out that for them to recruit highly qualified individuals to do research, more has to be done to improve aspects such as access to matching funds and improvements to research infrastructure.

When specifically talking about the two new principles, many universities pointed out that they are already in the process of implementing such measures locally. Two general points were made. One was that universities have been in the process of marketing their skills as researchers to the non-academic community and through the development of sophisticated fund raising efforts by the universities they consistently promote the research they produce. With the decrease in the levels of funding provided by the federal and provincial levels of government in the early and mid 1990s, universities by necessity have participated in the types of measures that the Council has described in the consultation documents. Second, all universities have pointed out ways in which they are already interacting with the community in which they reside.

One of the most frequent statements made concerning the principle of interactive engagement was that, while attempting to connect researchers examining the same topic has positive aspects to it, is not inevitable that larger groups create better research. As the University of Toronto submission stated, the tone and language of the consultation documents provided by sshrc emphasised research collaborations, but that there also needs to be a recognition within the transformation process that insights and knowledge arise also from the researcher working alone or in small groups.[68] In fact one of the most frequent recommendations was to increase the number of smaller grants to allow more individuals to do research which seems to run counter somewhat to creating networks.[69]

Many submissions also pointed out the steep transaction costs imposed by interactive networks of researchers and collaborators, including academics and non-academics. The amount of time that administrative matters take grows with the size of the group and thus takes away from the actual work of research.[70] Many submissions stressed there is a need for these costs to be dealt with, particularly with large networks or research teams.

With regard to the principle of maximum knowledge impact, certain concerns were consistently brought forward. The first centred on determining what is meant by the Council regarding the "dissemination" of knowledge. The Council proposed a number of ways to disseminate knowledge which were accepted as positive options but it seemed that the Council was only recognizing certain paths of dissemination while not giving credit to other forms.[71] Although the Council stated it would protect the core programs that included support for journals and conferences, they did not acknowledge the importance of teaching.[72] What also needs to be understood more clearly during the transformation process is how the level of dissemination will be measured. If the success of a research project or program has an accountability mechanism with regards to dissemination, what kind of impact does the research need to have to be considered a success? This does bring up the issue of commercialization and how this will play into the decision to provide funding to a similar program or research project. It may be too early in the process to expect the Council to have a clear understanding of this but it will need to be considered.

Another aspect of this principle concerns the amount of work and the recognition of this work. As the submission from the University of Regina stated: "if SSHRC is planning to place greater emphasis on collaboration, smaller grants, and communication initiatives that will not immediately result in concrete results (e.g., publications), will our own university follow suit in its criteria for merit and promotion."[73] Since work within the community, dealing with questions from the media as well as work with lay journals are not connected to the issue of promotion and tenure the way that other forms of knowledge dissemination are then the impetus to do this has to be dealt with. As already stated above researchers may do this for other reasons than simply materialistic and career ambition reasons, but when one is starting out on a research career this may be less of a motivating force. The Council is looking at this issue and ways in which rewards for this kind of work are being dealt with in other countries.[74] However, the issue of rewards and recognition of this work is chiefly in the hands of the universities. Thus, in order for this to take place these institutions would have to change. This is not only for monetary and promotional reasons but also for the reasons of time. Workloads will have a significant affect on this. This concern was echoed by some of the smaller universities. If change takes place here it may be more than evolutionary but rather revolutionary as what is expected from the academic researcher would be altered significantly by the recognition of their employers.

CONCLUSIONS

This chapter has examined the changes to the SSHRC as it moves from a granting council to a knowledge council. It has also looked at how the research community has changed and also at the values that have not changed in that community. It's focus has been on the nature of the change, its rationale, and the consultation process involved in the overall transformation process.

The analysis has shown that the submissions from researchers and universities had two major themes: protection of the SSHRC's core programs with no loss of funding; and a balanced approach. While they accepted the new principles it was with a cautious approval. The core programs that SSHRC administered, as a granting council, had to be protected as it was transformed to a knowledge council. This is an action the Council has promised to do but this promise will be ultimately dependent on the government to give it the net new resources for its new elaborated role. This is by no means a certainty as the parting words from the out going president of the Council indicated.

Marc Renaud's criticized the Martin Liberal government approach to funding of research as lacking a vision and not wanting to continue the approach to research funding of the Chretien Liberal administration.[75] Renaud is not concerned specifically about financial support for the Council as he states "money follows vision."[76] Renaud seems to be questioning the current administration's commitment to the innovation agenda of the Chretien Liberals. While this commitment can be questioned Renaud's comments may be due to the government's denial of his request for a two-year extension of his posting to implement the transformation. Whatever the reason for this, the departure of Renaud, the champion for the transformation of the Council, has meant that the research community may have some of its fears realized. The approval of the transformation was a cautious one specifically with regards to the commitment of the government to fund these new undertakings without harming the old core commitments. Without a champion to see the transformation through and to protect the core commitments the research community may see their fears realized.

The second theme is that the transformation process has to take a balanced approach. This means that the Council must understand and recognize the development of knowledge is a process that requires all types of approaches to research. From large teams to the individual researcher and from applied research to pure research, the ability to apply for funding needs to be available to all researchers. The ability of the researcher to ensure their independence is crucial to their willingness to accept change. This also means a recognition that although this process of transformation has been a top down approach, transformation must also come from the bottom up in the research community.

What also needs to be recognized is the complexity of the social science and research community. The sheer number of disciplines does not lend itself easily to creating clusters and structures which would be the social science equivalents to those fashioned for the CIHR. Just to fathom how many broad areas there would be is difficult because each area would quite literally bring forth another. Moreover, whereas the CIHR is expressly an applied multidisciplinary research institution the Council must provide a visible balance between basic and applied research. The transformation of the Council also has to balance top down approaches with bottom-up changes and restraints that exist within the research community.

Three basic conclusions flow from the analysis as a whole. First, both the SSHRC and the research community agree that there are indeed changes in the research process that justify the broad direction of change being pushed by the SSHRC. However, significant contradictions and tension points in the new knowledge council also exist. These tensions are historical with regards to keeping the independence of research vis a vis the state but they are also due to technological innovations which are changing how research is done.

The ability of the sshrc transformation to create the right environment for producing high quality research is still a question that needs to be answered. Are permanent interfaces better than chance encounters in enhancing the creativity process that researchers need? The new knowledge council may improve the dissemination of research but it seems that questions will linger about its ability to create better research than already exists.

Second, the chapter concludes that the sshrc was already becoming a knowledge council, defined in its own terms, well before the change in name implied in the current granting body to knowledge body exercise. The issues of dissemination of information and connecting researchers are not overly new and the Council acknowledges this. Universities have been celebrating the research of their academics in order to raise funds, both privately and publicly, and to also show a form of accountability to both government and the taxpayer. The Council has been on this path since the mid 1990s and the transformation is a continuation of this change. What is significant about this change is the Council's top down approach to influencing the evolution of research. The transformation to a knowledge council this way may be a natural progression of how research is being conducted in Canada but until the full transformation process has been enacted this will not be known.

Finally, the analysis has shown that these changes observed for the sshrc conform to the larger pressures and world views that the federal government has of all the granting councils and of science and government in general but that this view contains the considerable danger of requiring researchers to be the servants of too many masters in such a way as to satisfying few or none of them very well or as well as they could. What influences researchers to study topics and fields and the way they study them is wide and varied. However, having the independence to make these decisions is what researchers hold dear. The Council has and has always had a formidable task of balancing the interest of the government with that of the independence of the researcher and as it transforms to a knowledge council it will be ultimately evaluated on its ability to do this.

NOTES

1 I wish to thank Bruce Doern and Michael Howlett for their advice and comments on this chapter. Errors of omission and interpretation are mine.

2 The Social Science and Humanities and Research Council of Canada will be referred as either sshrc or as the Council.

3 sshrc, *1978–79 First Annual Report*, (sshrc, 1979), 10.

4 sshrc, *From Granting Council to Knowledge Council: Renewing the Social Science and Humanities in Canada*, Volume 2, (sshrc, January 2004), 3.

5 SSHRC, *1978–79 First Annual Report*, 10.

6 SSHRC, *From Granting Council to Knowledge Council: Renewing the Social Science and Humanities in Canada*, Volume 1, (SSHRC, January 2004), 10.

7 Ibid., 10.

8 Ibid., 11.

9 Ibid., 11.

10 Ibid., 10.

11 Ibid., 12.

12 Ibid., 12-13.

13 Ibid., 12, 14.

14 As the Council stated, "(the) … core values will not change. We must however reassess how best to continue delivering on these core values under changed circumstances." Ibid., 10.

15 Canada, *Social Sciences and Humanities Research Council 2005–2006 Estimates: Part III – Report on Plans and Priorities*, (Minister of Government Works and Government Services Canada, 2005), 14-16.

16 For the Negotiated Grants see SSHRC, *Annual Report 1978–79*, 17-18. For MCRI see http://www.sshrc.ca/web/apply/program_descriptions/mcri_e.asp.

17 SSHRC, Annual Report 1978–79, 18.

18 SSHRC, *The Year in Numbers: Expenditures and Competition Results 2003–2004*, (SSHRC, November 2004), 67.

19 2003–04 marked a return to the funding of master students by the federal government who abandoned this type of funding.

20 SSHRC, *The Year in Numbers*, 13.

21 SSHRC, Annual Report 1978–79, 22.

22 Ibid., 22-3.

23 J.R. Miller describes a good example of this. In 1981–82 when the government under the mandate of restraint created a fund of $11 million dollars for research in areas of Canadian Studies. This motivated by the Symons Report *To Know Ourselves*. Of this finding $2 million was allocated to SSHRC who requested and accepted this money. The reaction to this was described in the 1981–81 SSHRC annual report under the title The Year of the Debate. The Council's President Andre Fortier wrote, "[the] criticism we have received have made it clear now more than ever, that in fact we have two sets of loyalties: toward the researchers on one hand, and toward the government and the people of Canada on the other." See J.R. Miller, "From Massey to Metamorphosis?: Canada's Granting Councils in the Human Sciences," presented at Hildafest: The Work and World of Hilda Neatby, Saskatoon, 27 March 2004. Also see the Social Sciences and Humanities Research Council of Canada, 1981–82 Annual Report, 20-1.

24 Miller, Saskatoon, 27 March 2004.

25 See http://www.sshrc.ca/web/apply/program_descriptions/cura_e.asp#a.

26 SSHRC, *Annual Report 2001–2002*, (Social Sciences and Humanities Council of Canada, 2001–02), 32.

27 As stated the percentage numbers here do not include the Indirect Costs that are costs that SSHRC incurs administrating a number of programs such as Canada's Research Chairs program. For a complete breakdown of SSHRC's current budget see, SSHRC, *The Year in Numbers*, 10.

28 Canada, *Social Sciences and Humanities Research Council 2005–2006 Estimates: Part III – Report on Plans and Priorities*, 18.

29 SSHRC, *Annual Report 1978–79*, 19.

30 Ibid., 19-20.

31 Ibid., 19.

32 See http://www.sshrc.ca/web/apply/institutions_e.asp.

33 See http://www.sshrc.ca/web/apply/program_descriptions/aid_small_universities_e.asp.

34 See http://www.nce.gc.ca/about_e.htm.

35 See http://www.nce.gc.ca/about_e.htm.

36 SSHRC, *The Year in Numbers*, 12.

37 See http://www.chairs.gc.ca/web/about/index_e.asp.

38 These were the totals as of June 30, 2005. 1057 chairs total, natural sciences and engineering field 676, health 487, and social sciences and humanities 344. See http://www.chairs.gc.ca/web/chairholders/index_e.asp.

39 SSHRC, *Shaping the Future of SSHRC as a Knowledge Council: Strategic Plan 2006–2011*, (SSHRC, June 2005).

40 Interview with Christian Sylvain, Director, Corporate Policy and Planning, SSHRC, June 10, 2004.

41 SSHRC, *From Granting Council to Knowledge Council: Renewing the Social Science and Humanities in Canada*, Volume 1, 10.

42 SSHRC, *From Granting Council to Knowledge Council: Renewing the Social Science and Humanities in Canada*, Volume 2, 2, 4.

43 Ibid., 13.

44 SSHRC, *From Granting Council to Knowledge Council: Renewing the Social Science and Humanities in Canada*, Volume 1, 8.

45 For a discussion on replacing of retiring faculty with new faculty see Karen R. Grant, "A Conversation on the Future of the Academy with James Turk, PhD., Executive Director, Canadian Association of University Teachers," *The Canadian Review of Sociology and Anthropology*, 39.3 (2002): 264-7.

46 It is important to note that the Council is looking into this issue and has funded a report on it. Kerry Ann O'Meara, *Influences of Faculty Work and Academic Reward Systems: A Comparative Perspective*, (SSHRC, 2005). Available at http://www.sshrc.ca/web/whatsnew/initiatives/transformation/summaries/rewards_e.asp.

47 SSHRC, *From Granting Council to Knowledge Council: Renewing the Social Science and Humanities in Canada*, Volume 1, 8-9.

48 Ibid., 9.

49 Ibid., 9.

50 SSHRC, *Shaping the Future of SSHRC as a Knowledge Council: Strategic Plan 2006–2011*, (SSHRC, June 2005).

51 Ibid., 9 and SSHRC, *From Granting Council to Knowledge Council: Renewing the Social Science and Humanities in Canada*, Volume 2, 8.

52 Ibid.

53 SSHRC, *Striking the Balance: A Five-Year Strategy for the Social Sciences and Humanities Research Council of Canada 1996–2000*, (SSHRC, 1996), 8-9.

54 SSHRC, *From Granting Council to Knowledge Council: Renewing the Social Science and Humanities in Canada*, Volume 1, 7.

55 Interview with Christian Sylvain, Director Corporate Policy and Planning, SSHRC, June 10, 2004. Martha Piper, Building a Civil Society: A New Role for the Human Sciences, *Killam Lecture Series*, (Halifax, Trustees of the Killam Trusts, October 24, 2002). Available at http://www.killamtrusts.ca/english/pdf/Killam_Lec_02.pdf.

56 Ibid., 11-12.

57 Ibid., 11.

58 SSHRC, *From Granting Council to Knowledge Council: Renewing the Social Science and Humanities in Canada*, Volume 3, 2, and 18-20.

59 Ibid., 18-20.

60 The process at Simon Fraser University in British Columbia was an example of some the more extensive ones done. See http://www.sfu.ca/vpresearch/SSHRC%20Transformation/.

61 SSHRC, *From Granting Council to Knowledge Council: Renewing the Social Science and Humanities in Canada*, Volume 1, 21.

62 A good collection of the academic institutions responses is available at http://www.sfu.ca/vpresearch/SSHRC%20Transformation/Otherreports_files/Otherreports.htm.

63 University of Toronto, Institutional Response to SSHRC, (University of Toronto, 2004), 1. For other examples see McGill University, The SSHRC Transformation Consultation at McGill University, (McGill University, May 1, 2004), 1-2 or Leonard Diepeveen, From Granting Council to Knowledge Council: The Perspective from Dalhusie University, (Dalhusie University, 2004), 1.

64 Simon Fraser University, Report on Consultations Social Sciences and Humanities Research Council Transformation, (Simon Fraser University, May 2, 2004), 4.

65 Ibid., 8.

66 McGill University, The SSHRC Transformation Consultation, 6.

67 For one example see, University of Northern British Columbia, Transforming the Social Sciences and Humanities in Canada: A Report from the University of Northern British Columbia, (UNBC, May 1, 2004), 1-2.

68 University of Toronto, Institutional Response to SSHRC, 3.

69 For example see Canadian Federation for the Humanities and Social Sciences, Report on the Response of Scholarly Associations in the Humanities and Social Sciences, (CFHSS, September 7, 2004), 6-7.

70 For example see: McGill University, The SSHRC Transformation Consultation, 4.

71 SSHRC, *From Granting Council to Knowledge Council: Renewing the Social Science and Humanities in Canada*, Volume 1, 14-16.

72 University of Toronto, Institutional Response to SSHRC, 3. Also see McGill University, The SSHRC Transformation Consultation.

73 University of Regina, sshrc Dialogue, (U of Regina, February-April 2004).

74 See note 45.

75 Sarah Schmidt, "Top Researcher Blasts Liberal's Lack of Vision: Retiring Council Boss Claims They 'can't figure out where they're going," *The Ottawa Citizen*, (Ottawa, July 7, 2005), A3.

76 Ibid.

7 Changing Horses: Is the Innovation Strategy Working for the Mineral Sector?

DAVID ROBINSON

Canada's innovation strategy has taken shape slowly over the 17 years since the Canada-US Free trade pact was enacted in 1988. The broad outlines of Canada's current policy were widely discussed by 1990. This chapter examines a specific opportunity that was explicitly identified by 1991, and that is still awaiting federal action. The history of the Mining Supply and Service (MS&S) cluster in Sudbury provides a remarkably straightforward test of whether the Canadian innovation strategy as practiced will support "changing horses" – becoming an economy less dependent on natural resources, and more reliant on innovation and skills. The example reveals a troubling inability at both the federal and the provincial level to act on an obvious opportunity.

Sudbury is Canada's leading mining community. With a GDP that is much larger than the GDP of Prince Edward Island, (5.6 vs. 3.4 billion in 2002) and a population greater than the combined populations of the Yukon, the Northwest Territories and Nunavut, Sudbury has been called "one of the world's four great "mining city-states."[1] It sits on one of the ten largest producing mineral deposits in the world (and the largest in North America). It is the only city in the world with fourteen producing mines and two major smelters within the city limits. It is the only mining community in Canada with a research university.

Sudbury is also home to Canada's densest concentration of specialized mining supply and service firms, with over three hundred within city limits and more in nearby NorthBay. A 2000 report by Natural Resources Canada[2] found that 45% of Canada's MS&S firms were in just three communities: Toronto, Vancouver, and Sudbury. The Sudbury firms draw, on average, half of their revenue from outside of the immediate region and 11% from outside of Canada.[3]

For the last 15 years the Sudbury MS&S cluster has presented federal and provincial policy-makers with an opportunity to develop a high-tech, innovation-based export sector based on existing strengths in the resource sector. Industrialization based on Canadian resource wealth has been the goal of Canadian economic strategy since confederation. The Sudbury cluster also has the potential to drive economic development in one of Canada's most economically depressed regions. It provides policy analysts with a natural experiment that tests the capacity of the current policy regime to achieve the goals that were set for it in the early 1990s.

The first section of the chapter therefore describes the MS&S sector and its evolution in Sudbury. We need to establish that the MS&S sector really did present a significant opportunity for Canadian policy-makers. The second section describes the 15-year evolution of Canadian policy with respect to innovation since the implementation of the Free Trade agreement in 1989. It also sketches two recent strands in economic theory that lay behind that evolution, and describes how they have gradually been incorporated into the conventional wisdom of policy makers. To explain why progress has been so slow in one of the few sectors specifically identified by the key policy analysis of 1991 it is also useful to follow the convoluted process through which theory has gradually been translated into programs. The third section of the analysis then describes the very limited support for the development of the Sudbury cluster provided by federal and provincial governments in the fifteen years since the cluster was first described. The final section attempts to account for the very limited progress and draw lessons of that apply more generally. Conclusions then follow.

PROMISE: THE MS&S SECTOR

The MS&SD sector now employs more Canadians than mining does. The labour-saving technological change that is driving mining employment down around the world is increasing demand for capital equipment and technology. The supply industries now compete internationally and are becoming a significant export sector for advanced technology and services. As Table 1 suggests, mining supplies and services are provided by firms in many different industries. Firms are connected through their customers and their need for specialized knowledge of the mining industry, but the diversity of products and services has made it difficult for analysts to see them as a coherent entity.[4] Until the development in the 1980s of the Ontario Mining Equipment and Service Exporters, which later became the Canadian Mining Equipment and Service Exporters (CAMESE), no organization represented the MS&S sector.

A crucial element was added to the Sudbury cluster in the 1990s. David Peterson's Liberal provincial government announced it would transfer the Ontario Geological Survey (OGS) and offices of the Ministry of Northern

Table 7.1
Selected Canadian Mining-supply and Service Providers

Exploration financing	Engineering
Investment analysis	Project management
Due diligence	Mine construction
Legal services	Parts and equipment
Geophysics	Materials handling
Geology	Mineral processing
Geochemistry	Smelting
Analytical laboratories	Refining
Mapping	Ventilation
Remote sensing	Explosives
Drilling	Safety supplies
Communications	Automation and software
Community relations	Environmental management
Feasibility studies	Transportation

Development and Mines (MNDM) from Toronto to the campus of Laurentian University in Sudbury. Peterson hoped to create a critical mass capable of attracting additional industry by concentrating government assets related to the northern economy in northern Ontario. The presence of the OGS did make Sudbury a centre for exploration, and it stimulated mining-related research. There are now thirteen mining-related research institutes or centres at Laurentian, including the mining branch of the Canadian Mining Industry Research Organization. Active participation of the OGS and MNDM also made possible Laurentian's PhD program in Precambrian Geology.

ECONOMIC THEORY AND THE EVOLUTION OF CANADIAN POLICY

With the implementation of the Free Trade Agreement in 1989, industrial policy became a changed but still crucial issue for Canada. By 1989 at least 45 federal agencies were engaged in adjustment programs.[5] In 1992 Industry, Science and Technology Canada (the current Industry Canada) reviewed 44 studies conducted between 1988 and 1991.[6] One of the studies, *Canada at the Crossroads*[7] by Michael Porter and the Monitor Company of Boston, brought to bear the largest collection of new data, and was the only study to seriously examine the theory of trade and competitiveness, and was the only one to offer a synthesis that pointed to a consistent set of policy recommendations.

The study was commissioned by the Business Council on National Issues and the Government of Canada (represented by four ministries: Industry, Science & Technology, Employment & Immigration, Trade, and Consumer &Corporate Affairs). Although undertaken for Brian Mulroney's Conservative government, it became the basis of the economic policy of the Chretien Liberals in the 1993 election.[8] The innovation strategy of both the current federal government and the Ontario government in 2005 are direct descendents of the recommendations in *Canada at the Crossroads*.

Prescriptions

Porter's report was based on an analysis of the pattern of Canadian trade, a detailed study of 25 industries accounting for more than 37% of Canadian exports, and an audit of the institutional and public policy environment in Canada and its impact on the way Canadian firms compete. It also drew on the principle conclusion of Porter's most influential book, the *Competitive Advantage of Nations*.[9] In that work, Porter argued for policies based on an extension of the standard theory of comparative advantage.

The most significant and sustainable competitive advantage results, he argued, when a country possesses factors which are both advanced and specialized in a particular industry. Sustained international competitive advantage results from innovation and that "the factors most important to modern industrial competition and to national prosperity are created, not inherited."[10] Human capital, infrastructure, the institutional system, and patterns of industrial organization and attitudes are all factors of production created over time at great expense.

Porter emphasized that Canada's wealth was still precariously based on natural resources, which are inherited factors. In 1991 exports were concentrated in only five of the sixteen 16 broad sectors. Four of these were minimally processed natural resource-based products: metal and materials, forest products, petroleum and chemicals, and food and beverages.[11] In 1982 the four "clusters" provided more than 62% of Canadian export revenues. The only other large exporter was the auto industry, protected by national policy and international treaty.

Commodity prices have fallen relative to the prices of manufactures by an average of about 1% annually over the last 140 years.[12] Between 1971 and 2000 commodity prices dropped over 50% in real $US. Not only have prices fallen but Canada's competitive advantage has been undermined. Low-cost southern-hemisphere eucalyptus hardwood, for example, now competes with higher-cost Canadian softwood in producing pulp and paper, and fast-growing US plantation pine competes with slower-growing Ontario species in the lumber market. In 1950 Canada produced 95% of the "free world's" nickel, enjoying monopoly rents. By 1976, when employment in the Canadian industry peaked, Canada share had fallen to 43% and by 2002 Canada produced only 15% of the

world's nickel. Ores of nickel are now mined in about 20 countries on all conti-
nents, and are smelted or refined in about 25 countries.

Canada at the Crossroads also found that Canada had largely failed to develop sophisticated suppliers for its resource industries. "Few Canadian industries have obtained significant competitive advantage from healthy indigenous
related and supporting industries."[13] This failure put the resource sectors at
further risk in international competition. Of special concern for Porter was
that Canada has few internationally competitive machinery industries.[14]

Since the middle of the 20th century Canada has been increasing the share
of manufactures in its bundle of exports. In 2005, however, Jim Stanford,
chief economist for the Canadian Auto Workers began to call attention to the
fact that Canadian exports have become more resource intensive since 1998,
with falling investment in the manufacturing sector and increasing dependence on natural resource exports. A now increasing part of our export sector is producing commodities that are steadily falling in value. In contrast to
the Canadian economy, the US, Swiss, Danish and Japanese economies are
increasingly weighted towards firms producing unique products using
unique processes and the assets of these firms are increasing in value.[15]

Program: Innovation, Clusters, Advanced
and Specialized Factors

The barriers to upgrading[16] for Porter were in "essential areas such as science,
technology, education and training" that were in the public domain. Like many
analysts he was highly critical of Canadian management, but his emphasis was
on public policy. Key problems included the fact that Canada's R&D infrastructure was not well aligned with requirements for upgrading. Supporting industries were weak, and clusters were inadequately developed. To improve the
productiveness of R&D, Porter recommended that governments improve coordination, foster better linkages between public research institutions and industry, shift government research funding from government labs to universities
and the private sector, encourage greater specialization among universities,
both in research and in training programs, and stimulate the adoption of technology. In addition, governments should revise regional development strategies and other policies to foster the development of stronger industry clusters
by encouraging existing clusters and focusing on developing specialized factors.[17] With varying degrees of commitment and success, the Canadian government has acted on all of these recommendations.

Clusters

The concept of clusters is one of the key ideas in Porter's work and perhaps
the most contentious and difficult.[18] The concept initially described industries at the national level that succeed in international competition.

Table 7.2
Stages of Mining

Stage	Employment	Description
1	47 000	mining and quarrying
		This sector comprises establishments primarily engaged in extracting naturally occurring minerals. These can be solids, such as coal and ores; liquids, such as crude petroleum; and gases, such as natural gas.
2	87 000	smelting and refining,
		Primary metal manufacturing (manufacturing metal products by rolling, drawing, extruding, alloying or casting (NAICS 331 includes smelting and refining ferrous and non-ferrous metals from ore, pig or scrap in blast or electric furnaces.).
3	255 000	in non-metal semi-fabricated parts,
		This subsector comprises establishments primarily engaged in forging, stamping, forming, turning and joining processes to produce ferrous and non-ferrous metal products, such as cutlery and hand tools, architectural and structural metal products, boilers, tanks and shipping containers, hardware, spring and wire products, turned products, and bolts, nuts and screws.),
4		Fabricated parts and simple products, and fabricated metal manufacturing.
		and These establishments cut, grind, shape and finish granite, marble, limestone, slate and other stone; mix non-metallic minerals with chemicals and other additives; and heat non-metallic mineral preparations to make products, such as bricks, refractories, ceramic products, cement and glass.
5		Product assembly

Source: Natural Resources Canada. Key Facts 2002

Figure 7.1 uses Canada's mining cluster and its relationship to the MS&S sector to illustrate what Porter meant by a cluster. In 2003, Canada's minerals and metals sector employed about 389 000 in the first three of five stages of production (Table 7.2). The fourth and fifth stages occur to a large extent in other countries.

The shaded areas in Figure 1 indicate industries in which Canadian firms supply a relatively large share of industry demand. In some areas Canadian-based companies are world leaders. Canadian firms have captured a significant share of the world market for airborne geophysical equipment and related software, and thus Canadian data companies have a strong international presence. The Canadian consulting engineering industry, which

Figure 7.1
Schematic of the stages of the mining industry and
the associated mining supply and service sector

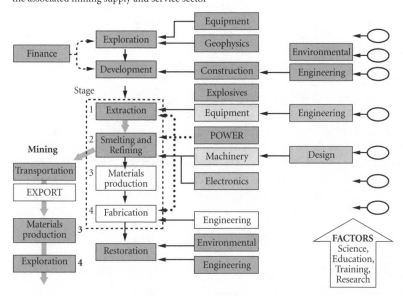

developed to service large government-funded infrastructure projects, markets project development services worldwide. Challenging mining conditions have helped to make the geophysical contracting industry competitive, and "stringent safety regulations contributed to the emergence of an internationally competitive explosives industry."[19]

Employment and the variety of products increase rapidly in the later stages of production. Figure 7.1 suggests the relative absence of value added production after smelting, and the weakness of Canadian, machinery suppliers. Despite its size and potential, the Canadian metal sector has limited depth and breadth.[20] The distinctive feature of *Canada at the Crossroads* was the emphasis on reinforcing and completing clusters of industries that produced traded goods.

Sudbury was singled out for special attention in *Canada at the Crossroads*. Although Porter observed that "few of Canada's resource-based industries have upgraded or widened their source of advantage."[21] the nickel industry is one of the very few exceptions. It had been "successful in developing advantage in advanced factors,"[22] and furthermore, "the nickel industry has benefited from the clustering of certain research and development activities, educational institutions and the Ontario Government's Ministry of Northern Development and Mines, in the Sudbury area."[23]

Over the course of the 1990's the concept of a cluster increasingly came to mean a geographically located group of companies and other institutions located close enough to each other to allow extensive interpersonal contact and for firms to benefit from a variety of externalities generated by the grouping. Growing clusters were thought to attract skilled people through offering greater opportunities. Entrepreneurs or individuals with ideas might migrate to the cluster from other locations, because a growing cluster signals opportunities. In *Canada at the Crossroads* Porter argued that innovation tends to be facilitated by the presence of a cluster, particularly where the cluster is concentrated geographically.[24]

Although it is not without serious critics[25] the cluster-based strategy has become enormously popular – "Clusters have become recognized as a potentially effective mechanism for enhancing competitive advantage, and governments around the world have sought to develop mechanisms to identify actual and potential clusters and to promote their formation and operation. Clusters enhance economic performance through increases in the productivity of member organizations, driving the pace and direction of innovation, stimulation of the formation of new businesses, and access to new knowledge and learning."[26] The cluster approach "promised a seemingly easy answer to the challenges created by increased international competition and the growing importance of innovation in the knowledge economy – particularly for smaller regions tied to traditional industries."[27]

The cluster approach was adopted by the federal government in 1994 and has guided the activities of several federal agencies, including Industry Canada, (providing funds for communities to identify their clusters), the National Research Council (investing in cluster building), the SSHRC, (funding a major research project on clusters), and the Ontario Provincial government, (funding biotech cluster in each region of Ontario, supporting research on clusters). Because the cluster approach has been adopted and has become part of the mental machinery of policymakers at all levels, a basic understanding of the approach is crucial for understanding the evolution of competitiveness policy and innovation policy since 1990.

There is no common definition accepted by all the agencies, researchers and consultants who use the term. I have pointed out in other published work that if cluster theory directs public resources, we should expect that the struggle for control of resources will lead to a struggle for control of the definition."[28] The simplest definition comes from Swann and Prevezer who define it as "groups of firms within one industry based on geographical area"[29] Porter, whose several definitions tend to dominate discussion, has increasingly emphasizes geographical concentration. He stresses that "clusters are critical masses – in one place – of unusual competitive success in particular fields"[30] but he also extends the notion beyond a single industry in that a cluster is "an array of interrelated industries and organizations sharing common technology, skills, information, customers and clients and sharing ideas of common concern to increase productivity and competition."[31] Clusters may also be characterized functionally as networks that provide advantages to the member firms. The OECD has a working definition that places greater emphasis on the knowledge dimension.[32]

The key element in all definitions is a collection of related firms. Figure 7.2: CDAW Cluster Model reproduces the cluster model used by Cassidy et al[33] to explore the success of the National Research Council's cluster-building program. The figure places the group of firms in a setting that includes customers and competitors. The success of the firms rests on local factor conditions and may be enhanced by a wide variety of supporting institutions, including government and industry organizations. The narrowest definition includes only the firms. The collection of over 300 mining supply and service firms in Sudbury is automatically a cluster by this definition. Wider definitions require that the cluster include an array of supporting institutions such as research facilities, standards associations, government offices, universities and colleges with specialized training and research programs. Senior policy makers and consultants sometimes look for softer indicators such as signs of self-consciousness, the presence of a cluster organization, or a reputation or brand.[34] Porter's 1990 conception of a cluster as a grouping of firms at the national level that succeeds in international competition makes performance integral to his definition.

Growing Political Support

The Chretien liberal government did move quickly from 1997 on to increase research funding for universities and to shift resources from government labs, but active promotion of innovation and of clusters did not take hold until almost ten years after the recommendations were published and seven years after they became Liberal Party policy. Liberal policy documents for 1997[35] and 2002 repeated key ideas from the 1994 Redbook, (and Porter's 1991 report), providing evidence that the ideas were persisting among Liberal policy-makers.[36] Interestingly, sections of the Redbooks based on the Porter analysis were being quoted in departmental discussion papers by 1998,[37] suggesting that Redbook policies were also insinuating themselves into the culture in the federal bureaucracy.

In 1998, for example, the National Research Council (NRC) and the Natural Sciences and Engineering Research Council (NSERC) funded the Innovations Systems Research Network (ISRN), a multi-year multi-researcher study of innovation systems and clusters. The Social Sciences and Humanities Research Council (SSHRC) funded a second round beginning in 2001. It is significant that the second round shifted the emphasis from innovation networks to the cluster model. When the second round wound up in 2005, ISRN researchers had examined 27 clusters or potential clusters across the country. Over the course of the project researchers met regularly with senior people from HRDC,

Figure 7.2
CDAW Cluster Model

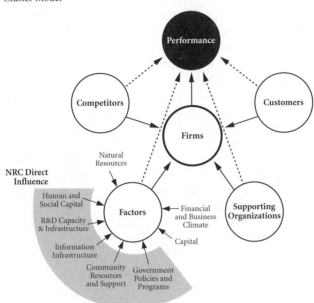

Industry Canada, Statistics Canada, and, in the Ontario government with the Ministry of economic development and technology. Links with the relevant departments in other provincial were also established.

For the researchers the ISRN was clearly an exciting project, but its role in the evolution of economic policy is particularly interesting. It helped established a national network of senior bureaucrats with a more or less common understanding of innovation and cluster development. The ISRN contributed directly to a process of cultural change within the federal government and to a lesser extent within some provincial bureaucracies. It was understood in this light by some of the senior bureaucrats and by some of the senior researchers involved.

A turning point may have been reached in 2002 when the federal government conducted a 10-month cross-country consultation ending in November with a "National Summit on Innovation." The summit was attended by the Prime Minister and over 500 influential Canadians. The stated objective of this time-consuming and costly process was to "engage partners from the private sector, non-government organizations, academia and government in shaping the priorities for Canada's Innovation Strategy, and to seek commitment from all sectors for a Canadian innovation and learning action plan."[38] An unstated objective was to engage a still largely uncomprehending public service and local political representatives in a set of policies that had originated outside of the bureaucracy. It had taken over a decade for policies that had been articulated by academics, supported by a large part of the business community, and adopted by a political party when it was out of power to be grafted onto the federal program machinery.

A key element of the National Innovation Strategy was the National Research Council's new responsibility to contribute to the development of at least 10 internationally recognized clusters by 2010.[39] Between 2000 and the present, the NRC has received over $300 million in four rounds of funding to establish and reinforce cluster initiatives across the country.[40] In 2005 the NRC published a report[41] on its cluster-building activities called Building Technology Clusters across Canada. The report states that "Stimulating the growth of community-based technology clusters across Canada is an important part of NRC's business" and that "NRC has played a critical role in the development of emerging and mature clusters across Canada such as Ottawa (IT), Montréal (biopharmaceuticals) and Saskatoon (plant biotechnology)."

Some of the clusters supported by the NRC are very large – the Montreal life-sciences and aerospace clusters employ 37,000 and 35,000 respectively. Others are quite small and speculative. The NRC is investing heavily in the Saskatoon biotech, nutricutical and bio-products cluster. According to the NRC report, Saskatoon is home to 35 companies involved in agricultural biotech and another 30 "nutraceutical and functional food companies" which, with the related public sector employs some 1,100 staff. The NRC will attempt to anchor a PEI bio-resources technology cluster by investing in a $31.5 million institute for Nutriscience and Health and it is providing $8.45 million to help Halifax develop a life-sciences cluster that now has "over 60 core companies." The NRC claims to have initiated the cluster-building process for a Newfoundland ocean technology cluster in 2001 and directed $20 million in federal funds to the cluster in 2002. As of October 2004 there were more than 40 ocean technology firms in St. John's, with 11 housed in a $6.5 million facility largely funded by the NRC. The NRC has been working on the New Brunswick "information technology/e-business cluster" since it first received ACOA funding in 2000. In 2005 the cluster had grown to 200 firms, 75% of which employ fewer than 20 people. The NRC has also made its mark in advancing Cape Breton's "nascent wireless systems cluster," helping to secure a $7.8 million project.

Surprisingly, the Sudbury cluster – with over 300 MS&S firms in 2005, with estimates of MS&S employment that range upwards from 8,000, and approximately 6000 more working in mining, has received no attention from the NRC. The oversight was not because the cluster was invisible. It had been identified by Porter in 1991, and in fact even earlier under Ontario premier David Peterson. It was not because the cluster did not fit the mandate of the NRC. The Sudbury cluster is clearly more promising than several that the NRC has committed resources to. Senior NRC officials have explained to the author that the NRC could not act in an area that was the responsibility of Natural Resources Canada.

A more convincing reason for the neglect was almost the lack of champions at the provincial level through the 1990's. The Ontario provincial government's views of innovation have shifted toward Porter's strategy very slowly over the last ten years. The 1997 (Conservative) budget papers, for example, expressed a commitment to not investing in innovation: "The Government's plan is to create a positive business climate to unleash the power of private-sector job creation – by cutting taxes" and went on "The Province's plan – cut taxes, invest wisely, and rely on the private sector for job creation and economic growth – will work for R&D just as it is working in other areas. Supporting R&D through tax cuts is one important way of creating good, long-lasting jobs."

The difference between provincial and federal approaches persisted through the 1990s. The Ontario Competitive City Regions (OCCR) Partnership begun in 1999, for example, brought together Human Resources Development Canada, Industry Canada and its Federal Economic Development Initiative in Northern Ontario (FedNor)), the Government of Ontario (represented by the Ministry of Economic Development and Trade), and other agencies. The Partnership funded a series of local symposia for communities with populations greater than 100,000, at least one university, and at least and one college. The symposia in North Bay and Sudbury in 2000–2001 were actively encouraged by Fednor staff to identify the economic clusters that could serve as the basis for growth. Direction from the province was virtually non-existent. In 2000, Industry Canada was actively promoting the cluster approach at the community level through its regional development staff. The province had no strategy to offer.

In 2001 the province began taking a more activist stance, responding at least in part to pressure from the business community. The Speech from the Throne announced a Task Force on Competitiveness, Productivity and Economic Progress, to be led by Roger L. Martin, Dean of the Joseph L. Rotman School of Management at the University of Toronto. The Task Force was to measure and monitor Ontario's productivity, competitiveness and economic progress compared to other provinces and the U.S. states and to report to the public on a regular basis. The task force was supported by an independent, not-for-profit Institute for Competitiveness and Prosperity headed by Martin and funded by the Government of Ontario.

Martin's appointment was evidence of the growing influence of Porter's 1991 study. Before becoming Dean of the Rotman School in 1998 Martin was a director the company that produced the report, *Canada at the Crossroads*. In 2000 he co-authored, with Porter, *Canadian Competitiveness: Nine Years after the Crossroads*, a review of progress in implementing the recommendations in *Canada at the Crossroads*. The Institute's first working paper *A View of Ontario: Ontario's Clusters of Innovation*.[42] It was a "comprehensive view of Ontario's industry clusters" and "the result of collaboration with Porter's Institute for Strategy and Competitiveness."

A change of government in 2003 returned the province to a more interventionist stance. The Liberal's Budget Speech in 2005 promised to create a Research Council of Ontario to coordinate and align research and commercialization investments. The language is eerily similar to that of the early 1990s. The Budget also projected over 500 million dollars of spending for a new Ontario Research Fund (ORF) to support scientific, technological and medical research in Ontario universities, colleges, research hospitals and institutions. The fund replaced a 1997 Ontario Research and Development Challenge which required matching funds from industry. Then in June of 2005 Premier Dalton McGinty appointed himself minister of Research and Innovation. Overall, the new government has signaled that it sees innovation leadership coming from public sector institutions rather than primarily from industry.

Although the decade after *Canada at the Crossroads* was one of growing political momentum for both an innovation strategy and the cluster approach, practical progress was much more limited. In *Canadian Competitiveness: Nine Years after the Crossroads* Porter and Roger Martin concluded that Canada was "most definitely slipping in competitiveness[43]. Moreover, many of the weaknesses relate to innovation in one form or another" and that "There is room for governments to show greater entrepreneurial acumen and zeal in providing support to clusters."

PROGRESS FOR THE MSS&S CLUSTER

The thrust of the preceding sections has been first, that developing industrial clusters has become Canadian policy and second, that there is an MS&S cluster in Sudbury that fits all the criteria for active promotion. The cluster was well established and showed significant growth potential even in 1991 when it was identified by Porter in one of the key documents in developing Canada's innovation strategy. The cluster presented an opportunity to build on Canada's existing strength in resource production to develop industries based on advanced technologies. It offered an existing concentration of "advanced and specialized factors." It promised to reinforce the dangerously weak Canadian machinery sector. It presented a unique opportunity to promote economic development in northern Ontario, one of Canada's most economically depressed regions. Decisions already made in the 1980s by the provincial government had laid the foundations for a research-intensive cluster.

The two most significant public initiatives associated with the MS&S sector after 1991 were, first, the development, by the Ministry of Northern Development and Mines (MNDM), of the Ontario Mining Industry Cluster Council (OMICC) in 2004, and second, progress toward creation of a Center for Excellence in Mining (CEMI – pronounced semi).

OMICC was created in 2004, by MNDM Minister Bartolucci, building on an initiative begun under the previous government. OMICC consists of "representatives of the mineral industry, academia, government and communities." Although it is called a "cluster" council it is in fact a mineral sector council. Representatives of MS&S firms, specifically the Canadian Association of Mining Equipment and Services for Export (CAMESE) at the national level and The Sudbury Area Mining Supply and Service Association (SMASSA) in Northern Ontario are grouped with "other key stakeholders" and not identified as central players. The evolution of OMICC makes it clear that the provincial government was prepared to listen carefully to the mining companies and saw the MS&S firms as a secondary issue. MNDN staff worked to ensure that the council represented the whole province and to make sure that Sudbury was not identified as "the cluster."

Nonetheless, the mandate OMICC is to "lever the current mineral industry assets to create a larger and more globally competitive cluster of mineral and related industries and organizations." The method is by bringing together the cluster of mineral-related industries and organizations. The boundaries of the so-called cluster are those of the province of Ontario, but within the council it is increasingly recognized that assets will have to be concentrated in the existing cluster.

The only recommendations by the OMICC Co-Chairs in February 2005 that were among the key items identified in *Canada at the Crossroads* were support for mining education and for R&D. Progress on the first was underway before the OMICC Co-Chairs reported. Porter had noted that provincial funding policies for post-secondary education discouraged specialization by universities[44] and inhibited the development of the relatively costly but necessary programs in science, engineering and technology fields. These policies prevented smaller universities from launching PhD programs that were industry-specific. Throughout the 1990s they prevented Laurentian University from developing programs around the mining industry. The effect was to inhibit the development of the research base for the mining industry in Sudbury. Research funding necessarily went to southern universities, inhibiting both the growth of the cluster and the economic development of the region. The problem has been addressed since 2002 and Laurentian has gone on to create programs in Precambrian Geology and Natural Resource Engineering. The recent Rae report on postsecondary education also supported differentiation, making room for linking post-secondary education to local clusters, a policy that can only be pursued by the provincial government.

The Center of Excellence in Mining Innovation has been presented as an initiative of OMICC although it was initiated and has been driven by FedNor, the federal agency for economic development in Northern Ontario. CEMI is intended to deal with the fact that "much of Canada's mining related R&D is being undertaken in an uncoordinated manner." It is significant that FedNor has been the driving force and that the Federal government is expected to be the most significant source of funds through the National Research Council.

Fourteen years after *Canada at the Crossroads*, a branch of Industry Canada is pursuing a cluster-based innovation strategy for northern Ontario and for the mining industry.

CEMI is still at the proposal stage. A business plan was released in May 2005. The plan calls for a national center of excellence in mining and exploration to be located in Sudbury. The rationale for locating CEMI in Sudbury has four parts: 1) the largest concentration of Canadian mining is in Northern Ontario; 2) Sudbury is the largest mining district in the world; 3) Sudbury has a concentration of supply and service firms; and 4) Sudbury has a concentration of internationally renowned research. The CEMI business plan shows that the Sudbury Cluster has finally been accepted in key parts of the federal and provincial bureaucracies. It is striking, however, that the NRC is still not participating directly.

An additional sign of progress is that the MS&S cluster is explicitly mentioned in the plan. While most of the proposed $100 million in funding for R&D is to be directed toward short-term initiatives identified by the mining industry, provision has been made for telerobotics and automation, projects not currently of interest to the Canadian mining industry. It is hoped that these initiatives will open markets for Canadian suppliers. In line with the current federal emphasis on commercialization, (a theme also strongly present in the studies at the beginning of the 1990s) the CEMI plan emphasizes commercialization and spin-off companies. Existing SMEs however, are largely ignored and the local MS&S cluster has no explicit role in CEMI.

CONCLUSIONS

Although the case for promoting the Sudbury cluster is easily made in retrospect, it took the two senior levels of government 14 years to recognize the opportunity flagged in *Canada at the Crossroads*. At the time this chapter was written in mid 2005 neither of the senior levels of government had committed significant resources to the project. The failure is puzzling when the NRC has already committed significant efforts to developing clusters that were arguably less promising in Nova Scotia and Prince Edward Island.

Jurisdictional issues certainly contributed to the problem. The strategic analysis was developed for the federal government, but the key responsibilities for natural resources and education are provincial domains. Within the federal government, agencies for regional development, science, and industry are within Industry Canada, but mining falls under Natural Resources Canada. Within the provincial government, responsibility is distributed as well, although the pattern differs. Mining and regional development are under the same Ministry, MNDM, but industrial development is the responsibility of the Ministry of Economic Development and Technology (roughly equivalent to Industry Canada). It is as though Fednor were transferred to the minerals branch of NRCCan.

Lack of capacity at the provincial level was also a barrier. MNDM had no staff economists as a result of cutbacks in the 1990s. Arguably the ministry had neither the capacity to recognize the opportunity nor the resources to campaign for federal support. It is unlikely that the ministry had the staff to develop the suggestions in *Canada at the Crossroads* into an economically coherent plan. In 2003, when the cluster process was begun in Ontario, the Minister and the Deputy Minister of Northern development and Mines virtually begged the mining industry representatives to provide leadership. Industry leaders responded that they wanted the ministry to continue to provide coordination. It is a feature of the Canadian confederation that "although the provincial governments collectively constitute a major factor in the Canadian economy, individually they are relatively minor when compared to the significance of the central government."[45] Even mighty Ontario relies on the federal government for data and analysis.

Part of the explanation of policy inertia lies in the very long time needed to make a new strategy part of the political culture. It may take a decade to harness the machinery of government. Although the ideas that were to become Canada's innovation strategy were described fairly completely by 1991 it is possible that building consensus and collecting information cannot be done much faster.

Even when both federal and provincial governments began to support clusters with funds and institutional changes, they had great difficulty identifying clusters to support. The practical solution adopted by the NRC appears to have been to deal with the clusters that organized themselves and were effectively championed by the province and/or municipality. This approach probably resulted in imperfect and somewhat politicized selection, but may produce relatively efficient interventions because it ensures that the resources of the community and the cluster are mobilized at the beginning of the NRC's participation.

Another partial explanation is that the Sudbury cluster lacked the governance machinery needed to represent it when the senior levels were looking for horses to back. The PEI cluster supported by the NRC, for example, was objectively less promising than the Sudbury MS&S cluster, but PEI has a provincial government with a premier and ten cabinet ministers serving a population smaller than that of the City of Sudbury. On the other hand, Northern Ontario was represented by a single minister with no direct say in industrial development, education, research, trade or any of the other issues central to the innovation strategies.

Wolfe[46] and Creutzberg[47] among others have argued that the ability of the national and even provincial governments to influence local economic development is declining and that local governance is becoming more important. This argument supplies the increasingly local cluster approach with the beginning of a political theory. The implicit theory is that growth increasingly depends on local governance, local intelligence, mobilizing local resources – in short on political development and autonomy.

There are signs that the Sudbury cluster was slow to be recognized simply because it was a resource extraction area. Over a century of generating resource rents that flowed to metropolitan regions and supported metropolitan commercial growth has established a vision of how the economy should work. In 2002 many public officials believed it was neither possible nor desirable to promote the MS&S in Northern Ontario. Even MNDM staff argued that the MS&S sector in southern Ontario deserved to be promoted by MNDN at least as much as the Sudbury sector, a remarkable view given that the MS&S sector in the south falls in neither of the Ministry's two areas of responsibility. The national organization of exporting MS&S firms, CAMESE, which continues to receive MNDM funding, actively opposed the formation of a local supplier organization. Northern Ontario suffered silently the kind of economic colonialism that Western Canada has struggled against.

Writing about New Brunswick, Donald Savoie concluded that "economic development in New Brunswick requires a constant pulling against gravity. Gravity does not come solely from the market forces or from the province's inherent inability to compete. It also comes from a federal government incapable or unwilling to accommodate regional interests in its policies other than those of vote rich Ontario and southern Quebec."[48] Savoie distinguishes northern and southern Quebec in this passage, but not Northern and southern Ontario. Northern Ontario in fact faces the double disadvantage of having two senior governments that tend to align with outside metropolitan interests.

The main lesson in the history of the Sudbury MS&S cluster are easy to extract if we try to imagine what might have happened if there had been an independent regional authority with its own economic analysis capacity, if there had been a Northern Ontario Economic think tank, or a PhD Program in regional economic development at Laurentian University. The implication for northern Ontario of *Canada at the Crossroads* would certainly have been recognized and elaborated. The strategy that is emerging with such difficulty in 2005 would clearly have developed earlier and would have been kept in front of decision-makers at all levels throughout the 1990's. At the end of the 1990s, when federal and provincial governments were prepared to act, deepening the Sudbury MS&S Cluster would have seemed both obvious and easy. This thought experiment suggests that a major barrier was the lack of brainpower committed to the problems of Northern Ontario.

Promoting the Sudbury MS&S cluster is perhaps the most direct possible response to the problem of Canadian underdevelopment. Ultimately the delay in promoting the Sudbury MS&S cluster may be precisely because shifting the focus from extraction to the MS&S sector required attacking the most basic distortion in the economy. Clusters in new industries are easier to identify and promote precisely because they are not embedded in an institutional structure and a configuration of interests committed to industrial strategies that have failed. As *Canada at the Crossroads* put it, "resource abundance contributes to a set of policies that reduce the incentives to upgrade and make it difficult to move beyond the factor-driven stage of development."[49] It also contributes to a set of attitudes that make it very difficult to imagine a different approach.

If resource dependency is the old horse and innovation-based supply industries are the new horse, Canada is not even trying to change horses yet. Federal and provincial governments have still to understand the need, they still have to make key decisions, and they still have to commit resources. So far the innovation strategy has failed to accomplish its goals in northern Ontario.

NOTES

1 The term is usually ascribed to John Baird, Executive Director of the Canadian Association of Mining Equipment and Service Exporters.

2 Natural Resources Canada. Canadian Suppliers of Mining Goods and Services: Links between Canadian mining companies and selected sectors of the Canadian Economy, September 2000, 25. http://www.nrca.n.gc.ca/mms/pdf/minegs_e.pdf.

3 D. Robinson, "Sudbury's Mining Supply and Service Industry: From a Cluster "In Itself" to a Cluster "For Itself," in David Wolfe and Lucas, eds. *Global Networks and Local Linkages: The Paradox of Cluster Development in an Open Economy.* (McGill-Queen's University Press, 2005).

4 The most striking example occurred in April 2002 when the Institute for Competitiveness & Prosperity published its first working paper, *A View of Ontario: Ontario's Clusters of Innovation.* The paper listed the clusters that the Institute had identified in each Ontario city. Neither mining nor the MS&S sector appeared on the list for Sudbury. The large number of MS&S employees were scattered across 17 NAIC codes, none of which alone had more employees than the metropolitan average.

5 Advisory Council on Adjustment 1989, *Report* (Ministry of Supply and Services Canada, Cat. No. C2-116/1989, 1989.

6 Industry Science and Technology Canada. *An Overview of Selected Studies on Canada's Prosperity and Competitiveness.* Ministry of Supply and Services Canada. C2-195/1992E 1992.

7 M.E. Porter, and the Monitor Company, *Canada at the Crossroads: the Reality of a new Competitive Environment.* Ottawa, Ont. Business Council on National Issues, and Minister of Supply and Services Canada, 1991.

8 D.A. Wolfe, "Innovation Policy for the Knowledge-Based Economy: From the Red Book to the White Paper," in Bruce Doern, ed. *How Ottawa Spends, 2002–2003: The Security Aftermath and National Priorities.* (Oxford University Press, 2002), 137-150.

9 M.E. Porter, *The Competitive Advantage of Nations,* (The Free Press. 1990).

10 Porter, *Crossroads,* 46.

11 Porter classifies food and beverages as production for final consumption, but points out that most of Canada's exports were relatively unprocessed products such as fish and wheat.

12 See for example E.R Grilli and M.C. Yang, "Primary commodity prices, manufactured good prices and the terms of trade of developing countries: What the long run shows," *World Bank Economic Review*, 2, (1988), 1-47.

13 Porter, *Crossroads*, 43.

14 Ibid., 15.

15 M.E. Porter and R. Martin, *Canadian Competitiveness: Nine Years after the Crossroads.* Paper present to the CSLS Conference on the Canada-US Productivity Gap. January 22, 2000, 7.

16 Porter in *Crossroads*, 5, proposed an analogue of Adam Smith's "progressive state," the "upgrading economy" – one that "relentlessly pursues greater productivity in existing products, using more efficient production processes, and migrating into more sophisticated and higher value industries."

17 Ibid., 93-6.

18 Porter was not the first to focus on agglomeration. Alfred Marshall (*Principles of Economics* [Macmillan. 1890]) described Industrial districts a hundred years before Porter. P. Maskell and L. Kebir draw out the differences among the three major conceptions, Marshallian industrial districts, Porter-style clusters, and innovation networks in, "What Qualifies as a Cluster Theory?," DRUID Working Paper No 05-09. http://www.druid.dk/wp/pdf_files/05-09.pdf 2005.

19 Porter, *Crossroads*, 44.

20 Ibid., 16, 53, 91.

21 Ibid., 43.

22 Ibid., 34, 41.

23 Ibid.

24 Ibid., 27.

25 See, for example R. Martin and P. Sunley, "Deconstructing Clusters: Chaotic Concept or Policy Panacea," *Journal of Economic Geography* 1, 3, (2003): 3-35.

26 R. Johnson, "Clusters: A Review of Their Basis and Development in Asia," *Policy and Practice* 6, 3, (2004): 3.

27 E. Cassidy, C. Davis, D. Arthurs, and D. Wolfe, "Measuring the National Research Council's Technology Cluster Initiatives." CRIC Cluster Conference. Beyond Cluster: Current Practices & Future Strategies. June 30-July 1, 2005, 4.

28 Robinson, "Sudbury's Mining Supply," 22.

29 G.M.P. Swann and M. Prevezer, "A comparison of the dynamics of industrial clusterings in computing and biotechnology," *Research Policy* 25 (1996): 1141.

30 M.E. Porter, "Location, Competition, and Economic Development: Local Clusters in a Global Economy," *Economic Development Quarterly* 14,1 (2002): 15.

31 M.E. Porter, "Clusters and the New Economics of Competition," *Harvard Business Review*, (Nov/Dec 1998): 23-33.

32 OECD, *Boosting Innovation: The Cluster Approach* (OECD, 1999).

33 Cassidy, et. al., "Measuring," 7.

34 Robinson, "Sudbury's Mining Supply," 10.

35 Liberal Party of Canada, *Securing Our Future Together: Preparing Canada for the 21st Century*, 1997.

36 A very high percentage of Redbook commitments have been carried out according to an assessment on CBC.ca, which tracked every promise in that pamphlet to see what action has been taken since November 2000.

37 See for example Natural Resources Canada, *From Mineral Resources to Manufactured Products: Toward a Value-Added Mineral and Metal Strategy for Canada*, 1998. http://www.nrcan.gc.ca/mms/pdf/val-e.pdf, or Environment Canada, *Progress in Pollution Prevention 1996–1997* Annual Report of the Pollution Prevention Coordinating Committee. Ottawa, Ont. 1998 http://www.ec.gc.ca/p2progress/1996–1997/en/minister.cfm.

38 Industry Canada, *Achieving Excellence: Investing in People, Knowledge and Opportunity: Canada's Innovation Strategy* (Industry Canada, 2002).

39 Cassidy, Measuring, 5.

40 Ibid., 5.

41 National Research Council, *Building Technology Clusters Across Canada*, 2005. NR16-85/2005E-PDF, 0-662-39995-1. http://www.nrc-cnrc.gc.ca2005.

42 Institute for Competitiveness & Prosperity, *A View of Ontario: Ontario's Clusters of Innovation*. WP No.1. April 2002.Ironically, the methodology used to identify clusters at the CMA level actually drew attention away from the Sudbury cluster that Porter had pointed to in 1991 on the basis of national data and interviews.

43 Porter and Martin, *Canadian Competitiveness*, presented new evidence that the Canadian economy was at risk. Data from the 1999 Global Competitiveness Report rated Canadian company operations and strategy as 12th in the world, far below Canada's standing in the microeconomic environment for business. Canadian ratings on Capacity for Innovation (20th), Product Designs (19th), Value Chain Presence (17th), Control of International Distribution (15th) and Extent of Branding (14th) are all similarly disappointing. In 2002, the last recorded OECD figure, our annual expenditure of GDP on R&D was 1.8 per cent, which is far below the U.S., France and Germany, and below the 2.33 per cent average of the total OECD.

44 Porter, *Crossroads*, 50, 93.

45 F.F. Schindeler, *Responsible Government in Ontario*. (University of Toronto Press, 1969)

46 D. Wolfe, "Community Participation and Emerging Forms of Governance in Economic Development Strategy" Paper prepared for the 2005 CPSA Annual Conference, London, Ontario, June 2-4.

47 T. Creutzberg, "Scalar Dimensions of Non-Market Governance in Knowledge Economies." Paper prepared for the 2005 CPSA Annual Conference, London, Ontario, June 2-4.

48 D.J. Savoie, *Pulling Against Gravity: Economic Development in New Brunswick During the McKenna Years*. (Institute for Research on Public Policy. 2001)

49 Porter, *Crossroads*, 29.

8 Commercializing Technologies Through Collaborative Networks: the Environmental Industry and the Role of CETACS

BERT BACKMAN-BEHARRY
AND ROBERT SLATER

This chapter examines the role of a unique public policy instrument, the Canadian Environmental Technology Advancement Centers (CETAC), which were established over ten years ago by Environment Canada with the mandate to facilitate the commercialization of environmental technologies and to thereby foster international competitiveness through the commercialization and application of such technologies.[1] The centers, established in Ontario, Quebec and Alberta as not-for-profit, private sector corporations, with private-sector oriented management and their own Boards of Directors, work in cooperation with provincial governments, environmental industry associations and the private sector. However, they operate at arms length from governments. They therefore fit in a unique space in the public-private sector model of arms-length governance and operations.

The centers' core funding has been provided by Environment Canada. Over the past 10 years this has been reduced by 60%. Projects have been supported by other government and private sector funding, allowing the centers to continue their public policy focus on facilitating small businesses to commercialize environmental technologies. The three centers have adapted their services to meet the needs of the markets in their respective geographic areas, but follow a similar network-based collaborative business model for capacity building and market development for small to medium sized enterprises (SME's).

Over the last decade, this unique, but little-recognized experiment in public/private sector partnership, has established a sound track record in successfully supporting hundreds of SME's to commercialize environmental technologies and to promote the adoption of sustainable development and pollution prevention practices in various industry sectors – such as the manufacturing sector in Ontario, the agricultural sector in Quebec and the oil and gas sector in Alberta.

This chapter is organized into five sections. The first section deals with the initial establishment of the CETACs. The second and third sections deal, respectively, with basic features of the global environmental industry and the Canadian environmental industry. This is followed by a discussion of the innovation and technological commercialization dynamics in the environment sector. The final section examines the CETAC approach and its track record. Conclusions then follow.

The chapter argues that an industry sector focus has been critical to the CETAC's success in facilitating small businesses to commercialize technologies. Further, the value added of the CETAC approach to the commercialization of new technologies is that it is practical, non-bureaucratic and client-based. It demands experienced management, strong industry networks and an appropriate governance structure. There are thus practical lessons to be learnt from the application of this network-based model in the environmental sector.

THE ESTABLISHMENT OF THE CETACS

Environmental Policy Evolution

In the early 1980s, Environment Canada initiated studies to better understand what was termed the 'environmental industry sector.' At that time, this was seen as the goods and services that were required to meet environmental quality objectives related to air and water pollution control and the management of domestic and industrial waste. It soon became clear that the sector was much more than pollution control and included the transformation of industrial processes so that less energy and raw material were consumed and less waste generated. There was the realization that this was a policy driven business and that the principal determinants of its size, character and rate of development were laws, regulations and their enforcement.

This gave rise to new thinking on the design of products and services offered by both the private and public sectors. There was much enthusiasm for the notion that those countries, governments, businesses, universities, etc. that could work out how to do this first would have a comparative advantage that would serve them well in a world with a likely fifty per cent increase in population within the next fifty years. During the period of the 1980s, the policy focus also shifted from domestically driven issues to ones that originated on the global stage. Solutions to problems such as the thinning of the ozone layer, climate change, and toxic chemicals were developed by international organizations and implementation became the responsibility of nation states.

In 1987, the politics of the environment shifted as a result of the UN commissioned Brundtland report, entitled "Our Common Future."[2] This report introduced the concept of sustainable development that "meets the needs of the present without compromising the ability of future generations to meet their own needs." Also, in calling for cooperation with industry, it helped legitimize the 'jobs and environment' argument, supplanting the earlier 'jobs or the environment' view. This shift coincided with a rise in the 'top of mind' ranking in Canadian public opinion polling of the 'environment' as the most important issue, supplanting economic considerations for the first time. The environment became a frequent topic for Prime Ministerial speeches, engagements and state visits and new laws were proclaimed.

This culminated in the "UN Conference on Environment and Development" in Rio de Janeiro in 1992 where the largest single assembly of heads of government and heads of state in human history was convened. They signed Conventions on Climate Change and Biodiversity, adopted a set of principles to guide the actions of individual states and agreed to Agenda 21 as a work plan for sustainable development for the 21st century.[3] They also announced more initiatives in support of sustainable development than has probably ever been announced in any 4-day period.

The environmental industry sector and its prospects represented a readily understandable and exciting manifestation of this new energy and sense of purpose. In Canada, the Department of Industry formed an Environmental Affairs Sector with the mandate to develop a strategy to promote the industry. Statistics Canada started to collect data and Environment Canada launched the first GLOBE conference and industry trade show in Vancouver in 1990. Later, as a result of Canadian initiatives, industry trade shows were held in parallel with diplomatic meetings on the Biodiversity Convention to emphasize the connection between policy and business opportunities.

FORMATION OF THE CETAC'S

These factors led to the issuing, in 1992, of a contract between Environment Canada and Industry, Science and Technology Canada (now Industry Canada) to Doyletech Corporation to assess options for strengthening Canada's supply capability in the environmental industry. It resulted in a report based on a survey of Canadian companies engaged in the supply of products and services for environmental applications, as well as on a survey of other constituencies such as the investment community and regulatory authorities that establish environmental rules and standards and enforce them.[4]

The report found that the major barriers to a stronger supply capability were regulatory and financial in nature. Other barriers that were identified were related to "technical" and "market" issues but were not rated as highly as the first two. The report recommended the establishment of a facility (or facilities or a network of facilities) that would assist firms in overcoming such barriers and that would meet the following criteria:

- Linkages to the R&D community, the investment community and to the regulatory authorities.
- The ability to assist firms in technology assessment, scale-up and commercialization.
- The ability to function on a national basis; and be
- Partially funded by the private sector and other levels of government and operating at arms length from government.[5]

In 1993, three Canadian Environmental Technology Advancement Centers were established in Calgary, Alberta (CETAC-WEST), in Toronto, Ontario (OCETA) and in Sherbrooke, Quebec (Enviro-Access), with the mandate to facilitate the commercialization of environmental technologies and to thereby foster international competitiveness through Canada's commercialization and application of such technologies. Each of the CETAC's was provided with an initial funding for core operations from Environment Canada at $1 million annually, with a four-year commitment.

The CETAC's were established as not-for-profit, private sector corporations, with their own Boards of Directors and operating at arms length from government. Three experienced CEO's, with extensive private sector backgrounds were recruited (and remain to the current time) and the centers were provided the freedom to execute on their common mandate in the light of the unique circumstances in their respective marketplaces. Five years after their inception, Environment Canada, as part of the federal fiscal budgeting process, significantly cut the core funding to each of the CETAC's by 60 per cent to $400K annually, an amount that is annually reassessed but which still remains for the current fiscal year 2005–2006. In 2004, funding at this level was assured by Environment Canada for the next three years.

THE FUNDAMENTALS OF THE GLOBAL ENVIRONMENTAL INDUSTRY

The Global Environmental Industry – Size and Definition

Global market estimates for the size and growth of the environmental industry are varied due to the difficulties in defining and measuring the industry and the lack of universally accepted criteria for defining the boundaries of the industry. The industry covers a heterogeneous set of goods and services, from those used to clean up pollutants ("end of pipe" technologies), to those that prevent pollution, to those that clean up past environmental damage (e.g. soil remediation). An added complication is the interest in including renewable energy, and clean technologies and products (e.g. fuel cells) in the definition of the environmental industry. This leads to considerable difficulty in making reliable comparisons of studies performed by different organizations, even within the same country.

Consequently, estimates for the size of the global industry in 2002 ranged from over US$ 550 billion[6] to US$ 800 billion.[7] To put the Canadian market in context, Statistics Canada estimated that Canadian revenues from environmental-related activities in 2002 were less than 3% of the global market.[8] The global market itself is estimated to grow to almost US$1 Trillion by 2010.[9]

In the global market, the OECD countries currently dominate. The largest established markets for environmental goods and services are in the North America, Western Europe and Japan, which account for roughly 85% of global expenditures. These markets are expected to grow relatively slowly at rates around 2% compared with expected growth in emerging markets' in the order of 6-10% per year (Ibid).

The US is estimated to be the largest producer and consumer of environmental goods and services. It generated over $220 Billion (US) in revenues in 2002, while Western Europe and Japan accounted for roughly $165 Billion and $92 Billion (US) in revenues respectively.[10] Although major new market demands are expected from emerging nations in Asia (particularly from China and India) and Latin America, tariff and non-tariff barriers could restrict this environmental trade.[11]

Greatest Global Demand for Environmental Products and Services

The greatest global demands for environmental goods and services are in the water and waste water management, and in the waste management segments, which account for almost 80% of global expenditures.[12] The water and waste water segment includes the provision of equipment and services related to the analysis and assessment of needs, and the design, installation and operation of partial or complete water-related systems. Water and waste water treatment present significant business opportunities, with the global water market estimated at about 45% of the global environmental market.[13]

Cleaner technologies upstream in production processes (despite difficulties in categorizing them) are having important impacts in reducing pollutants. The water and waste water segment mainly depends on public expenditure (for example in some OECD countries accounting for almost 70 per cent of demand). However, it also depends on the manufacturing segment compliance with environmental regulations. It is the most mature environmental segment for large global firms and the barriers to entry are mainly related to costs.[14]

The waste management segment includes the provision of products, systems and services that reduce the quantity of solid waste produced or that collect, treat and dispose of solid waste. It is the second largest segment in almost all OECD countries and often includes waste recycling technologies and products. New modes of treating solid waste especially hazardous waste and recycling (paper, plastic, packaging etc.) are expected to grow over the next few years and to benefit from rising disposal charges in the medium term. In the longer term, the emerging regulatory approach in developed countries, which favours pollution prevention and waste minimization strategies, as well as cleaner technologies, are expected to reduce clean-up and recycling volumes.

Market Drivers in the Environmental Industry

The single, most important driver for growth in the global environmental industry is the policy driver – environmental legislation and regulation, combined with regulatory enforcement. This is a policy-driven business. Without this driver, it is highly unlikely that enlightened self-interest would drive businesses to invest in pollution prevention or control measures. In addition, legislation must be coupled with enforcement for business to pay attention.

Supporting drivers include: growing industrialization, market place demands, environmental awareness and legislation in emerging markets; liberalization of environmental technologies trade via bilateral and multilateral efforts; greater global interest in sustainable development; and broader application of environmental "best practices" by multinationals. Nevertheless, the key driver is the strength of legislation and of enforcement.

Industry Structure

The global environment industry is characterized by a large number of SMEs together with a small number of large companies that dominate a few market segments. The supply side is very diverse (from divisions of large chemical firms to individual consultants) and has a different structure of activities and size distribution in different countries.

Large firms are more common in the German industry, while small firms are more important in Canada, the US, Italy and Switzerland.[15] In addition, there is a higher degree of diversification (in terms of the range of environmental products and services produced) by the larger companies in the more mature environmental segments (e.g. water and waste water). A recent announcement by General Electric that they were promoting their business line for green products and services with a sales target of over $20 billion annually and a research investment of $1.5 billion per year by 2010 may suggest that a turning point has been reached in the sector.[16]

The dominance of SMEs in the Canadian environmental industry can be illustrated by the fact that, in 2002, small establishments with less than 100 employees made up 93% of all establishments and accounted for 54% (or $8.5 Billion Cdn.) of total Canadian environment industry revenues.[17]

Changes in Industry Structure

The structure of the global environment industry is changing, with a shift from suppliers with "end of pipe" equipment and clean-up services to those with integrated and "clean" environmental technologies. This structural change is being driven by the increased policy and regulatory focus on integrating clean environmental technologies into industry production processes.[18] This policy focus, in turn, reflects greater societal concerns in the developed nations about clean water, clean air and climate change.

In the longer term, as regulatory emphasis moves upstream to the production processes of "polluting" industries, these demands will likely result in suppliers of environmental goods and services providing more complete packages – from research, design and equipment production, to providing services related to the installation and application of equipment. This trend will impact SMES, which, because they are small and niche-oriented, will likely face consolidation, acquisition, or greater opportunities for cooperative arrangements with larger firms intent on producing "packaged" products.

Growth Opportunities and Competition

From a global perspective, the water and waste water management and waste management segments are expected to continue to provide solid growth opportunities for innovative technologies and entrepreneurial firms. In the developed nations, rising demands are forecast for clean technologies and for green energy (e.g. biomass, wind, solar etc.).

A large proportion of business environmental investment expenditures is made by manufacturing firms, energy production firms and utilities. Within manufacturing, the major purchasers of environmental goods and services are the traditional processing industries such as chemicals, iron and steel, metals, and pulp and paper. Within energy production, the major purchasers of environmental goods and services, or the "receptor industry" are the oil and gas integrated and mid-sized companies.

These industries have made high levels of investment to meet regulations and reduce pollution, and, for business reasons, make the shift towards clean technologies when required to do so by public policy. Such expenditures to meet environmental requirements would make the most business sense when they also provide economic benefits from process modifications, such as reducing the consumption of raw materials and energy – hence the increased interest in energy and eco-efficiency business opportunities.[19]

The demands of the Kyoto Protocol are also expected to create business growth opportunities, particularly for more eco-efficient production processes in those countries that have ratified the Protocol, such as Canada. Reflecting these demands and also the higher demands from Asia and Latin America, the environmental industry has become highly competitive, with governments actively supporting the development of local firms, particularly in export market penetration. The creation of the CETAC's over ten years ago was an attempt at the Canadian federal level to support the growth of an indigenous industry.

THE CANADIAN ENVIRONMENTAL INDUSTRY

Canada's Position in Global Market

Based on the Statistics Canada 2002 survey of the Canadian environmental industry, that used a broad definition of the industry and which focused on the end use of the goods and services, Canada has a relatively low global profile, with revenues from environmental-related activities estimated at $16 Billion (Cdn.) in 2002. Revenues were only slightly lower for the production of environmental goods such as equipment compared with the production of environmental services such as consulting.[20]

Industry Structure

According to Statistics Canada, there were roughly 8000 Canadian firms that produced environmental goods and services, either as the sole line of business or together with other activities. In fact, the estimated $16 Billion in environmental-related revenues represent 54% of the total revenues reported by firms that made up Canada's environmental industry in 2002. The total employment of these businesses was roughly 160,000 people, including those that performed environmental and non-environmental activities. SMES continued to dominate the Canadian environment industry, and firms employing less than 100 employees represented 93% of all firms.[21]

Comparisons of the industry in the years 2000 and 2002 show that there was an increase of almost 500 firms, primarily the result of the growth of the "Consulting Services" sector. Firms that sell "eco-efficiency" technologies that decrease material inputs, recover valuable byproducts and reduce energy consumption, continue to grow at a faster rate than average within the industry.[22]

Provincial Environmental Revenues and Exports

As in previous years, Ontario and Quebec generated the greatest environmental revenues in the year 2002, with Ontario accounting for $6.9 Billion and Quebec accounting for $3.1 Billion. Next in line were Alberta at $2.3 Billion and British Columbia at $1.9 Billion.[23]

Export markets in 2002 represented 9% of total Canadian environmental revenues, at $1.4 Billion. The US was by far the dominant export market, accounting for 80% of all exports, followed by Europe and Asia. With respect to the resident provinces of the three CETAC's, StatsCan estimated that the level of environmental exports was roughly 11% in Ontario, 8% in Quebec and 7% in Alberta.[24]

INNOVATION AND TECHNOLOGY COMMERCIALIZATION IN THE ENVIRONMENTAL SECTOR

The Innovation and Technology Commercialization System

The innovative capacity of a nation can be described as its ability to sustain its global competitiveness over time. The three main contributors to a nation's overall innovative capacity are viewed as: the common innovation infrastructure (e.g. research in basic science); the cluster-specific conditions that support innovation in particular groups of interconnected industries (e.g. regulatory drivers or technical skills in the environmental technology industry); and the strength of the linkages between these two factors (e.g. the ability of firms to connect basic research with the creation of environmental products or services that are needed by customers).[25]

Therefore the "innovation system," though broadly used to describe the process of transforming knowledge into new products and services, involves more than science and technology. It integrally requires a sound understanding of customers' needs and meeting those needs in specific markets through the commercialization of products and/or services by the private sector.

Figure 8.1 depicts the innovation system and the two key drivers of commercialization – technology push and market pull. The extensive linkages between the elements of the system are also shown.

The focus of this chapter is on the commercialization of environmental products and services, defined as the processes by which economic value is extracted from knowledge through the production and sale of new or significantly improved products and services According to the Conference Board, in order to commercialize successfully, a nation must excel in four areas – research, funding, institutions (e.g. infrastructure) and people (e.g. management skills). The strength of the linkages between these areas is seen as critical to the success of the entire commercialization system.[26]

Challenges in the Commercialization of New Technologies

The most fundamental business challenge for any private sector organization in introducing any new technology is that of creating value for the customer. Even if the technology at the research phase has demonstrated the promise to create value for the customer, the question still remains on how much of that

Figure 8.1

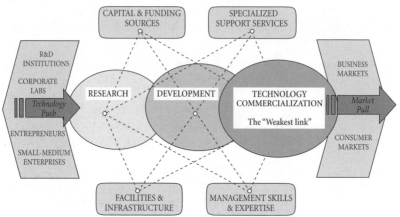

value the innovative firm will be able to capture. As has been emphasized repeatedly, understanding the mechanisms by which value will not only be created but captured, is critical for a concept or invention to become a successful commercial innovation.[27]

In addition, even after understanding the mechanisms by which value to the customer is captured, the firm in question, in order to execute on its strategy for value capture, must have the internal capabilities, distribution networks and other resources necessary to lever its knowledge. For example, for firms in the information technology and biotechnology sectors, the speed of commercialization and the time to market are key success factors.

Although the path from innovation to commercialization of technologies is much more complex with multiple feedback loops and linkages to developments outside the core skills of any one company, the diagram above illustrates, in a somewhat idealized fashion, the key stages of technology progression. The critical challenge in commercialization starts at the stage of "technology development" or the transition from a prototype to a commercial product that meets the market needs. This is the so-called "Valley of Death" stage that challenges all small, resource-constrained enterprises such as those that dominate the environmental industry in Canada.[28]

At this stage, product or service specifications appropriate to an identified market are identified and production processes are defined, allowing estimates of product/service cost. This is where initial verification of a commercial concept occurs, through further prototype work, through the identification of an appropriate market and possibly through the creation of intellectual property. It is at this stage that the worlds of research and development (R&D) and those of business and finance must interact to validate a business case and start to attract capital sufficient to permit initial production and marketing ("product and market development").

Figure 8.2

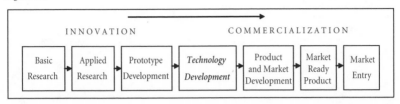

There are major skills and culture challenges at this stage. The worlds of the technologist (e.g. in the environmental sector) and the manager/investor are very different and each has different training, expectations, information sources and culture. The technologist's interests tend to be primarily in the realm of the technically innovative. The manager's interests are primarily in networking with complementary expertise, accessing other peoples' money, bringing new products to market and investing money to make a profit, regardless of the technology.

The Death Valley gap is therefore much more than money. Equally critical are considerations of market prospects, time to market, people competencies and cultures, and getting the best quality projects that would maximize the chances of commercial success.[29] The primary focus of the CETAC's work is on providing safe passage through the Death Valley gap for SME's in the environmental industry.

Peculiar Challenges in Commercializing Environmental Technologies

New technologies face high barriers to adoption relative to existing technologies for several reasons, including the perception of higher risk, a lack of experience with the new technology among managers and/or regulators or the fact that decision-makers may simply not be aware of the new technologies. Environmental technologies add an extra dimension of complexity in moving from innovation to commercialization.

This is partly the result of the fact that environmental resources are largely in the public domain where the private sector may be unable to capture all the benefits of the new technologies (i.e. in economic terms, the benefits are "non-appropriable"). Environmental technology development therefore fits in the gap between public and private goods.[30] As the diagram below suggests, in such a space, partnerships and collaboration are essential – a realization that is at the heart of the CETAC's modus operandi.

An added dimension of complexity is that environmental projects involve multiple stakeholder groups with divergent interests. There is no single bottom line and no single technology is likely to emerge that is perceived by all stakeholders as superior in all respects to competing alternatives.

Figure 8.3

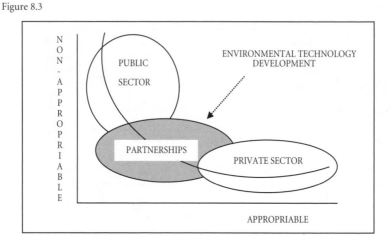

The challenge of divergent stakeholder interests increases with the interest in "sustainable development." Since the introduction of this concept in the 1987 Bruntland Report, there has been increasing interest in simultaneously creating economic value for firms and the economy, reducing the dependence on raw materials and improving environmental protection. This new paradigm is reflected in the strategic thrust of public policy towards sustainability, on a global stage.

Structural changes are therefore slowly occurring, as the regulatory and public policy focus shifts away from "end of pipe" pollution clean-up solutions to requiring the integration of "clean" eco-efficient technologies (that improve economic efficiency as well as reducing environmental pollutants) earlier into industry production processes. One of the implications of this policy shift on the potential supply of environmental solutions is the drive to new technologies rather than incremental changes to existing technologies.

However, such so-called "eco-efficient solutions" may be resisted by decision-makers (e.g. corporate or regulatory) used to simpler solutions or to whom environmental protection is not a high priority. For the firms that are in the business of commercializing such technologies, this means that understanding the marketplace, regulatory trends, and customer niches including market segmentation and technology adoption rates, have become very important and much more complicated.

One of the advantages of the old paradigm was its relative simplicity of cleaning up pollution after the fact. There were few decision variables and a limited number of criteria (mainly cost) by which alternatives could be evaluated. In the new paradigm, there are an expanding number of decision variables (e.g. on economics, energy usage, short vs. long term impacts etc.) that lead to a more complicated decision-making process.

Moreover, with the increase in the number of decision variables, comes a further expansion in the number of stakeholders, with different values and priorities. This expands the number of criteria by which alternatives would be assessed. In addition, the limited truly collaborative experience between the now larger interested parties (e.g. including a receptor industry such as forestry, and regulators, economic development experts, economists, environmental activists and the environmental suppliers etc.) could present a major challenge to technology commercialization.

The expansion in the range of stakeholders and their multiple interests means that the process of commercializing environmental technologies involves, in addition to the normal challenges of marketing and financing, many linkages and networks of new relationships that need to be cultivated and managed by environmental technology suppliers. These challenges become enormously more complex when local suppliers attempt to access global markets with different regulatory regimes.

In summary, the four key challenges that have been demonstrated to bedevil small firms in commercializing technologies (network relations, marketing, management and financing) are considerably magnified in the commercialization of new environmental technologies, particularly those that attempt to bridge economic efficiency with environmental protection.[31] A recent study on the barriers to the deployment of environmental technologies in the Canadian oil and gas industry has confirmed the higher degrees of difficulty in commercializing and deploying environmental technologies relative to other technologies.[32]

THE CANADIAN CETAC APPROACH AND ITS TRACK RECORD

Formation and Performance of the CETAC's

Since 1993, the three CETAC's have had considerable experience in working with small Canadian firms, helping them to commercialize environmental technologies. They have established significant credibility in Eastern and Western Canada with hundreds of small to medium sized enterprises (SME's) in helping them to commercialize environmental technologies in various industry sectors (e.g. manufacturing sector in Ontario, agriculture sector in Quebec, oil/gas sector in Alberta).

By such means they have also created direct business opportunities for SME's. In addition they have also located in some areas (e.g. upstream oil and gas facilities) where conventional low efficiency technologies were ripe to be supplanted with higher efficiency technology should it be developed.[33] These represent future business opportunities for SME's in the CETAC network.

It is difficult to claim that the efforts of the CETAC's were solely responsible for the success of their client small firms and there are no long-term quantitative measures of the CETAC's performance since inception. However, client surveys have been overwhelmingly positive, demonstrating a strong market pull and value-added of the services. For example, a review by Doyletech Corporation of CETAC-WEST's relevance since its inception, based on surveys of clients and other technology providers, noted that the organization was unique in providing a wealth of commercialization assistance "under one umbrella" and concluded, among other things, that it was filling a gap not well served by other technology commercialization organizations and was making significant contributions to Canada's national environmental and innovation strategies.[34]

Although the three centers have adapted their specific services to meet the needs of the markets in their respective geographic areas, they follow a similar network-based collaborative business model for capacity building and market development for SME's. This collaboration is essential because of the complexity of stakeholders and interests involved in the commercialization of environmental technologies – such as regulators, receptor industries like agriculture and energy, industry associations, angel investors, SME suppliers etc.

Equally importantly, the CETAC's have built strong linkages with other government programs that complement their activities, notably the National Research Councils' Industrial Research Assistance Program (IRAP), Environment Canada's Technology Advancement and Pollution Prevention initiatives, Natural Resource Canada's Technology Early Action Measures Program (TEAM), Sustainable Development Technology Canada (SDTC) initiatives and the initiatives of Western Economic Diversification Canada (WED). These programs are used to complement and strengthen the CETAC's programs, such as linking the technology and R&D emphasis of the IRAP Program with the capacity building emphasis of the CETAC's.

Role of the CETAC's in the Technology Commercialization Continuum

The diagram below outlines the technology commercialization continuum from "technology push" to "market pull." Though technology push and market pull are both important, it is the market that determines success and it is the private sector that drives innovation and commercialization. The CETAC's operate in the "space" represented by the triangle – providing a range of services that facilitate "Innovation" and the "Commercialization of Technologies" by SME's and acting as catalysts between the technologies and markets.

Figure 8.4

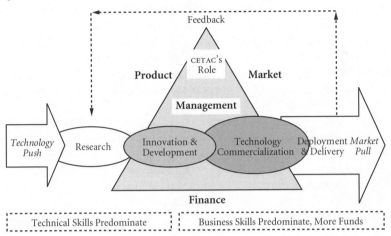

As a product/service moves from left to right along the continuum from research to market acceptance, the nature and magnitude of the necessary skills and funds changes. At the "technology push" stage, research funds and scientific and technical skills are paramount. However, in order that the product be commercialized, a much broader range of skills is needed (business and management skills now paramount) and considerably more funds are necessary (e.g. for technology demonstrations, marketing, product distribution etc.).

The CETAC's focus is on filling the gaps between research and the deployment of products and services into the market. The critical capabilities' gaps faced by the CETAC's customers, SME's, are represented by three sides of the triangle – understanding the needs of the "Market," developing the "Product" that meets those needs, securing the appropriate "Financing" – and in the centre of the triangle, ensuring rigorous "Management" for market entry and development. The CETAC's utilize a network-based collaborative model to provide those capabilities to SME's that are necessary to commercialize environmental technologies.

The CETAC's Business Model – How They Do Business

The CETAC's act as both catalysts and brokers between the technologies and markets, providing a continuum of services that facilitate innovation and the commercialization of technologies by SME's. Innovative capabilities are shaped by innovation supply (e.g. inputs such as technology, skills, capital) and demand (e.g. outputs valued by markets such as environmental quality, efficiency etc.). Recognizing that the markets and the private sector drive innovation, the three CETAC's have operationalized their approach to filling the gaps between research and the deployment of products/services using the three-phase business model that is later described.

The primary goal of the business model is to strengthen the capacity and competitiveness of SME's for technology commercialization and to promote sustainable development practices (e.g. those that promote economic efficiency and environmental benefits) in receptor industries such as manufacturing and oil/gas in the various regions of Canada. This goal is achieved by the CETAC's networking these small businesses with expert business skills, sources of financing and end user markets, using a range of tools developed by the CETAC's. Their model embraces an end-to-end systems approach to working with and mentoring firms and networking them to the "right people" at the practical, grassroots levels, to assist SME's to commercialize their technologies.

The value of this network-based collaborative model derives from CETACs as a third party managing the linkages within an extensive network of industry and government contacts that have been developed over the past decade. It is important, from an organizational development perspective, to note that all the three CETAC's are still led by their founding CEO's, These individuals came into the job with extensive industry relationships and, through leveraging such relationships and new experimentation, have strengthened their linkages over the last decade.

The contacts or partners of these leaders are in the innovation chain – at the innovation supply end (e.g. the SME's that develop and market environmental technologies), at the innovation demand end (e.g. the industries that use the environmental products/services) and at the intermediary stage (e.g. business experts with the practical expertise to assist environmental firms, government program managers, regulatory agencies etc.).

Since the three jurisdictions in which the CETAC's operate are different, in terms of economic drivers and market needs and since the cultures of the respective CEO's are different, their specific tools and programs for their client SMEs are different. Although these programs are tailored to their respective markets, they still reflect a neutral, partnership approach to public policy execution.

What the CETAC's Deliver – Three Levels of Value-Added

Figure 8.5 shows the outputs of the CETAC's business model and illustrates their three levels of value-added. Greater or lesser attention is given to any specific value-added area by each CETAC based on the needs of the specific clients and the business environment in those markets (e.g. regional priorities, availability of complementary local programs and funding etc.).

The Appendix at the end of this paper illustrates representative success stories of the three CETAC's at each of the three levels of value-added.

Figure 8.5

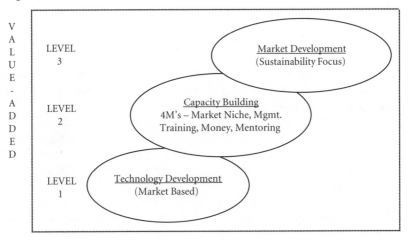

NEEDS OF SME'S

The impacts of the CETAC's performance over the last ten years in Canada have been to facilitate the commercialization of innovative environmental technologies by small firms in Canada and to support environmental sustainability at three levels, as illustrated in the diagram:

Level 1 – Market-Based Technology Development: The CETAC's are constantly seeking promising innovations in the environmental sector. Each year, they meet with hundreds of SME's across Canada and evaluate business opportunities with these companies, which include start-ups as well as companies that are already investing in new environmental technologies. For the early-stage SME projects at the "concept" level, expert guidance is provided to the entrepreneur on key areas of improvement to facilitate the development of a market-oriented concept or technological solution. The perspective is that of the market and of investors, reflecting the traditional gaps in understanding by small businesses. The outputs at this level are in the nature of due diligence evaluations by expert third parties of the market, the management and financial aspects of the project and identification of the "next steps" to advance the business. The intent is to improve the overall quality of the emerging opportunity by ensuring that the entrepreneur has grasped a sufficient understanding of the business marketing and financial fundamentals.

Level 2 – Capacity Building: For those business opportunities that seem viable, further services are aimed at building the capacity of the SMEs such that they can sustain the viability of their businesses over the longer-term. There is a critical need to build the capacity and competitiveness of smaller Canadian firms, which are often the technology innovators. The CETAC services are predominantly in the four critical areas of weaknesses of SMES – market niche identification, accessing financing, business management and financial management – and the emphasis is on bringing effective solutions to environmental problems as well as contributing to economic growth. The CETAC provides mentorship to the client entrepreneur throughout the capacity building process. This requires in-depth knowledge of the business context in which the environmental technologies fit, access to sources of early-stage financing such as angel investors, a thorough evaluation of the technology as well as its potential domestic and global markets, plus a sound appreciation of the management and governance needs of the particular business. Using their network-based collaborative approach, the CETAC's abilities to call on specialized expertise in the target sectors at a reasonable cost is one of the unique features of their business model. The services include the CETAC advisors' abilities to direct clients to a number of private and public financial institutions to obtain the financing for technology development and commercialization of their innovations.

The CETAC's have developed customized tools to assist in the capacity building process such as the "Entrepreneur to CEO Workshop" of CETAC-WEST or the "Business Match-Making" service of Enviro-Access, or "aboutRemediation.com" and Canadian Brownfield Network of OCETA. Clients operate in areas as diverse as drinking water supplies, energy management systems for buildings, hazardous wastes and GHG emissions reductions.

Level 3 – Market Development: The highest level of value-added support by the CETAC in commercializing environmental technologies is at the market development stage where the Centres act as non-profit, third-party catalysts that broker relationships between innovation suppliers (SMES) and end user customers in the markets (that create the demand for environmental products/services). At this level, the CETAC is much more externally focused and are using its extensive networks to help create market opportunities that generate both economic and environmental benefits. In other words, it is actively working the markets as brokers with a public policy mandate to achieve sustainable development. Technology demonstrations are often an integral component at this level of support.

This support is provided in two principal ways, both with the objective of facilitating the adoption of sustainable development and pollution prevention practices: (1) direct support to SMES that supply environmental solutions – and linking those SMES to target end-user customers that need their services; and (2) direct support to end-user SME customers that require environmental solutions, such as manufacturing operations – and linking those with appropriate suppliers of environmental technologies.

Prominent examples of the CETAC's initiatives at this level are Enviro-Access's "Enviroclubs," OCETA's "Toronto Region Sustainability Program" and CETAC-WEST's "Eco-Efficiency Program in the Upstream Oil and Gas Sector" – as outlined in the Appendix.

CONCLUSIONS

The domestic environmental industry sector has been instrumental in helping Canada reach national and international environmental targets and has developed to the point where it now contributes over 3% to the GDP. It has moved beyond pollution control to develop technologies which consume less raw material and energy and produce less waste while still offering a good or service of comparable or superior quality. This improvement in efficiency of production contributes to both competitiveness and sustainable development.

The sector is dominated by a large number of SMEs and they are largely responsible for the development and commercialization of new technologies which are deployed by other, frequently larger, corporations. The critical challenge for an SME in technology commercialization starts at the transition from a prototype to a commercial product or service. Many fail to make this transition which has been referred to as the "Valley of Death." Environmental technologies add an extra dimension of complexity in moving from innovation to commercialization.

The Canadian Environmental Technology Advancement Centers have a primary focus on providing safe passage for SME's as they make this transition. They are independent, not for profit organizations each with their own Board of Directors and CEO. They utilize a network-based collaborative model and offer three levels of value added service: from market based technology development, where the emphasis is on ensuring that there is a viable market for the proposed technology; to building the capacity of the enterprise so that it has the right attributes for success in the field; through to actual market development by working directly with the manufacturers and processors to locate opportunities to reduce pollution and improve competitiveness.

The CETAC centers provide linkages with government program and policy organizations such as the National Research Council, Natural Resources Canada and Environment Canada and have facilitated investment decisions from both the private sector and Sustainable Technology Development Canada.

We have argued that have been a number of central factors governing their success. First, their unique governance structure allows them to bridge public and private sector interests in the commercialization of environmental technologies. They work in cooperation with provincial governments, environmental industry associations and the private sector, but operate at arms length from governmental control. This is a distributed network sensitive to client needs rather than the conventional, centrally directed model. Second, the stability and industry credibility of their experienced leadership have provided knowledge of technology commercialization as applied to the environmental sector and has brought networks developed over decades to the service of clients. Third, the design of their programs is based on the recognition that not all SMES are created equally. A large percentage of the SMES in the environmental sector might have less than 5-10 employees and these micro-firms will have unique cultures, learning styles and financial conditions requiring tailored solutions. And finally, we have shown that the continuous support and recognition from their collaborators is important and at the same time there is a need to be opportunistic and entrepreneurial in adapting to new policy directions and funding sources.

Applications of the CETAC's Network-based Business Model –
Selected Success Stories

1. "MARKET DEVELOPMENT" PROJECTS (LEVEL 3)

Prominent examples of the CETAC's initiatives at this level of Market Development include:

- CETAC-WEST's "Eco-Efficiency Program" in the Upstream Oil and Gas industry, and funded by Alberta Energy, TEAM, WD, NRCan, Environment Canada and industry sponsors. With a limited execution in the Upstream Oil & Gas sector, it is already estimated to reduce GHG emissions by 125,000 tonnes/yr. It has the potential for a further reduction of 6.1 Megatonnes over the next 15 years, moving Canada significantly forward in meeting its Kyoto commitments.
- OCETA's "Toronto Region Sustainability Program," developed to promote the adoption and implementation of pollution prevention planning in SME manufacturing facilities in Toronto and funded by Environment Canada, the Ontario Ministry of the Environment and the City of Toronto. Through the use of pollution prevention planning, the Program minimizes the generation of toxics, sewer discharges, smog precursors, GHG and hazardous wastes. Program clients have significantly improved their environmental performance, reduced risks and costs and reduced their regulatory exposure. It is estimated that the aggregated payback for clients is 11 months.
- Enviro-Access's "Enviroclubs" that build awareness of environmental management and help manufacturing SME's within a region to implement profitable pollution prevention projects by reducing their technical and financial risks. This initiative is funded by Environment Canada, Canada Economic Development and IRAP. By the end of fiscal 2004, this initiative is estimated to have reduced the generation of 190 tonnes of hazardous wastes, 1.3 tonnes of Volatile Organic Compounds (VOC) and 570 tonnes of GHG.

2. "CAPACITY BUILDING" PROJECTS (LEVEL 2)

Examples of the CETAC's initiatives at this level of Capacity Building include:

- The Enviro-Access's Web Site, which serves as the principal mechanism for the promotion of environmental technology and expertise available in Quebec and Atlantic Canada. Information is presented using, for example technology and company fact sheets and university expertise in R&D. For the fiscal 2003–2004, the site had generated over 2 million visits, with an average of 200,000 visits per month, an increase of 3.7% compared to the previous year.

- OCETA operates the aboutRemediation.com (AR) website, Canada's premier resource and network on sustainable brownfield redevelopment and effective remediation of contaminated lands. AboutRemediation.com provides news, initiatives, resources, tools, technologies and case studies for stakeholders involved in remediation and brownfield redevelopment. Practitioners promote their business partners. The website attracts some 700,000 visits per month and is linked to comparable sites in both Europe and the U.S. aboutRemdiation.com and the Canadian Urban Institute recently launched the Canadian Brownfields Network (CBN) in response to the National Round Table on the Environment and Economies recommendation to create a national brownfields network. The CBN facilitates linkages, builds capacity and coordinates the exchange of ideas, expertise and success stories.
- CETAC-WEST's "Entrepreneur-to-CEO Workshop," now in its tenth year, is an intensive five-day management training workshop that is expressly tailored to the needs of SME's in commercializing environmental and related technologies. The workshops attract an average of 40 participants and provide in-depth case studies and training in areas such as market segmentation, financing, managing for growth and intellectual property. Since 1996, over 500 participants have benefited from these workshops.

3. "MARKET-BASED TECHNOLOGY DEVELOPMENT" PROJECTS (LEVEL 1)

Examples of initiatives at this early stage of concept and technology development include:

- OCETA has worked to support Stantec Global Technologies over several years. Stantec is marketing the Goodfellow EFSOP® product (Expert Furnace Systems Optimization Process). This is a sophisticated system to measure off-gas composition from industrial processes and employs continuous fume analysis, flow and temperature measurements along with real-time process data, to optimize combustion and to control post-combustions systems. OCETA has previously produced a Technology Profile for Stantec on EFSOP® use in the steel sector for electronic arc furnaces and ETV Canada has undertaken a detailed evaluation of the Process and issued a performance claim ETV certificate. OCETA is now partnering with Stantec, Unisearch and the University of Toronto in the development for new industrial applications of EFSOP®. The consortium has been successful with a request for $4 Million funding from SDTC to support this consortium initiative.
- Enviro-Access provided strategic support to Odotech, a company that came into being through the development of new technologies for quantifying odours at the *Ecole Polytechnique de Montreal*. Enviro-Access's supported the company in preparing its business plan, producing a development strategy,

identifying business partners and completing a first round of financing. Odotech now offers integrated solutions for managing odour problems. The company's instrumentation and software make it possible to measure and quantify the impact of odours, thereby facilitating the application of quantitative norms for odour and the establishment of quality control standards relative to odours generated by products and processes. Olfactory nuisance levels can thereby be reduced in the vicinity of various industrial or agricultural facilities.

- CETAC-WEST's support to Environmental Power Technologies Ltd. (EPT), started in 1995 with the company founder's request for help in marketing and accessing financing. The EPT technology reconditions fire-retardant phosphate esters that are used as lubricating fluids in compressor turbines. The fire-resistant qualities prevent incineration of the used lubricant that therefore must be disposed in landfills. The impact of the EPT technology is to lower lubricant requirements by significantly extending the life of these lubricating fluids, to reduce operating costs by reducing the need for maintenance shutdowns and the need to replace parts, and to reduce the need for costly and environmentally harmful disposal. CETAC-WEST has assisted the company with marketing feasibility studies, that included applying the technology to turbines used in electro-hydraulic systems. CETAC-WEST also helped EPT with its business strategy, to secure financing and to develop a market penetration strategy to extend its client base. The company has now grown significantly, with a client base that includes the US Navy, major pipeline companies and electrical utilities in the US and overseas.

NOTES

1 Thanks are due for the support and guidance provided by the CETAC CEOs, Joe Lukacs of Calgary, Ed Mallet of Mississauga, and Manon Laporte of Sherbrooke. The views expressed are soley the responsibility of the authors.

2 G.Bruntland, *Our Common Future: The World Commission on Environment and Development* (Oxford University Press, 1987).

3 United Nations Sustainable Development, Agenda 21, *United Nations Conference on Environment and Sustainable Development*, Rio de Janeiro, Brazil, June 2-14, 1992 (United Nations Division of Sustainable Development, 1992).

4 Environment Canada and Industry, Science and Technology Canada, *Building a Stronger Environmental Capability in Canada*. A report prepared by Doyletech Corporation, Ottawa, 1992.

5 Ibid., 3.

6 US Department of Commerce, Office of Environmental Technologies Industries, "Industry Facts" (US Department of Commerce, 2002).

7 Industry Canada, Environmental Industries Branch, "Canada's Environment Industry – At a Glance" (Industry Canada, 2003).

8 Statistics Canada, "Environmental Industry Survey: Business Sector, 2002" (Statistics Canada, Catalogue No. 16F008ʙxɪᴇ, 2003), 1.

9 Industry Canada, "A Decade of Change-Canadian Environmental Industry Competitiveness Analysis." Report prepared by Aegis Management Consulting Group, 2003.

10 US Department of Commerce, Office of Environmental Technologies Industries, "Industry Facts."

11 US Department of Commerce, Office of Environmental Technologies Industries, "Global Environmental Technologies- Trends, Markets and Prospects," *Export America* (US Department of Commerce, 2002), 24.

12 Industry Canada, *A Decade of Change – Canadian Environmental Industry Competitiveness Analysis.*

13 US Department of Commerce, Office of Environmental Technologies Industries, "Industry Facts."

14 ᴏᴇᴄᴅ, *The Global Environmental Goods and Services Industry* (ᴏᴇᴄᴅ, 1996), 7.

15 Ibid., 10.

16 General Electric, "General Electric Unveils Ecoimagination Plan," ɢᴇ News Release, May 10, 2005.

17 Industry Canada, Environmental Industries Branch, "Environmental Industry Survey: Business Sector, 2002," 1.

18 ᴏᴇᴄᴅ, *The Global Environmental Goods and Services Industry*, 23.

19 Conference Board of Canada, "Why Energy Efficiency." Briefing on Regulatory Policy and Taxation, 2005.

20 Statistics Canada, "Environmental Industry Survey: Business Sector, 2002."

21 Ibid.

22 Statistics Canada, "Environment Industry: Business Sector," Stats Canada Daily, September 21, 2004.

23 Statistics Canada, "Environmental Industry Survey: Business Sector, 2002," 17.

24 Ibid., 25.

25 Michael Porter, S. Stern and Council on Competitiveness, *The New Challenge to America's Prosperity: Findings From the Innovation Index* (Council on Competitiveness, 1999), 5.

26 Conference Board of Canada, *Six Quick Hits For Canadian Commercialization* (Conference Board of Canada, April, 2005), 2.

27 L.M. Branscomb and P.E. Auerswald, "Between Invention and Innovation." Paper prepared for the U.S. National Institute of Standards and Technology, November 2002.

28 Ibid.

29 Ibid.

30 See T.P. Seager and K.H. Gardener, "Barriers to the Adoption of Novel Technologies," in E. Levner, J. Linkov, and J.M. Proth, eds. *Strategic Management of Marine Ecosystems* (Kluwer, 2004), 48-68, and E.V.Larson, I.T. Brahmakulam, Building a New Foundation for Innovation (Rand Corporation, 2002), chapter 4.

31 See J. Pellikka and M. Virtanen, "The Problems of Commercialization in Small and Medium Sized Information Technology Firms." Paper presented at the 13th Nordic Conference on Small Business Research, 2004.

32 See Deep Blue Associates, *Barriers to the Deployment of Environmental Technologies in the Upstream Oil and Gas Industry.* Report prepared for the Petroleum Technology Alliance Canada, Calgary Alberta, January 2005.

33 CETAC-WEST, "The CETAC-WESTerner – Eco-Efficiency Workshop Issue – Opportunities to Extend Our Resources" (CETAC-WEST, Summer, 2005).

34 Doletech Corporation, *An Assessment of CETAC-WEST's Relevance Ten Years After Inception*, November, 2003.

9 Source Water Protection in Canada: Local Innovation and Multi-Level Governance

CAREY HILL

The Great Lakes Basin Sustainable Water Resources Agreement was released for public comment on June 20, 2005, six months after the US President designated the Great Lakes a 'national treasure.' By executive order a 10-member Cabinet level Task Force led by the Environmental Protection Agency (USEPA) was established to coordinate state and federal initiatives. Ontario members of the Lake Ontario Lakewide Management Plan team have participated in these efforts to lay the groundwork for a Great Lakes Strategic Plan. These efforts provide an opportunity to reflect on source water protection in Canada and to consider how policies adopted locally, provincially, nationally and internationally have impacted some of Canada's source waters, including those shared with the United States.

Only in recent years have the United States Environmental Protection Agency (USEPA), Canadian provinces, and the Canadian Council of Ministers of the Environment (CCME) begun to formally recognize the importance of source water protection for drinking water quality. Justice O'Connor's report on the Walkerton Inquiry in Ontario also drew attention to the importance of source water protection as an aspect of the multi-barrier approach with 22 targeted recommendations. While local actions offer innovations, from bi-national to federal, provincial, and community efforts, source water protection requires multi-level governance.

This chapter compares and contrasts two cases of source water protection in Canada. It examines local innovation and multi-level governance in the area of surface water sources[1] including the source of Toronto's water, Lake Ontario, and the three watersheds located in the Coast mountains that provide water to the city of Vancouver. The chapter argues that source protection is an important and vital component of drinking water protection but that it must be viewed in the context of a broader multi-barrier approach. Further, the chapter highlights two innovations with respect to source water protection, Vancouver's protected watersheds and Ontario's proposed source water protection legislation.

As previous chapters in this volume have shown, innovation as a policy field or concept typically focuses on the development by industry of new products and processes. Cast in this light it can readily be linked as well to sustainable development concepts and in particular to sustainable production by firms. When the issue of multi-level regulation and governance is added to this initial view of innovation, one of the commonplace reactions is that innovation is more likely to occur if layers of regulation can be reduced.

In the area of source water protection, however, and arguably in environmental protection as a whole, innovation and multi-level regulation, take on more complex meanings and realities. First, policy innovation can mean simply but importantly sustained improvements in protection through a series of legal, regulatory and technical steps and practices. Second, the reality of multi-level regulation can either support such innovation or constrain it and thus there is no automatic assumption that multiple levels of governance harm it. Indeed, multi-level regulatory cooperation is highly likely to be needed.

The chapter examines these different dynamics in three stages. First, it looks at source water protection as needing a multi-barrier approach. The second and third sections of the chapter then analyzes historically the Vancouver and Toronto case studies. The fourth section compares the two cases more directly and then conclusions follow. The chapter argues that the necessity of the multi-barrier approach for drinking water protection is instructive for environmental regulation. Cooperation and involvement of several levels of government can provide lines of defense to protect source waters from contamination. The Toronto case demonstrates that multi-level regulation can produce regulatory innovation at several levels. The Vancouver case highlights the local nature of watersheds and the innovation that can occur while underscoring the need not to rely too heavily on one level or one type of drinking water protection.

SOURCE WATER PROTECTION

A multi-barrier approach to drinking water protection is generally accepted as most conducive to public health.[2] The first barrier in the multi-barrier approach is source water protection.[3] Source water protection involves limiting discharges into the source water to avoid microbiological, chemical, and radiological contamination. Common causes of contamination include agricultural and urban runoff, sewage effluent, landfills, pulp mills, mines and chemical plants, for example. At its limit, source protection involves closure of the area surrounding the source water to humans thereby limiting exposures related to industrial, recreational, residential, or other activities. Benefits of source water protection include lowering risk by limiting contamination and reducing the costs associated with treating contaminated water. Treatment costs are "inversely related to the proportion of the watershed protected by forests, wetlands and other open space."[4] Furthermore, the non-governmental sector in Ontario argues that the economic benefits of source water protection "override the costs" of implementation.[5]

Watersheds "describe an area of land that drains downwards towards lower elevations," and usually refer to surface water resources.[6] For example, river sources such as those located in the Capilano watershed are buttressed on all sides by forested land. If forestry activities occur in the watershed this can affect the levels of soil and other particles (i.e. turbidity) that find their way into the water, as well as levels of chemicals for fire retardation or pesticides that may be sprayed in conjunction with tree-planting or fire practices. Watershed-based source water protection "offers communities a method of reducing vulnerability of drinking water to contamination before it enters into a community's water distribution system."[7] This approach involves several steps including determining the boundaries of the watershed, undertaking an inventory of the potential sources of contamination, mapping the aquifer, developing a management plan, involving the public, and developing continuous evaluation and monitoring, as well as identifying alternative sources of drinking water.

Most watersheds are open to the public from swimmers to industrialists. In fact, many are used for industrial, recreational, agricultural, energy, and sewage disposal purposes as well as for drinking and bathing. As discussed later in this chapter, Lake Ontario is susceptible to contamination from a variety of sources. Recently, exposures to antibiotics and other pharmaceuticals in water have raised concerns. Pharmaceuticals and personal care products (PPCPs) are found in sewage effluent. The long-term impacts of these are not well-understood and conventional treatment methods may be ineffective.[8]

PPCPs can be considered both point and non-point sources of pollution. Other point sources of pollution include pulp and paper mills, chemical plants, dry cleaners, landfills, sewage treatment plants and mines. Non-point sources (NPS) such as agricultural and urban runoff, roads, shipping and pesticides also exist. The challenges to protect source water from poor land-use planning, natural resource management and changes in climate are considerable. The need to address climate change was included in the recent 2005 draft agreement signed by the 8 governors and 2 premiers of the Great Lakes Basin.

As described above, watershed protection occurs in a local context and is dependent upon the source location, surrounding natural resources, source size, and its accessibility to the public. While the local context is where source protection occurs, the regional and international context may drive protection efforts. Impetus for this can include spillover effects, benchmarking by advocacy groups or governments, and shared sources. Joint agreements between countries to protect shared sources can arise out of a mutual need to protect the source for continuous and future use. The Great Lakes Water Quality Agreement is one such example.

INNOVATIVE VANCOUVER:[9]
LOCAL WATERSHED CONTROL
FOR SOURCE WATER PROTECTION

The diffusion of innovations literature identifies innovation as "the degree to which an individual is relatively earlier in adopting new ideas than other members of his [sic] social system."[10] The efforts of Vancouver, British Columbia in protecting its source water can be viewed as innovative by any measure. This section describes and examines this innovativeness drawing lessons for later adopters. One key finding is that innovativeness in one aspect of the multi-barrier approach may lead to laxity in another. The importance of viewing the barriers for drinking water protection as multiple and complex is thus emphasized. In this case, innovation can be understood as sustained improvements in protection as a result of legal steps and practices.

Today, the Vancouver metropolitan region obtains its water from three natural watersheds nestled in the "North Shore" mountains, part of the Coast Mountain range. The water system is operated by the Greater Vancouver Water District (GVWD), which is a creature of the Greater Vancouver Regional District (GVRD), a regional agency directed by a council of representatives from 21 local municipalities and 1 electoral area.

The Capilano River watershed was the first source of drinking water for the city located across the first narrows, across the ocean's inlet, from the City of Vancouver. The water system was privately built and operated but became a public utility in 1891 when it was purchased by the City. In 1905, some very diligent city councilors went to the provincial capital and asked to lease the watershed in order to protect its "pristine quality."[11] On April 3, City Solicitor Arthur McEvoy and Alderman George Halse attempted to secure a 999 year lease on the watershed, source for the Vancouver Water Works. The provincial government refused the 999 year lease citing monetary value of the timber resources.[12] Later that same year, Vancouver Mayor Buscombe managed to negotiate a 50 year lease for a portion of the watershed amounting to 75 to 100 square miles at a cost of $2400 per year.[13]

In order to further protect the watershed, the city began buying up parcels of private land and by 1926 when the province reversed its earlier decision, the city had bought up 13 000 acres of subdivided and unsubdivided lands.[14]

Table 9.1
Vancouver's Watersheds

	Capilano	*Seymour*	*Coquitlam*
Watershed Size	19,800 ha	12,600 ha	21,200 ha
Year Added to GVWD	1926 (1889)	1926 (1907)	1931
Percentage of GVRD supply	40 percent	40 percent	20 percent as BC Hydro owns most of the rights to the water

The lease entitled the city to the land in the Capilano and Seymour watersheds for 999 years while ending logging in the lower watersheds. The third watershed used by New Westminster had already been protected by the Dominion government's Order-in-Council of March 4, 1910 that created a "reserve of 55,670 acres of land around the Lake for protection and preservation of the water supply."[15] The Coquitlam Lake watershed lies within the Railway Belt and jurisdiction over this watershed was decided by the Judicial Committee of the Privy Council in 1910 in favour of the Dominion over the province of British Columbia. In 1913, the federal government and the province agreed that administration of water within the railway belt would be transferred to the province.[16] The Seymour watershed was added in 1907 to address the growing city's need for an additional supply of water.

Vancouver's watersheds are distinguished from others around the world because of the City's foresight in closing them to the public and, for the most part, to commercial and industrial access.[17] Environmental groups and agencies have identified Seattle, Boston, New York, San Francisco, Portland and Denver as source protection leaders. Vancouver's protection stands apart because of its timeliness, and its degree. While today Seattle now owns nearly all its watersheds, it has not always had the level of control over its watersheds that Vancouver gained early on. Similarly, while the efforts of Boston, New York, San Francisco and Denver are laudable, parts of their watersheds remain open to contamination from private, residential or recreational threats. Vancouver's watersheds are closed to the public. Access is limited to City workers caring for the watersheds and operating the water system and within the Coquitlam watershed to designated BC Hydro employees.

While the extent of control over the watersheds today is unique, the GVWD had its resolve tested in the 1950s. In 1952, the provincial government recommended that a highway be built from North Vancouver to Squamish through the Capilano watershed. At the time, residents had to take the ferry from Squamish as no roads connected it with the lower mainland. Chief Commissioner E.A. Cleveland warned about building a highway through the watershed explaining that it "would greatly increase the possibilities of pollution to the water supply and add to the forest fire danger."[18] The road never materialized and today Squamish residents have access to the lower mainland along a coastal highway rather than one through the still-protected watershed.

Fifty years later, the issue of a highway through the watershed resurfaced. Getting to Squamish was the concern in the 1950s, and getting just beyond Squamish to Whistler for the Olympics was the new concern. In 2002, the provincial government suggested four possible highways including one through the Seymour watershed and one through the Capilano watershed. Several organizations and groups including the North Vancouver District Mayor and the Society Promoting Environmental Conservation (SPEC) noted their concerns.[19] The province decided to upgrade the sea-to-sky highway rather than build any of the four proposed projects citing costs. The resolve of the city to protect its watersheds in the face of development supported by the province is an example of actions that form part of the larger innovation story of watershed protection in Vancouver.

With respect to the multi-barrier approach, source protection is a first line of defense followed by disinfection. Chlorination as well as more recent technologies of ozonation and ultraviolet kills bacteria while filtration removes particles that contribute to bacterial and other contamination. Somewhat ironically, Vancouver's conscientious efforts to protect its pristine watershed have at times led to delays in responding to threats to public health or using the best available technologies.[20] The city of Vancouver was one of the last major cities in Canada to chlorinate its drinking water. It did so in 1943. It has also delayed filtration of its water sources which are expected to occur for the first time in 2007. Most major cities in North America chlorinated their water by 1920, owing in part to the United States Public Health Service regulations on inter-state carriers in 1914.

In 1937, Dr. C.E. Dolman of the BC Provincial Board of Health refused to certify the Vancouver's water to foreign shipping on account of its refusal to chlorinate. The GVWD and the public, lead by E. A. Cleveland, argued that chlorination of the protected watersheds was not necessary. In 1942, the federal government took advantage of its new powers gained as a result of the war ordering Vancouver to chlorinate its drinking water. Dr. Ian Mackenzie, Minister of Pensions and Health and a Vancouverite explained that chlorination was necessary to kill bacteria, and that, even though Vancouver's water source was protected, "We would chlorinate the water if it came from heaven."[21] A correspondence between Cleveland and the Chairman of the war's Provincial Civilian Protection Committee clarified that the late Medical Health Officer for Vancouver, Dr. McIntosh, favoured chlorination "as the only recognized method of offsetting the contamination present in Vancouver water."[22] In reply, Cleveland explained that he "[could] not recall ever having heard Dr. McIntosh refer to chlorination."[23]

In response to considerable public opposition in Vancouver, the federal government moved to refer the question to the Supreme Court as a reference case. However, by November, it ordered the water chlorinated with the threat that refusal would result in its administration of Vancouver's water system. The threat worked and the city of Vancouver agreed to accept the chlorination order. The federal government paid for the chlorinating machinery which the city eventually bought at a considerably reduced price. Chlorination finally commenced in October, 1943, but was probably not fully online until sometime in 1944. It should be noted that this situation was highly unusual as drinking water is considered to be a provincial jurisdiction.

When the war ended, and the federal government's chlorination order expired, Cleveland who had been a tireless advocate of the closed and protected watersheds wrote a paper providing arguments to end chlorination which included the testimonies of several American experts. There is little evidence that the chlorinators were turned off, but there is considerable correspondence indicating local residents requested an end to chlorination, some even claiming they had become sick because of it.[24] The federal government's intervention during the war was highly contentious yet ultimately improved the safety of Vancouver's drinking water.

Following the war, a series of events led to significant change in the watersheds. In 1948, the province passed the Forest Act and officially adopted the concept of 'sustained yield management'.[25] In 1952, chief commissioner E.A. Cleveland, tireless advocate of the closed watersheds and self-proclaimed anti-chlorinationist, died. T.V. Berry was appointed Water Commissioner and under his leadership a timber harvesting program was begun in the watersheds.

While the GVWD has maintained its longstanding commitment to prohibit housing or industrial development in its watersheds, it has not always viewed logging of the watersheds as a comparable threat. Between the late 1960s and mid-1990s logging was permitted in the watersheds, ranging from clearcutting in early years to selective harvesting more recently. Under the original 999 year lease negotiated with the province, forest management practices were not permitted. In February 1963, Commissioner Berry recommended to the Minister of Forests that the lease be amended. On March 7, 1967, the provincial government signed the Amending Indenture to the lease which permitted the sale of logs from the watersheds.

In the late 1980s, logging in the watershed became controversial. Environmentalists and the BC Medical Association expressed concern that mudslides in the watershed may be connected to logging.[26] The fear is that deforestation will lead to greater runoff of soil into the watershed, and that increased turbidity of the source water will render disinfection less effective. In response, the GVWD has asserted that some logging is necessary to avert intensive fires and insect infestations that could lead to greater contamination of the resource though this explanation would not seem to explain more extensive clearcuts in the 1960s.[27] This reversal of its position offers a lesson about the complexity of source water protection and the need for multi-level regulation.

In 1989, the GVWD undertook major deliberations to plan a long term water quality and quantity strategy for the region. This began with a comprehensive assessment of watershed policies and management programs. There had not been a technical review of watershed management since the 1960s. The GVWD noted that watershed "philosophies and social concerns have changed in the past two decades."[28] The same firm that conducted the watershed management review was also charged with examining drinking water quality in the region. At a city council meeting, the manager of GVRD's water department explained that while Vancouver's water quality had generally not changed over the past 3 decades, the review was the result of a combination of factors including changes in capacity to test water quality, in federal government standards, and in public awareness about the environment.[29] The review found that Vancouver's water did not meet all of the Canadian Drinking Water Guidelines. High turbidity, lack of rechlorination, and excessive bacteria levels in summer and fall put the water supply at risk of waterborne diseases. This review coupled with major turbidity events in 1990 raised public awareness of the issue. The Western Canada Wilderness Committee called for a moratorium on logging and a public inquiry in December.[30] The British Columbia Medical Association also called for an inquiry.

In response, the GVWD moved to initiate a public consultation process in 1991. As part of its planning exercise, the district initiated extensive public consultations via public meetings, survey research, and newspaper inserts, both to educate citizens about the problems with water quality and the costs of different improvements and to solicit their preferences. In 1992, the provincial government introduced the Safe Drinking Water Regulation under the Health Act. This included binding standards for coliforms, and stated that water purveyors must deliver potable water to consumers. This regulation appears to have had little impact on the GVRD. It is notable that the GVRD failed to meet both the Canadian Guidelines and the provincial Regulation during some periods of high turbidity. In 1994, following public consultation and review, the GVWD passed a motion to build rechlorination stations and commence filtration on the Seymour source, as soon as possible.

However, by 1998, the GVRD Board voted to postpone construction of some aspects of the plan to improve Vancouver's drinking water quality, including the Seymour filtration plant, in order to save money. Although the GVRD's water committee voted to proceed with the original timetable at the urging of regional health officials, the Board reversed the committee's decision stating that the costs saved were worth the "minute risk."[31] The 1994 schedules had the Seymour plant slated to be built by 2003 but construction did not commence until 2004, delaying completion until 2007.

Amidst these delays, the Ontario Walkerton tragedy occurred in May 2000. For Vancouver residents, concerns about risks of waterborne disease were further heightened as just 5 months later Health Canada released research linking turbidity events in Vancouver's watersheds to gastrointestinal illness including 17,500 visits to physicians and 85 hospitalizations annually.[32] For BC residents, reports by the Auditor General (1999) and Provincial Health Officer (2001) contributed to increased interest in BC's lax drinking water regulations.

In 2001 in response to Walkerton, the provincial government passed amendments to the Safe Drinking Water Regulation. The new standards resulted in a decision by the GVRD board to cancel the Capilano Ozone Project in favour of filtration on the Capilano water source as well as the Seymour source. The new Seymour-Capilano Filtration Plant is scheduled to be operational by 2007. The Coquitlam source, on which the GVWD completed a $40 million ozonation plant in 2001 and which suffers from far fewer turbidity events, is not scheduled to be filtered until 2025 at which time Vancouver's drinking water is expected to meet one hundred percent of the Canadian Guidelines.[33]

In 2001, the NDP government passed the Drinking Water Protection Act, but the Act did not come into force before the newly elected BC Liberal government convened a Drinking Water Review Panel to review the legislation. An amended Drinking Water Protection Act came into force in 2003.

One of the highest priority recommendations of the Drinking Water Review Panel was the strengthening of drinking water source protection measures. It also recommended that the BC government create a single lead agency for drinking water protection. Neither of these happened. *The Drinking Water Protection Act* (2003) includes provisions for source water assessments but only if the Provincial Health Officer recommends these. While Vancouver's water is protected because of local initiative, much of the province's source waters are threatened by increasing urbanization, intensive agriculture and expansion of forest activities. With respect to source protection, the Panel's recommendations are worth noting. It suggested that the provisions of the drinking water act pertaining to source protection should prevail over other acts. Moreover, local governments should have greater influence and authority in relation to watersheds and groundwater supply areas. As well, the Panel argued that there needed to be clear establishment of liability in the Act and that non-point sources should be controlled using multistakeholder processes and regulatory instruments, where necessary.

Vancouver's control of its watersheds is clearly innovative. It adopted this practice early noting the water's "pristine quality" and held fast to its resolve for over a century. However, the case demonstrates the need to comprehensively implement the multi-barrier approach and not to depend too heavily on any one aspect. While Vancouver has made groundbreaking efforts starting a century ago, the province of British Columbia has been slow to enact laws or regulations addressing source water protection.

TORONTO'S LAKE ONTARIO: INNOVATION AND MULTI-LEVEL GOVERNANCE

In contrast to Vancouver's closed watersheds, Toronto's drinking water comes from Lake Ontario, open for business and recreation. Source protection for

Lake Ontario is primarily governed by the Great Lakes Water Quality Agreement. Ontario's Ministry of the Environment is in the process of developing source water protection legislation it suggests will complement this. The city of Toronto is also active in implementing the Canada-Ontario Agreement, recently introducing a sewer-use bylaw that is more stringent than any in Canada. Source water protection for Lake Ontario is evidently a situation of multilevel governance.

When the Great Lakes Water Quality Agreement was signed between Canada and the United States in 1972, neither side used the concept 'source water protection' even though their efforts certainly fall within that scope. The Great Lakes are sources of water for nearly three-quarters of Ontarians. While source protection has received renewed interest since the Walkerton tragedy, protection of the Great Lakes has been ongoing for many decades. Efforts to protect the Great Lakes have primarily been local with respect to limiting discharges from municipalities and, even moreso, international with respect to joint Canada-US efforts to clean up these important sources of drinking water.

The Great Lakes Water Quality Agreement (GLWQA) exists under the 1909 Boundary Waters Treaty of Canada and the United States. The International Joint Commission is the dispute resolution agency under the agreement. When the GLWQA was first signed in 1972, the GLWQA aimed to improve water quality and since then it has included ecological protection among its goals. It was revised in 1978, 1987 and most recently in 1999. The Great Lakes Charter was signed in 1985 and the recent draft agreements signed by the governors and premiers of the Great Lakes Basin suggest that attention to this issue has been sustained.

The status of Lake Erie as 'dead' and the obvious presence of algal growth in Lake Ontario provided the impetus for the GLWQA. Moreover, the US had entered the 'environmental decade' following its first ever Earth Day. From 1972 to 1978, Environment Canada and the USEPA as the lead agencies for the GLWQA focused on the need to reverse eutrophication. Eutrophication can be defined as water pollution caused by excessive nutrients stimulating the growth of aquatic plant life and often resulting in the depletion of dissolved oxygen. Its reversal involves the reduction of phosphorus accomplished primarily by detergent bans and sewage treatment. The efforts undertaken as a result of the GLWQA had a significant impact on Lake Ontario with reports suggesting citizens noticed the reduction in algae.[34]

The revision of the GLWQA in 1978 involved some discussion of the differences in philosophy between the two lead agencies. Botts and Muldoon note that the USEPA pushed for Canada to adopt similar regulations especially with respect to sewage treatment pointing to US success in implementing the Clean Water Act. Initially, the Water Quality Board, which acts as principal advisor to the Commission, had reported that a larger proportion of Canadian locales were served by 'adequate sewage' treatment but the US efforts under the Clean Water Act greatly expanded the sewage treatment facilities and techniques in the US. Thomas Jorling, USEPA Assistant Administrator for Water and one of the negotiators said that Canada's attempts to 'tailor the discharge to the assimilative capacity of the receiving water' was like allowing the equivalent of only primary treatment whereas the US required the "best practicable treatment."[35] Scholars have noted the legalistic regulatory approach adopted by the US versus the high degree of discretion in Canada.[36] Even today, only Ontario is in the process of adopting legislation directly addressing source water protection whereas nearly a decade ago the US included requirements for source water assessments in its 1996 amendments to the Safe Drinking Water Act.

Alongside the GLWQA, the federal government entered into Canada-Ontario Agreements with the province to ensure implementation. Ontario agreed to implement sewage treatment upgrades if the federal government agreed to pay for capital improvements. The Ontario Water Resources Commission which existed prior to the development of the Ministry of the Environment in the 1970s had the expertise to address the sewage treatment upgrades and the federal government had the funds. This agreement had been signed 8 months before the renewed GLWQA was signed.

Canada suggested the "ecosystem management" approach that formed the basis of the revised 1978 GLWQA.[37] The definition of the ecosystem included the interacting components of air, land, water and living organisms within and around the Great Lakes. The success in reversing eutrophication had drawn attention to a new problem that had less obvious indicators, toxics. While citizens could view the ugly algael growth caused by phosphates, toxics were not so apparent.

In 1986, the province announced the Municipal/Industrial Strategy for Abatement (MISA) program though it was not fully implemented until the late 1990s. This strategy provided a means to implement the Canada-Ontario Agreement Respecting the Great Lakes Basin Ecosystem, and, in particular, the commitment to managing persistent toxic substances. The MISA program was developed as the "most ambitious water pollution control program in Canada" to limit and monitor the levels of persistent toxic substances from industrial direct discharges entering Ontario's waterways.[38] Today, the program focuses on 9 sectors ranging from pulp and paper to electric power generation with regulations developed between 1993 and 1995. The regulations state that effluents cannot be toxic to fish and water fleas. There are two limits for monitoring, a daily limit which the plant is not to exceed and a monthly average. Plants must provide an annual report to the public and must report quarterly to the MOE. Records must be kept for 3 years.

Concern with toxics and an ecosystem emphasis persist today with Lake-wide Management Plans (LaMPs). The Lake Ontario Lakewide Management Plan (LaMP) is a "binational cooperative effort to restore and protect the health of Lake Ontario by reducing chemical pollutants entering the lake and addressing the needs of the fish and wildlife living in the watershed."[39] The LaMP includes participation from Environment Canada, the USEPA, the Ontario Ministry of Environment, the New York State Department of Environmental Conservation, Fisheries and Oceans Canada, the US Fish and Wildlife Service and the Ontario Ministry of Natural Resources. In 2004, the LaMP management committee was expanded to include Fisheries and Oceans Canada, US Fish and Wildlife and Ontario Ministry of Natural Resources. For Lake Ontario, air quality is an important consideration. Atmospheric deposition is a "major source of critical pollutants entering Lake Ontario" including pesticides, PCBs, dioxins and mercury in precipitation.[40] Binational monitoring efforts include the Lake Ontario Atmospheric Deposition Study, Lake Ontario Aquatic Foodweb Assessment and the Interagency Laboratory Comparison Study. Toronto and Region is identified as one of the areas of concern (AOC) and its focus is on wet weather flow management and habitat protection.

In 1985, the Great Lakes Charter was signed by the 8 governors[41] and 2 premiers[42] of the Great Lakes Basin in cooperation with their federal governments. The Charter reaffirmed the need to cooperate and to address the pollution of the Great Lakes, particularly toxics. In 2001, the Annex was signed to the GLWQA re-emphasizing the eco-system approach but also outlining the need to prohibit diversions and manage any exceptions. The draft 2005 implementation agreement includes a need for new minimum standards of water use regulations across all basins, formally recognizes the federal governments and the International Joint Commission, and, in the case of Ontario, provides it with a "stronger voice." The Pembina Institute and others have criticized the most recent agreement as not being strong enough with respect to 'no net loss' of water, and its impact remains to be seen.

International cooperation with respect to Lake Ontario's water quality has lead to provincial programs and municipal actions. Recently, the city of Toronto has introduced a sewer-use by-law that reduces the limits on waste discharges, requires mandatory pollution prevention (P2) plans and includes enforcement and compliance provisions. Chapter 681 of the Municipal Code was amended in July 2000 with additional changes in 2003. Industries and companies involved in metal finishing, industrial laundry, gas stations/auto repair, photofinishing/printing, dental/medical labs, soap and detergents, rubber and plastics must submit a pollution prevention plan for a six-year period with goals for the three-year mark. Upgrades must be submitted every two years. Companies that came into existence after the bylaw was amended must submit a plan within one year of existence. If a company or individual is non-compliant, a compliance agreement must be made. Fines for contravention range from $5000 to $100 000 depending on number of offences, section violated, and whether an individual or a corporation commits the violation. The city of Toronto consulted with the public, Environment Canada, the Ontario Ministry of the Environment and the World Wild Life Fund in developing the bylaw. The Sierra Legal Defense Fund pointed to this bylaw as the "toughest in the country."

Local efforts are important as wastewater is one of the major challenges for source water protection. In 2002, the National Pollutant Release Inventory listed the City of Toronto Ashbridges Bay Treatment Plant as having the largest release of pollutants into Lake Ontario at 3,856, 950 kilograms with the wastewater treatment plants of other cities among the top ten.[43]

In his 2003 report, Justice Dennis O'Connor identified source protection as a 'missing element' in terms of a source to tap approach in Walkerton. In response, and in keeping with its commitment to implement all the recommendations of the Walkerton Inquiry, the MOE developed the White Paper on Watershed-based Source Protection Planning in 2004. In this paper, the Ontario Ministry of the Environment explains that proposed source protection legislation would complement existing programs.

The proposed Ontario legislation, the Drinking Water Source Protection Act,[44] uses the existing 36 Conservation Authorities as the basis for planning for the watershed regions including the development of Source Protection Planning Boards and Committees. Source Protection Planning Boards would overlap with Conservation Authorities and be responsible for reviewing the work of Source Protection Planning Committees composed of multi-stakeholders. The SPPC would undertake technical assessment to gather information on water use/demand and potential sources of contamination, as well as identify management actions. As the White Paper explains, "The purpose of the Source Protection Plan would be to indicate the management actions that are required to protect the quality and quantity of sources of drinking water over the long term."[45]

In addition, concerns with water-taking are in contrast to the Vancouver case where a protected watershed does not permit commercial uses of the water. In December 2003, the Ontario MOE announced that it intended to apply charges on water-taking for commercial purposes, something it had not done in the past. In this vein, the proposed legislation requires source protection plans to address water budgets noting how water enters and leaves the watershed and the quantity of water.

The Ontario strategy has included stakeholders in an advisory capacity. Two committees provided recommendations with respect to the proposed legislation, an "Implementation Committee" and a "Technical Experts Committee." The strategy also takes into account the need for local planning. The legislation is expected to be introduced in the legislature in the fall of 2005. Some organizations[46] have already expressed concern that progress of the legislation has been delayed. In response, the Environment Minister has noted the complexity of the legislation and its innovativeness as barriers to rapid adoption.[47]

INNOVATION AND MULTI-LEVEL
GOVERNANCE: THE TWO CASES COMPARED

In Canada, source water protection has recently received attention, and, in most cases, it is 'ad hoc' with each locale providing its own leadership.[48] Ontario's efforts to develop legislation with respect to source water protection are pioneering. In a contrasting way, Vancouver's effort at protecting its sources was also innovative. Closure of the watersheds was possible but, at times, difficult, in the Vancouver case. For Toronto, closure of the watershed was not possible and protection has centered on cooperative restoration efforts. These two cases demonstrate several lessons about innovation and about source water protection challenges. Moreover, they point to areas for future research.

Do local or international influences matter in source water protection? These cases suggest both do. International cooperation remains necessary as the challenges posed for a large body of water such as Lake Ontario are considerable. The need for a multi-stakeholder approach has been recognized by several scholars of watershed-based source protection. It can be argued that additional levels of government increase the attention paid to a problem.

The resolve of the local level cannot be ignored. If the city of Vancouver valued the "pristine quality" of its water less most of the three watersheds would likely be logged today, and there would probably be a highway through at least one of these. The level of source protection afforded and fought for over the last century is unique and should be lauded. The caveat, of course, is that one level of protection is not enough. Federal intervention was required for Vancouver to chlorinate its drinking water some 2 decades after other major North American cities. Vancouver's innovation in protecting nature may have led it to take other threats less seriously and to lag in technological innovations. It should be noted that Vancouver has become an adopter of drinking water technologies and is in the process of building a state-of-the-art filtration plant scheduled to be online in 2007. Its resolve with respect to source protection is probably stronger than ever.

While Vancouver has been a leader in source water protection, British Columbia chose not to develop source water protection regulations or laws, though source assessments can be required if deemed necessary by the Medical Health Officer. Most experts believe this is not likely to occur. The Drinking Water Review Panel set up to make recommendations on the proposed Drinking Water Protection Act advised source protection as one of its primary recommendations. This should have come as no surprise as several of the appointees were concerned with and experts on source water issues. The Panel recommended that source protection aspects of the proposed act should prevail over other acts. Ontario stakeholders have made a similar recommendation with respect to the proposed legislation. They have suggested that source water protection regulations should have paramountcy over other laws and regulations. BC chose not to move on this with implementation as a primary concern. How would determinations be made when one regulation or law came into conflict with another? This is a relevant concern for provincial governments who have responsibility for natural resources as well as for safe drinking water. It also underscores the need for multi-level co-operation and ways in which regulations at one level of government may lead to practices or laws at another level.

In the Toronto case, cooperation began at the international level leading to federal-provincial cooperation and municipal participation. Is it any surprise that the 'most ambitious water pollution control program program' gives rise to the 'toughest sewer-use bylaw in the country' or that the province of Ontario later moves to further protect the source water with a specific act addressing source water protection?

The Ontario Ministry of the Environment has recently noted its reasons for delay with respect to the source protection legislation include its complexity which is likely to lead to effects across sectors. If source water protection legislation is implemented in this way and able to trump other legislation and regulations, it will certainly be innovative. Other jurisdictions will want to watch how this plays out. It is not clear from the draft legislation that paramountcy is being considered. In its current state, the Minister can determine if regulations and measures decided upon by source protection planning boards go beyond the intended legislation. It is instructive that the USEPA decided to prescribe source water assessments rather than the comprehensive legislation Ontario is considering adopting that includes mandatory and voluntary measures identified by local committees.[49]

There does appear to be a regulatory gap with respect to provincial legislation on this issue. Whatever the MOE decides with respect to the issue of paramountcy, the attention that has already been focused on the problem of source water protection is considerable and a move forward. The MOE has consulted with the public, raised awareness and included stakeholder groups. The process may be a further lesson to examine, and is in line with a multi-stakeholder approach recommended by watershed experts.

In addition to examining the Ontario process in-depth, the cases suggest several areas for future research. The impacts of American legislation and co-operative agreements such as the Great Lakes Water Quality Agreement on Canadian environmental policy need to be examined further. Moreover, our decision not to adopt a US regulatory style model even when prodded to by US negotiators provides avenues for research and consideration of the counterfactual. Recent work by the Sierra Legal Defense Fund has given several Canadian jurisdictions failing or barely passing grades with respect to wastewater treatment (2004). The Americans, by contrast, have made significant efforts after the passage of the Clean Water Act and with federal funds to improve sewage treatment in the United States even going so far as to sue jurisdictions that did not abide by the standards. A better understanding of wastewater regulations and the extent of success of the Americans and others including what can be done to limit and improve sewage effluent would go far in helping to protect the source of many lakes and rivers in this country. Consideration of multi-level governance in this area also seems promising.

CONCLUSIONS

While innovators are presumed to be the "cosmopolite," venturesome, and willing to "leave the village to learn,"[50] the Vancouver case suggests that innovators can also be heavily invested in their geography and surroundings and thereby take unique action to protect it. Rather than leaving the village, they fortify the fortress. Perhaps it is this type of innovator that may eventually turn into a laggard, slower to adopt new technologies developed elsewhere. It is this innovator that points to the need for multi-level cooperation.

By contrast, Toronto with Lake Ontario as its source is a late adopter of source protection measures, at least by North American standards. Within Canada, Ontario can recently be seen to be an innovator in terms of source water protection legislation. In their commentary on the Ontario White Paper, the Ontario Water Works Association and the Ontario Municipal Water Association emphasized, "Source protection should not be viewed as replacing treatment of drinking water but rather as simplifying and optimizing treatment measures as part of a comprehensive strategy of drinking water protection. Accordingly, while source protection is the first barrier for protection of drinking water, it is not the only one."[51] The Vancouver case underscores the need for local protection and the local nature of source waters. However, it also points to the need for protection at other levels. The Toronto case demonstrates how regulations or practices at one level will require action and regulations at other levels and allow for additional and sustained protection. The Great Lakes Water Quality Agreement pushes Ontario to adopt 'ambitious' by Canadian standards water pollution control with MISA, and the need to comply with MISA leads Toronto to develop the 'toughest sewer-use bylaw' in the country. Now, the province is filling in another regulatory gap by developing what is an innovative source protection law informed and supported through stakeholder participation.

In the Toronto case, multi-level regulation appears to support innovation. With respect to Vancouver, innovation at the local level must be celebrated but also underscores a need for complementary efforts at other levels. The Vancouver case reflects the importance and innovation that source protection offers, but it also contains the caveat that source protection is not a solution, but a first line of defense. Ontario's effort post-Walkerton is significant and innovative in its use of legislation to protect water sources. The two cases illustrate an important strength of multi-level governance: innovation can come from different levels at different times.

NOTES

1 Most Canadians (74%) get their water from surface water sources.

2 Health Canada, *From Source to Tap: The Multi-barrier Approach to Safe Drinking Water.* Federal-Provincial-Territorial Committee on Drinking Water of the Federal-Provincial-Territorial Committee on Environmental and Occupational Health. May 16. 2002. See also Steve Hrudey and Elizabeth Hrudey, *Safe Drinking Water – Lessons from Recent Outbreaks in Affluent Nations* (IWA Publishing, 2005).

3 Other aspects of the multi-barrier approach include water treatment (disinfection and filtration), maintaining the water distribution system, as well as comprehensive testing and monitoring.

4 Paul K Barten and Caryn E. Ernst, "Land Conservation and Watershed Management for Source Water Protection" *American Water Works Association Journal* 96, 4 (April, 2004): 121-35, 121.

5 Theresa McClenaghan and Darryl Finnigan. 2004. Protecting Ontario's Water Now and Forever – A Statement of Expectations for Watershed-Based Source Protection Planning from Ontario Non-Governmental Organizations. Canadian Environmental Law Association and Environmental Defence. November 10, 2004, 16.

6 Ministry of Environment, *White Paper on Watershed-Based Source Protection Planning.* (Ontario, 2004): 7.

7 Darren Timmer. "Source Water Protection in the Annapolis Valley, Nova Scotia: Local Capacity in a Watershed Context." MA Thesis, University of Guelph., 2003, 5.

8 Glen R. Boyd, Helge Reemtsma , Deborah A. Grimm , Siddhartha Mitra, "Pharmaceuticals and Personal Care Products in Surface and Treated Waters of Louisiana, USA and Ontario, Canada" *The Science of the Total Environment* 3, 11 (2003): 135-49, 136. Coagulation, flocculation and sedimentation have been shown to be ineffective while oxidation with chlorine and ozone, activated carbon and membrane filtration may remove some antibiotics.

9 Some of this section is taken from C. Hill, Intergovernmental Regulation: A Study of Safe Drinking Water Policy Implementation in Canada and the United States, PhD dissertation, University of British Columbia, Department of Political Science, Expected 2005. and C. Hill and K. Harrison, "Intergovernmental Regulation and Municipal Drinking Water" Paper presented to the CRUISE conference on Multi-level Governance, Carleton University October, 27-28, 2004.

10 E. Rogers. *Diffusion of Innovations.* (Free Press, 1962), 2.

11 *Vancouver Province*, "Refuses Lease of Capilano Lands – Government Turns Down the Proposal" April 7, 1905, 1.

12 Ibid.

13 James W. Morton, *Capilano – The Story of a River* (McClelland and Stewart Limited, 1970), 79.

14 E.A. Cleveland, "The Water Supply of Greater Vancouver" *Journal of the American Water Works Association* 24, 6 (1932): 795-821, 818.

15 Ibid., 819.

16 Ibid., 805.

17 12 percent of Vancouver's watersheds are owned by the City with 88 percent leased for 999 years. It is important to note that watershed lands have been identified within statements of intent by the Squamish, Tsleil-Waututh, Musqueam and Sto:Lo nations within the BC Treaty Commission's negotiation process.

18 *Vancouver Province*, "Squamish Road Start in '52 Opposed by Water Board." September 6, 1951.

19 Glenn Bohn, "Highway plan threatens to spark war over watershed: Seymour route would cost 3.85 billion – also faces political hurdles," *Vancouver Sun*, September 10, 2002.

20 C. Hill and K. Harrison, "Intergovernmental Regulation," 7.

21 *Vancouver Sun*, Ottawa's Sham Fight Against Sham Bacteria," October 6, 1942.

22 Vancouver Archives. Letter dated November 26, 1942, reply from Chief Commissioner E.A. Cleveland, Greater Vancouver Water District to WC Mainwaring, Chairman of the Advisory Council Provincial Civilian Protection Committee.

23 Ibid.

24 Several letters to this effect can be found in the GVWD correspondence for this period at the Vancouver Archives.

25 Alan Etkin, "When Common Sense Fails: Public Debate Over Watershed Management in British Columbia – A Case Study." Simon Fraser University; MA Thesis, 1994, 50.

26 Ibid., 76.

27 Greater Vancouver Water District, *Watershed Management Evaluation and Policy Review Final Summary Report*, Prepared by Economic and Engineering Services, 1991.

28 Ibid.

29 Etkin, "When Common Sence Fails," 83.

30 Ibid., 86.

31 Jeff Lee, "GVRD postpones water projects," *Vancouver Sun*, January 31, 1998, A3.

32 J. Aramini, M McLean, J Wilson, J Holt, R Copes, B Allen, and W Sears, *Drinking Water Quality and Health Care Utilization for Gastrointestinal Illness in Greater Vancouver,* Health Canada, Population and Public Health Branch, October, 2000.

33 Greater Vancouver Water District, Minutes of a Meeting of the Greater Vancouver Water District Administration Board, June 29, 1994.

34 Lee Botts and Paul Muldoon. *The Great Lakes Water Quality Agreement: Its Past Successes and Uncertain Future.* (Institute on International Environmental Governance, 1996).

35 Quoted in Ibid.

36 See Kathryn Harrison, "The Origins of National Standards: Comparing Federal Government Involvement in Environmental Policy in Canada and the United States" in P.C. Fafard and K. Harrison, eds, *Managing the Environmental Union: Intergovernmental Relations and Environmental Policy in Canada* (School of Policy Studies, Queen's University), 2000, 49-80, and Barry Rabe, "Federalism and Entrepreneurship: Explaining American and Canadian Innovation in Pollution Prevention and Regulatory Integration," *Policy Studies Journal* 27, 2, (1999): 288-306.

37 Botts and Muldoon, *Great Lakes Water Quality Agreement.*

38 Damian Dupuy, "Technological Change and Environmental Policy: the Diffusion of Environmental Technology," *Growth and Change*, 28, (Winter 1997): 50.

39 Environment Canada and USEPA, *Lake Ontario Lakewide Management Plan Update.* 2005. Available at www.binational.net.

40 Environment Canada and USEPA Environment Canada and USEPA. *Lake Ontario Lakewide Management Plan Update,* 2004, Available at www.binational.net.

41 Illinois, Indiana, Michigan, Minnesota, New York, Ohio, Pennsylvania, and Wisconsin were signatories to the agreement.

42 Ontario and Quebec were signatories to the agreement.

43 Environmental Defence and Canadian Environmental Law Association, *Great Lakes, Great Pollution: Canadian Pollutant Releases and Transfers to the Great Lakes.* (Pollution Watch, June, 2005).

44 The Nutrient Management Act has also been enacted and regulations are currently being developed to address agricultural activities that generate impacts on drinking water sources. Ontario's Environmental Protection Act and Environmental Bill of Rights may also provide some protections for drinking water sources. See Richard Lindgren, "Tapwater on Trial: Overview of Ontario's Drinking Water Regime." Paper prepared for the Third Annual Conference on Water and Wastewater in Ontario, May 5-6, 2005, Canadian Environmental Law Association.

45 Ministry of Environment, 2004, *White Paper on Watershed-Based Source Protection*, 19.

46 The Canadian Environmental Law Association, Environmental Defence, Conservation Ontario, Ducks Unlimited Canada, the Ontario Municipal Water Association and the Ontario Water Works Association joined in writing a letter urging the government to act quickly.

47 *Globe and Mail*, "Activists fear back-pedalling on water protection," May 23, 2005.

48 Timmer, "Source Water Protection."

49 It must be underscored that the EPA is a federal agency whereas the Ontario Ministry of Environment is provincial. Some US states certainly go beyond the Source Water Assessments required by the SDWA since 1996.

50 Donald M. Berwick, "Disseminating Innovations in Health Care," *Journal of the American Medical Association* 289 (2003): 1969–75.

51 Ontario Water Works Association and Ontario Municipal Water Association, Submission on the White Paper on Watershed-Based Source Protection Planning. Prepared by Joseph F. Castrilli, Judy A. Macdonald, and Gary Scandlan, 2004.

10 Information Disclosure as an Environmental Policy Instrument and a Self-Regulatory Tool

STEPHAN SCHOTT
AND COADY WING

An increasing number of governments have been experimenting with the use of environmental information disclosure programs, including the United States, Indonesia, and China.[1] And in addition to publicly managed programs, some governments are also faced with the implications of privately operated disclosure programs over which they have little control. Some industries have also begun setting their own standards, guidelines, and targets. These approaches often involve the development of voluntary codes by industry associations, standards organizations, and third party NGOs.[2] The Canadian Chemical Producers' Association's *Responsible Care* strategy is a good example of this type of self-regulation, and has become a model for industries in many other countries.[3]

In many ways, this growth in information disclosure is a byproduct of the advances in information technology made over the last 10-15 years. The advent of the Internet has drastically decreased the costs of disseminating, tracking, and managing information and data relevant to a huge number of social situations. But despite the growing interest in the use of information-based policy instruments, it is not yet clear how disclosure schemes actually affect environmental outcomes. Indeed, the very purpose of information disclosure programs is often unclear and confusing.

Disclosure strategies are sometimes justified on the grounds that the public has a *right to know* how the actions of different individuals and firms affect the environment. But this *right to know* rationale suggests that information disclosure is not so much an instrument for achieving environmental objectives as it is a vehicle for addressing ethical concerns. If information disclosure is to be useful as an environmental policy instrument, it must somehow affect the environmental decisions of the firms and individuals most responsible for environmental damages.

To this end, disclosed information about environmental issues may create peer pressure, stimulate a consumer response, or provoke NGOs and governments to take stronger action. In this decentralized regulatory environment, monitoring and enforcement are no longer performed solely by government bodies, and policy targets are, to some extent, endogenous to the nongovernmental policy process. This comes with both pros and cons. On the one hand, this new policy environment creates more uncertainty about outcomes and about the magnitude of environmental improvements. On the other hand, the increase in information may allow governments to avoid implementing ineffective and inappropriate targets and policies. Furthermore, regulators can gain important insights by encouraging information disclosure or relative performance criteria, rather than directly regulating the entire industry or specific firms.

Although there are clearly some potential benefits associated with the use of information disclosure strategies to achieve environmental goals, they are not appropriate under all conditions. The use of information disclosure for regulatory purposes should be grounded in a thorough understanding of the strategies and incentives of firms to reveal, share and publish information. The nature of regulation and the role of regulators changes with the type of information disclosure strategy being pursued: mandatory disclosure calls for a different role than situations in which entire industries decide to voluntarily disclose information and to create their own codes of conduct. Disclosure can reduce the burden of environmental regulation, or it can make it more complicated. In some cases, it may also necessitate more rigorous antitrust regulation.

Given these concerns, Tietenberg has argued that information provision represents a third phase (following command and control regulatory strategies and market based instruments) in the way that governments have attempted to manage pollution problems. Tietenberg observes that beyond any sort of ethical agenda, "the typical information disclosure strategy involves four separate functions: (1) establishing mechanisms for discovering environmental risks, (2) assuring the reliability of the information, (3) publicizing or sharing the information, and (4) acting on the information."[4] Although this set of functions is a good initial starting point, it does very little to aid policy makers who need to know when information disclosure programs can be useful, how disclosure strategies are likely to effect the operation of other regulatory instruments, how different program features and different types of information influence the expected impact of information disclosure, and how information disclosure might shape the behavior of firms and consumers. Existing work on the use of information disclosure instruments is often concerned with the operation and effectiveness of specific

programs. While this sort of analysis is valuable, it does not provide a theoretical basis for addressing the important policy questions mentioned above.

Our objective in the chapter is to clarify the different types of information
disclosure program models available to governments, to identify some of the
ways such programs might be used to improve environmental outcomes, to
provide a simple theoretical framework that can be used as starting point for
policy analysis, and to discuss some of the regulatory implications of information disclosure strategies. In the first section, we develop a taxonomy of
different models of information disclosure programs, and use it to consider a
sample of existing programs. The second section then presents a simple theoretical analysis of information disclosure in the presence of different informational constraints, and under different levels of industry heterogeneity.
Particular attention is given to the role of public perception in determining
the decision to disclose environmental data. Next, we turn our attention to
the implications of disclosing different types of information in government-
controlled programs. Then, in the fourth section, we evaluate some of the
regulatory implications associated with the various forms of information disclosure strategies. Finally, we discuss some conclusions about the use of environmental information disclosure and present some suggestions that we feel
can help improve policy analysis related to information-based instruments.

A TAXONOMY OF INFORMATION DISCLOSURE PROGRAMS

Before developing a more theoretical framework for analyzing information
disclosure strategies, it is important to consider some of the similarities and
differences associated with existing programs. In this section we classify several different forms of already implemented information disclosure programs, and discuss their role in changing the environmental business
practices of firms and industries. Table 10.1 categorizes different possible information disclosure programs by distinguishing between mandatory or voluntary information provision, by the type of information revealed (ranked
or non-ranked), and by the driver or processor of information disclosure.
Some examples are provided for illustrative purposes, but this is by no means
a comprehensive list of information disclosure programs.

Firm-specific Information Disclosure and Corporate Social Responsibility

Individual companies increasingly publish non-financial information as
part of the corporate social responsibility (CSR) movement. The Economist magazine recently published a survey on CSR, which defines two dimensions of business practices: raising or reducing profits, and raising or

Table 10.1
A Taxonomy of Information Disclosure Programs

	Mandatory		Voluntary	
	Ranked	Non-ranked	Ranked	Non-ranked
Government-imposed	Indonesia's Proper Prokasih, China's Green Watch	TRI, SFIP, NPRI		ARET
NGO-based	UK's Factory Watch, Score-card in U.S.	NPI	UK's Factory Watch, Scorecard in U.S.	NPI
Membership-based		Responsible Care, Electricity Producers		
Firm-specific			Sustainability, Standard & Poor, UNEP	Corporate environmental reports

reducing social welfare.[5] Underlying the CSR movement is the argument that good management raises both social welfare and corporate profits. Indeed, the appeal of CSR is that the appropriate business decisions can achieve results that both serves the public interest and maximizes shareholder value.

However, the CSR framework can also be used for less benign purposes. Firms might simply contribute to charity or other social projects because they need to improve their reputation after having received negative media attention. If they do this at the expense of their day-to-day business activities, the notion of a double-dividend falls apart. An interesting observation by *The Economist* is that business leaders in favor of good corporate citizenship rarely demand the removals of barriers to competition. Instead, they argue for regulation that restricts competition in the name of environmental or social causes. The Economist refers to this practice as "pernicious CSR" and concludes that "CSR is little more than a cosmetic treatment ... [that] will distract attention from genuine problems of business ethics that do need to be addressed," and that "correcting market failures is best left to government."[6] Although we agree that the CSR movement (and information disclosure more generally) is susceptible to these sorts of manipulations, we also feel that the correction of market failures comes at a cost and requires sufficient amounts of information. Indeed, the very reason for employing information disclosure strategies is that governments may not have the information to correct market failures. In this sense, asymmetric information is a source of both market failure and government weakness, and information disclosure may be crucial in correcting market failures.

In light of concerns about what The Economist has termed "pernicious CSR," several attempts have been made to rank/evaluate the quality of CSR reports produced by individual firms. The most recent report – *Risk and Opportunity* by SustainAbility, Standard & Poor, and the United Nations Environmental Program (UNEP) – presents a list of the top fifty socially responsible companies, most of which are multinationals from Europe. This type of ranking is of questionable value because of problems associated with:

- Comparing different industries and the objectives of different firms;
- The verification of reported non-financial data;
- Monitoring the implementation of stated targets and objectives; and
- Evaluating the trade-off between profits, environmental protection and social justice (the so-called "triple bottom line").

Although these problems make cross-industry rankings of self-reported non-financial information somewhat meaningless, such disclosure and ranking efforts do tend to reward companies that are more open about their problems and that provide a vision that deals with the social and environmental impacts of their business practices. Shareholders also seem to prefer companies with a clear vision that openly addresses possible environmental and social risks. A Canadian example of this is Suncor, which currently exhibits greater transparency regarding the impacts of its business practices and future plans than its Canadian competitors.[7]

Membership Programs

Membership in industry associations such as the Chemical Producers, the Electricity Producers, or the European Aluminum Producers usually requires achieving industry standards, and meeting minimum requirements for business conduct and environmental and social performance. Once a company becomes a member, it may also be required to disclose and share information. It is worth pointing out, however, that formal disclosure rules need not be in place for industry associations to be understood as a form of information disclosure. As long as membership is contingent on maintaining a given level of environmental performance, any firm that is a member of the association has revealed some information about itself: specifically, that it performs as well or better than the requirements of membership. Generally speaking, industry environmental associations pursue several objectives, including:

- Sharing information;
- Assuring coordinated development of innovative approaches;
- Avoiding free riding on industry leadership;
- Improving the image of the industry as a whole; and
- Preempting regulation.

In order to be successful an industry organization needs to be perceived as making continuous progress and having self-regulatory capacity. But even when these conditions are met, there are several risks and potential implications that should be considered when contemplating the environmental value of industry associations. First, it is not obvious to what extent environmental improvements should be attributed to the strategies of industry associations (even extremely successful ones like *Responsible Care*), and to what extent they should be understood as part of general trends in business practices and technological innovations. Second, industry associations present an implicit risk to competitive markets. By design, industry associations attempt to foster *cooperation* between individual firms. This same cooperative spirit could be used to limit competition and to better control markets. Third, and most importantly, the decentralized and voluntary nature of self-regulating industries raises questions about how far firms can be expected to pursue socially optimal targets. Simply put, we do not have a solid idea of how much we can expect from voluntary codes and industry initiatives, and how much must be done through more intrusive regulatory measures.

Government Sponsored Programs

Government information disclosure programs can take a variety of forms. They can be mandatory and ranked, as they are in South East Asian countries, such as China and Indonesia. Or they can be mandatory and non-ranked, as they are in the United States and Canada. There are also some programs, like the Canadian Accelerate Reduction/Elimination of Toxics (ARET) initiative, that are government sponsored but voluntary. In general, mandatory programs collect and publish information that is more or less reliable (depending on the auditing system and the reliability of data verification). Some of them process the information and create rankings of firms. These types of strategies are clearly intended to draw attention to the relative performance of firms, and to stimulate peer pressure and public reactions. These programs are only likely to work if:

- The potential reputational losses faced by firms are significant;
- There is a certain level of heterogeneity of firms; and
- There is considerable public pressure.

When reputation loss is not costly, or firms can make other claims (such as job security) to counteract bad publicity from published environmental data, mandatory programs might be fairly ineffective. But if reputations are damaged by disclosed information, and this damage matters to a large number of polluting firms, mandatory schemes can be very successful and efficient. This seems to be the case in Indonesia with the Proper Prokasih strategy of BAP-EDAL.[8] As we discuss in a later section, there are cases in which substantial monitoring and enforcement costs can be saved, because firms have an incentive to voluntarily comply with certain regulations or to move up in rank. This type of disclosure program can also be expected to improve the transparency of the regulatory agency as well. As Afsah, Laplante, and Wheeler (1997) point out, environmental agencies that implement disclosure strategies are also revealing their "ability to process information reliably and enforce existing regulations."[9]

Some environmental agencies do not expose themselves as much, or do not rank published or collected information. Instead they rely on the public or the legal system to interpret and use the disclosed information. In many ways, this is the case for the Toxic Release Inventory (TRI) program in the United States. Concerned citizens or NGOs can sue individual firms or industries, when the latter are out of compliance or pollute above industry standards. In Canada, the National Pollutant Release Inventory (NPRI) has raised public awareness, but has not been the driving force of changing business practices and improving environmental performance. Environmental improvements in Canada are still considered to be the result of direct government regulation.[10]

NGO Administered Programs

NGOs often use published information to inform the public or parties that are directly affected by the actions of firms, or to directly pressure specific companies or industries. They use both voluntarily supplied as well as mandatory information for these purposes. In some cases they use raw data to create their own rankings and interpretations of published data. By conducting this type of data analysis and presentation, NGOs add another dimension to the complexity of information disclosure programs. Because they represent a particular point of view, the involvement of a particular NGO might strengthen the ability of information disclosure programs to achieve socially desirable outcomes, or it might lead them in less desirable directions. For instance, from a total welfare perspective, it may not be desirable to boycott the worst polluting firm if that firm faces different production costs, adjustment horizons or social problems, but a single issue NGO may pursue this type of action.

VOLUNTARY INFORMATION DISCLOSURE: A THEORETICAL FRAMEWORK

The relative dearth of theoretical explanations of information disclosure makes it difficult for policy makers to determine when different sorts of information disclosure strategies might be useful, how they might interact with existing policy instruments, and what outcomes they might yield. In this section, we present a simple theoretical framework that could be used to guide policy analysis related to specific situations.

The framework focuses on the likelihood and implications of voluntary information disclosure under a variety of market conditions. In general, voluntary disclosure strategies operate at lower cost and may be easier to manage than mandatory disclosure regimes. However, there are risks associated with the quality of information, the decision to disclose, and the practicality of dissemination techniques that make voluntary disclosure more feasible in some cases than others. We argue that, under certain conditions, voluntary disclosure may approximate mandatory disclosure, or at least deviate from it in predictable and manageable ways. As such, an understanding of the incentives and dynamics at work in voluntary information disclosure offers significant insights into mandatory schemes.

In order to derive the true value of information disclosure instruments, we need to distinguish between different types of uncertainty and asymmetric information. The success of any environmental policy or regulatory strategy (be it government mandated regulation or industry initiated self-regulation) depends on public perception and on the incentives of the regulating body to implement new targets or environmental goals. This is particularly true in situations where information about the costs of environmental damage and of emission reductions is known only with uncertainty. Global warming is a perfect case in point. Different policies have been implemented in various countries and regions despite large uncertainty about climate change impacts from greenhouse gas emissions. When dealing with climate change, governments' decisions to pursue greenhouse gas reductions and to follow international agreements depend heavily on the level of public concern in their jurisdiction. Given these concerns about public perception and informational constraints, this section sets up an informal model that evaluates the implications of several variables on the decision of individual firms to disclose information. The key variables evaluated in the model are:

(1) Public Perception
(2) Heterogeneity of firms (complete homogeneity or identical firms, and heterogeneity)
(3) Private information about firms' costs
(4) Industry information about firms' costs (firms know each other's costs but the public and the government only have incomplete knowledge)

Defining Key Contextual Features

Throughout this theoretical discussion, we use terms such as *disclosure and release* to refer to the dissemination of environmental information about individual firms through a centralized reporting system of some kind. In practice, the reporting system is usually a website or regular publication that contains the same information about participating firms.

We use the phrase *homogeneous firms* to describe an industry in which each firm is responsible for the same amount of environmental damage, employs the same production processes, faces the same costs of reducing their environmental impact, and is subject to the same market pressures and incentives. In contrast, *heterogeneous firms* denotes an industry in which one or more firms is distinct in some way: they may cause less environmental damage, have access to different technologies or processes, find it less costly to improve their environmental performance, or face different economic incentives or pressures than other firms in the industry. Such heterogeneity could be limited to a single *different* firm, or it could be widespread in the sense that no two firms are exactly alike.

Within each industrial context, different informational conditions can influence the way voluntary information disclosure might occur. Regardless of the amount of information available, we assume that the public always has some perception of the environmental performance of an industry. For simplicity, we also assume that firms are able to observe this *public perception at zero cost* through the normal course of their business. It is also important to note that the level of public perception is almost certainly influenced by the disclosure of information. Indeed, the impact of an information disclosure strategy depends in large part on the degree to which public perceptions are determined by available information. In a voluntary disclosure setting, a firm's decision to reveal information about its environmental practices is driven by the *reputational gains and losses* that it may receive or incur as a result of its decision. Conceptually, potential gains or losses in reputation can be thought of as the distance between actual environmental performance and public perceptions of environmental performance, and between the environmental performances of individual firms. As we discuss more fully later in this section, the way a particular firm evaluates the possible reputational benefits or costs associated with information disclosure is affected by the industrial structure and informational constraints that it faces.

Beyond public perception and reputational incentives, we consider three informational conditions: perfect information, and two types of asymmetric information. In the context of our discussion, *perfect information* implies a situation of complete transparency. Firms have complete information about the production, environmental damage, technology, processes, costs, and incentives of every firm in the market. Because the public is also privy to all of this information, public perceptions about the environmental performance of the industry and its firms exactly match actual environmental performance. Implicitly, *perfect information* represents a case in which there is simply nothing left to disclose.

The first type of asymmetric information is the extreme opposite of perfect information. We use the term *private information* to describe a situation in which all information about individual firms is hidden. Firms know about their own situation but know very little about the other firms in the industry. Because this information is also hidden from the public, public perceptions about the environmental performance of a particular industry may be different than actual performance.

The second type of asymmetric information involves cases in which information about the production, environmental damage, technology, costs and incentives of firms is well known *within* the industry, but is hidden *outside* the industry. As before, public perceptions about environmental performance may be distinct from the actual performance of firms in the industry.

Perfect Information

Under conditions of perfect information, information disclosure – whether voluntary or mandatory – is unlikely to change the behavior of any of the actors in a situation. In this scenario, there is no confusion or misconception about the environmental damages caused by the firms in an industry. Perceptions of environmental performance exactly mirror their real counterparts, and firms are not able to extract any reputational advantage by releasing information that is already widely known. Interestingly, the condition of perfect information yields the same outcome as an extensive, mandatory information disclosure program: it represents the removal of all informational barriers and imperfections. Although the condition of perfect information is somewhat difficult to imagine in the real world, this discussion underlines the fundamental point that the usefulness of information disclosure is derived from market failures related to informational asymmetries.

It is also worth noting that in an industry with perfect information (or something close to it) firms may tend towards homogeneity simply because they can be expected to utilize the most efficient and effective business practices. New practices would be observable by everyone and would be copied by the entire market if they were actually beneficial. Since perfect information is similar to a successful and comprehensive information disclosure program, increased industry homogeneity may be an unintended byproduct of the use of information disclosure strategies.

Private Information

Unlike conditions of perfect information, information disclosure has the potential to alter the behavior of both the public at large and the firms within the industry. Here, the firms have information about the public's perception of their environmental performance and about their own actual performance. This allows them to gauge the potential for reputational gains associated with the disclosure of environmental information. In essence, firms are more likely to release information if their actual performance exceeds public perception.

However, because firms lack information about the performance of the other firms in the industry, they are less able to evaluate how they are performing in relation to other firms. When public perception is above a firm's actual environmental performance, the firm is reluctant to disclose any information, because it does not want to reveal that it is actually performing worse than public perception and it could be even worse than other firms in the industry. If public perception is at or below the level of the firm's actual performance, it would be advantageous to the firm to signal to the public that it is actually performing better than the public thinks. The problem with private information is, however, that firms do not know if actual industry performance is much better than their own. A firm that discloses, therefore, is afraid it would invite better performers to embarrass it once it starts the disclosing process.

When an industry is heterogeneous, a firm that performs better than public perception could have the worst environmental performance in its industry. If this information were revealed, the firm would probably incur reputational losses. Since information about the heterogeneity of the industry and their environmental performance relative to their competitors is as hidden from the firms as it is from the public, firms will be reluctant to be the first firm to disclose information, unless they are significantly above public perception.

This incentive to avoid making the first move can result in an equilibrium where voluntary disclosure does not occur, and in which public perception diverges quite a bit from actual environmental performance levels. It is important to recognize that even a small number of information disclosing firms can have a tremendous impact on the reputation of every firm in an industry. In a case in which a minority of firms reports environmental information, the public may assume that the non-disclosing firms perform worse than disclosing ones. More succinctly, in a voluntary disclosure scheme, disclosing firms are likely to be the top environmental performers, because if other firms were superior they would have an incentive to disclose. Convincing some firms to make the first move, then, is crucial to the success of voluntary information disclosure with private information.

Industry Information

This third informational constraint involves situations in which firms are completely informed about the performance and activities of the other firms in the industry, but the public is not similarly informed. This condition alleviates the tendency for firms to uniformly follow the risk-averse, non-disclosure strategy that they might under the constraints associated with hidden information. By comparing their performance to both public perceptions and the actual performance of the other firms in the market, firms that share industry wide information are able to more fully evaluate the potential reputational gains or losses associated with disclosure.

Firms in a homogeneous industry have nothing to fear from their relative environmental performance because every firm performs at the same level. Firms are likely to disclose information as long as their real performance exceeds the public's perception of their performance. Unlike the "avoid the first move" strategy predicted in the hidden information case, it would not be surprising if firms in this scenario engaged in a race to disclose information to the public. Beyond improving their reputation and correcting public perception, early disclosers might experience additional reputational gains associated with being a transparent, forward looking, trustworthy, industry leader (as is the case with public recognition of csr).

Heterogeneity makes the decision to disclose somewhat more complicated. Instead of basing their decision solely on the gap between public perception and the real level of environmental performance, individual firms must also consider their relative position within the industry. Provided their performance exceeds public perception, the top environmental performers are likely to disclose. The outcome is less clear for firms with lower performance levels: if they attribute greater importance to relative performance (they are concerned about standing out as a poor environmental performer) than to the simple matter of being better than public perception, then they may choose not to disclose. However, each additional disclosing firm would seem to increase the likelihood that the remaining firms will disclose. If some firms disclose and some firms do not, the logical assumption on the part of the public is that the non-disclosing firms are worse performers than the disclosing firms. Since the firm now bears reputational costs simply for not revealing its environmental performance, a disclosure strategy and a possible change in business practices that brings environmental improvements becomes increasingly attractive.

A Recap of Voluntary Disclosure

The theoretical discussion above is by no means a definitive account of information disclosure, but it does highlight the utility of evaluating the likelihood of disclosure in terms of industrial structure and the presence of certain types of informational weaknesses in a particular market.

If public perception is equal to or below actual industry performance, some firms (or all firms in the case of complete homogeneity) should have an incentive to voluntarily disclose information, when firms know where they stand relative to other firms in their industry. The larger firm heterogeneity, the more firms will be reluctant to disclose, because they fear being ranked. Although firms might perform better than public perception, they might not wish to come in last among the firms that decide to disclose. The fact that some firms are not disclosing will create public pressure, but the public pressure might not be strong enough for some of the dirtier firms (that perform significantly below public perception) to significantly alter their direction. If this is the case, further regulatory action is required.

When public perception exceeds actual industry performance we have a dilemma for the public and the industry. In the homogenous case no firm should disclose, unless there are gains from being perceived as an industry leader or a more transparent firm. Thus none or only a few firms are likely to disclose, and no updating of public perception occurs. With heterogeneity and industry wide information the best performers will disclose and we will receive information that can be used to update public perception. As more firms disclose, public perception converges to the actual performance of the industry. A large number of firms that perform below the old inflated public perception level will fall below the line now and worsen their reputation.

In light of the previous discussion, it is worth considering the essential gains from voluntary disclosure programs. The first and most obvious point is that information disclosure should be seen as an instrument for improving the distribution of information in a particular market. Disclosure is a tool for aligning perceptions about performance with real performance levels. It is certainly not a tool for aligning the incentives of polluters and victims. Information instruments rely on the market importance of reputation and an institutional capacity to properly verify and disseminate information. As such, they may be of limited usefulness in industries with low public exposure (although one might also argue that low exposure simply indicates the presence of extreme informational asymmetries). Ensuring that information is trustworthy and is received by its intended audience are non-trivial concerns that will weigh heavily on the eventual power of the instrument.

Another less obvious conclusion is that information disclosure is rarely if ever a static endeavor. The key variables here – public perception, real performance levels, relative performance levels, and the reputation of firms and industries – are dynamic and are at least partially determined endogenously. We have suggested some of the ways in which disclosure might affect not only the reputation of individual firms, but also the level of heterogeneity that exists in a particular industry, and other ways undoubtedly exist as well. This endogeneity represents the real complexity involved in the use of information to achieve policy goals: subtle changes in the type and amount of information available to different actors can radically alter their behavior, or very large amount of efforts can result in very little substance.

CHOOSING WHAT TO RELEASE
IN MANDATORY PROGRAMS

The nature of the information released can range from raw data to firm and industry rankings and scoring systems, to associational or membership criteria. These different ways of presenting disclosed information surely influences the way it will affect the behavior of both individual firms and the public. Rather than simply plunging into the use of information disclosure programs, governments are advised to carefully assess the implications of releasing different types of information in different types of markets. The previous section focused on the decision of individual firms to disclose information in voluntary settings. This section considers the implications of different types of information that might be released by government mandated information disclosure programs.

Raw Information

The release of raw information involves releasing the quantity of a particular pollutant released by a given company in a given time period. Initially, this seems like the ideal form of information to disclose. It directly increases the information available in the market, and it allows interested individuals and organizations to observe and compare the environmental performance of any firm on the list. The problem, of course, is that this approach implies that all pollution and all firms are alike and are comparable. Raw pollution information contains no explanation of the pollution reduction costs of the individual firms, nor does it account for differences in the level of output of different firms. While careful analysts could adjust their conclusions to account for output differences, they are less likely to have information about the pollution reduction costs of specific firms. The risk is that public pressure will be directed towards firms with the highest aggregate pollution, whether that pollution is efficient or not. In the worst possible scenario, this sort of information disclosure could run counter to the objectives of market based instruments like tradable emission permits.

Beyond its interaction with other environmental policy instruments, the effectiveness of raw information in stimulating public pressure also depends on the legal framework of the country. In the United States, where private legal action is very common, raw information could stimulate direct, organized campaigns against high polluting firms. In a less litigious country, such as Canada, public pressure is more likely to take the form of broad based protests, boycotts, and shaming strategies. Raw information might be less useful in this context because it requires participants to undertake the costs of analyzing the data without the incentive of any direct payoff.

Rankings and Scores

Rankings and scores involve transforming raw data into some measure of the quality of an entity's environmental performance. Since they can be created in ways that account for differences in reductions, costs and output levels, firm and industry specific rankings or scores can resolve some of the problems associated with the release of raw data. If this sort of transformation is done, there is no reason why information disclosure should be inconsistent with the operation of market-based instruments or emissions taxes.

In societies where private legal action is not common, ranked and/or scored data might also be more effective in promoting public pressure. Because rankings have already been analyzed and presented in an understandable way, interested organizations and individuals do not have to undertake analysis costs, and can quickly and easily evaluate the environmental performance of a particular firm. Ironically, given that it is much more aggregated, this type of information disclosure can be much less ambiguous than raw information. They contain an inherent judgment of the behavior and actions of particular firms and industries and are clearly intended to pressure firms to "do better."

Association/Certification

Associational information disclosure involves granting a particular firm the right to a particular label in return for employing an approved production method or business practice. In many ways, this sort of information disclosure is probably the most invasive and most powerful type of mandatory information disclosure. In general terms, it is an attempt to make previously invisible production techniques visible to consumers. Associational information disclosure is distinct from raw and ranked/scored data in that it requires substantially less collective action on the part of the intended audience. Instead of trying to generate public pressure on firms with poor environmental performance, associational devices simply allow consumers to differentiate between environmentally "good" and "bad" companies.

REGULATORY AND POLICY IMPLICATIONS OF INFORMATION DISCLOSURE

With perfect information about firms' emissions, their production costs and technologies, and the damage costs of emissions, we do not need information disclosure programs. In a situation like this, where informational constraints are minimal, environmental objectives are probably better served by the introduction of taxes or incentives, or the creation of an emissions trading system with a fixed cap set at the optimal level of pollution. Perfect information, however, can hardly ever be achieved. Damage costs can often only be vaguely estimated, and information about the abatement and production costs of firms is difficult and costly to obtain.[11] And even with close to perfect information, firms will not always comply with emission regulations. Monitoring and enforcement is, therefore, also required. This is costly and never achieves perfect results. In a world of uncertainty and asymmetric information, information disclosure could be a valuable and important policy instrument.

Voluntary information disclosure is free to the public and government regulators. Mandatory programs, on the other hand, are costly to run, because they must not only ensure that every firm that is obliged to disclose actually does so, but also verify that disclosed information is correct. It is crucial to recognize the fact that voluntary disclosure programs provide us with information about firms that decide not to disclose as well as information about those firms that actually do disclose. After analyzing the industry structure and the reaction of the industry to public perception and contextual variables (such as public pressure, the legal system, government rankings, etc), consumers of voluntarily disclosed information can infer a great deal about firms that chose not to reveal information. Furthermore, only the information from firms that are disclosing needs to be verified, which makes this a much more economic program to run in many cases. Finally, voluntary disclosure lacks the authoritarian characteristics of a command-and control instrument, in which the government alone dictates environmental objectives and rules of conduct.

When Do We Need A Mandatory System?

In our theory section we found that individual firms are reluctant to disclose under conditions of private information. In these cases, public perception could diverge quite significantly from actual industry performance. Even when public perception is lower than actual industry performance firms might be reluctant to disclose. Governments could gain significant informational insights if it implemented a mandatory system in situations of private information. Furthermore, the lower public perception is, the more pressured governments will be to introduce mandatory programs. Once information is disclosed, the public might adjust their perception upwards, and might be satisfied without any further regulatory action. If public perception is adjusted downwards, or the public is not satisfied with the disclosed environmental performance level, it might induce pressure through a variety of mechanisms. Ultimately, the effectiveness of an information disclosure program in achieving environmental change depends on the ability to pressure firms into changing their business practices. We have argued that firms will undertake improvements in their environmental practices, if there are strong reputational losses from being considered to be an underperformer (as in Indonesia's Proper Prokasih), if there are economic fees and incentives (as in China's system),[12] or if the legal system allows sanctions to be imposed (as in the United States). In a country where none of the above incentives are strong enough to induce change, information disclosure programs such as the NPRI in Canada are still valuable. They release information that will inevitably improve regulatory decisions. The information helps firms in the industry to evaluate where they stand, and it helps align public perception with actual performance levels. In addition, this might start a form of rivalry between firms to become better environmental performers. The latter could be desirable as long as it does not lead to improving environmental performance with no regard for costs, employment and consumer prices.

In some cases, it might be more economic to have a temporary mandatory program or to reward those industry leaders that first decide to disclose information. Once some firms disclose other top environmental performers (or the entire industry in the case of complete homogeneity) will follow, and public perception will be updated, and will move closer to actual industry performance. Under this scheme not all the firms' information needs to be verified because some firms will decide not to disclose.

We are faced with a social dilemma, however, if public perception is better than actual performance. In this scenario firms are very reluctant to disclose. Only the very best performers are likely to come forward, and then only if they are certain of their superiority. The government and the public both are quite satisfied as well. Without negative public sentiment, there is no pressure on the government to act. With industry-wide information this might promote collusion to maintain the artificially high public perception. The industry might decide to form an association and control information release, as well as the future direction of the sector. This would probably improve public perception even further and worsen the dilemma. Mandatory programs organized by industry organizations have the perverse ability not only to preempt mandatory government regulation, but also to control the interpretation and possible ranking of information. Most of them do not rank individual firms, but set membership standards and requirements instead. This may be a strategy for increasing market power over non-members, while keeping information about members semi-private.

To Rank Or Not To Rank

Governments that encourage voluntary programs or install mandatory programs need to decide whether to interpret information and possibly rank disclosing firms, or to simply release raw data. Rankings only make sense for industries with a considerable level of heterogeneity among firms. If information is private a ranking system will discourage firms to disclose voluntarily. In this case, a regulator could address this reluctance either by starting a mandatory program or by rewarding leadership (provide incentives to the first firms that disclose).

Raw information disclosure can be rather misleading. The reaction of firms and the public to raw information is uncertain. As discussed earlier, reactions seem to depend on rivalry between firms, sanctioning possibilities, the level of public engagement, and/or the interpretation of courts. A ranking system could provide government guidance and realign information disclosure programs with other policy targets and instruments such as emission taxes or pollution permits. Voluntary participation in an emission trading scheme, for example, could be considered by a regulator in the ranking of a relatively dirty firm. In addition, governments may want to consider the public demand for more transparent raw data versus its demand for the convenience of pre-analyzed rankings or scores. Here, the intended use of the information is also important. In general, raw data is probably more useful for formal, legalistic responses to information disclosure, while rankings and scores are more suited to more decentralized social responses, government imposed sanctions or other regulatory action.

Competition Between Firms

Depending on the situation, information disclosure might have anticompetitive implications or may improve competition between firms. Firms could use information disclosure and environmental improvement programs to erect barriers to entry. Competitive industries with different technologies could be prevented from entering the market because they do not belong to an industry association or they do not meet self-imposed industry standards or regulations.

In some cases there are incentives for the industry to avoid information disclosure, i.e. when public perception is better than actual industry performance. Particularly when there is industry wide information it could lead to collusion of firms to conceal information in order to sustain the divergence between public perception and industry performance. This kind of secret cooperation could also lead to increased market manipulations or sharing of profits, particularly in industries with only a few companies. It is worth noting that outside the environmental sphere, industry wide coordination of business practices are generally viewed as anticompetitive: it may be naive to assume that coordination under the rubric of environmental performance is not simply a cover for more malicious intentions.

Once information is disclosed it could reduce the heterogeneity of firms. This could reduce product diversity (a possible disadvantage), but could also increase competition by making it more difficult for firms to segment the market through product differentiation. Firms would have to compete with increasingly similar technologies, cost structures and products, and consumers would be less inclined to identify with a certain brand or production technology. Under these conditions firms might find it more difficult to extract consumer rents.

CONCLUSIONS

Information disclosure is crucial for effective, fair and appropriate regulation of polluters. It does not need to be perfect or complete. The increasing ease of information disclosure and dissemination, increasing rewards for firms that voluntarily disclose reduce the need for mandatory programs. Only in cases of insufficient industry-wide information do governments perhaps need to encourage disclosure with incentives, the supply of partial information about the industry structure, or temporary mandatory schemes.

Information disclosure not only benefits the public, but also helps individual firms realize how they perform in relation to other firms. This in itself is a very valuable effect, because it can encourage other firms to disclose and might induce under-performing firms to change their business practices.

The operation and implications of information disclosure programs are complex: their outcomes are affected by the behavior of multiple actors, and depend on public perception, information asymmetries, government incentives, and industry structure. This makes it difficult to predict what changes information disclosure programs will bring. As a result, disclosure strategies are most applicable to situations where it is difficult to agree on specific targets, there is insufficient information available, and where victims are entitled to pollution compensation determined by courts.

One thing is certain, however. Information disclosure will update public perception and bring it more in line with actual industry performance. This will prevent governments from being complacent when public perception is too optimistic, and forces them to act on unsatisfactory industry environmental performances. The main danger of information disclosure strategies is the potential for increased industry collusion on the type of information disclosed, the control of public perception, and the manipulation of market competition. The prevention of the latter is a major task for governments and NGOs, and calls for careful integration of environmental and competition policy.

NOTES

1 There are various categories that each firm is allocated to. See for example S. Afsah, B. Laplante, and D. Wheeler, "Regulation in the Information Age- Indonesian Public Information Program for Environmental Management," Unpublished Working Paper 1997, and S. Pargal and D. Wheeler, "Informal Regulation in developing Countries: Evidence from Indonesia," *Journal of Political Economy* 104, (1996): 1314-27.

2 See K. Webb "Understanding the Voluntary Codes Phenomenon," in Kernaghan Webb, ed. *Voluntary Codes-Private Governance, the Public Interest and Innovation* (Carleton Research Unit for Innovation, Science and Environment (CRUISE 2004)): 3-31.

3 See J. Moffet, F. Bregha and M.J. Middelkoop, "Responsible Care: A Case Study of a Voluntary Environmental Initiative," in K. Webb, ed. *Voluntary Codes-Private Governance, the Public Interest and Innovation*, (Carleton Research Unit for Innovation, Science and Environment (CRUISE 2004)): 177-207.

4 Ibid., 590.

5 The Economist, January 20, 2005. "The Good Company: A Survey of Corporate Social Responsibility."

6 Ibid.

7 Suncor was ranked 37th (the first time in the top 50) in "Risk and Opportunity" by SustainAbility, Standard & Poor, and UNEP.

8 See S. Afsah, B. Laplante and D. Wheeler, "Regulation in the Information Age, for an accurate description of the programme, its rationale and its impact."

9 Ibid.

10 STRATOS, "Enhancing Public Access to Corporate Environmental Performance Information," Report submitted to Environment Canada (Oil, Gas and Energy Branch), 2002.

11 Theoretically it is possible to inspect every firm and estimate how its production costs vary with different emission levels. This is very costly and in some cases not even feasible because of confidentiality restrictions and the possibility of firms hiding information when inspectors schedule to visit.

12 See a recent article by H. Wang and D. Wheeler, "Financial Incentives and Endogenous Enforcement in China's Pollution Levy System," *Journal of Environmental Economics and Management*, 49, 1 (January 2005): 174-96.

APPENDICES

APPENDIX ONE

Canadian and Comparative Science and Technology Data

GERD=Gross domestic expenditures on research and development; BERD=Business enterprise expenditure on research and development; HERD=higher education expenditure on research and development. Triadic patent families means that the patent has been registered at the three main national patent offices (the USPTO, EPO and JPO)

Figure 1
GERD as a Percentage of GDP, Top OECD and Non-OECD Countries, 2001

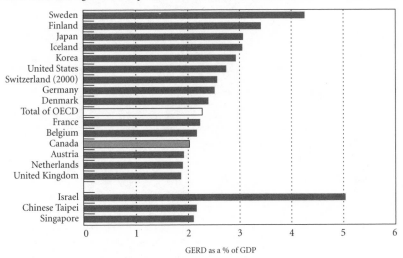

GERD as a % of GDP

Source: OECD, *Main Science and Technology Indicators*, 2004/1, July 2004.

Figure 2
Canada's GERD by Major Source of Funds, 1993 to 2003

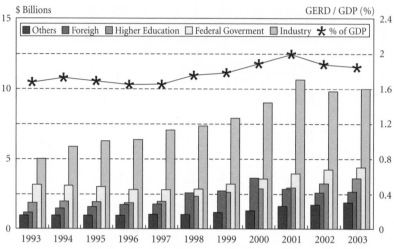

Source: Statistics Canada, *Science Statistics Service Bulletin*, Vol. 28, No 2, Cat. No. 88-001-XIE, January 2004.

Figure 3
Estimate of Canada's R&D Expenditudes by Source of Funds and Performing Sector, 2003

		Source of Funds						
Performer	Total	Federal Government	Provincial Government	Business Enterprises	Higher Education	PNPs	Foreign	Percent by Performer
				($ millions)				
Total	22 450	4 368	1 256	9 952	3 603	641	2 630	100
Federal Government	2 174	2 114	6	54	0	0	0	10
Provincial Governments	305	0	305	0	0	0	0	1
PROs	26	1	14	10	0	0	1	0
Business Enterprises	12 060	330	53	9 150	0	0	2527	54
Higher Education	7 831	1 919	861	730	3 603	616	102	35
PNPs	54	4	17	8	0	25	0	0
Percent by Source	100	19	6	44	16	3	12	—

Source: Statistics Canada, Estimates of Canadian Research and Development Expenditures (GERD), Canada, 1992, to 2003p, and by Province 1992 to 2001, Cat. No. 88F0006XIE No. 3, January 2004.

Figure 4

BERD as a Percentage of GDP, Top OECD and Non-OECD Countries, 2001

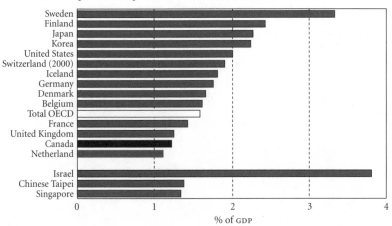

Source: OECD, Main Science and Technology Indicators 2004/1, July 2004.

Figure 5

HERD as a Percentage of GERD, Selected OECD Countries, 2001

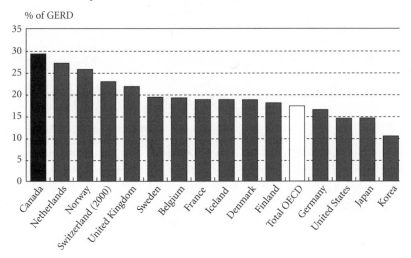

Source: OECD, Main Science and Technology Indicators 2004/1, July 2004.

Table 1
Triadic Patent Families[1]: As Percentage of GDP[2]
according to the residence of the inventors, by priority year

	1991	2000
Finland	1.69	3.99
Japan	3.30	3.90
Switzerland	3.95	3.68
Sweden	2.18	3.68
Germany	2.21	3.01
Israel	1.35	2.88
Netherlands	1.84	2.13
Denmark	0.98	1.90
United States	1.57	1.67
European Union	1.30	1.61
France	1.51	1.51
Belgium	1.16	1.43
United Kingdom	1.19	1.33
Austria	1.03	1.32
Singapore	0.47	1.08
Luxembourg	0.79	0.89
Norway	0.63	0.76
Korea	0.24	0.73
Australia	0.48	0.70
Canada	0.47	0.65
Italy	0.58	0.59
Iceland	0.52	0.56
New Zealand	0.35	0.50
Ireland	0.50	0.44
Hungary	0.24	0.29
Slovenia	0.09	0.25
Chinese Taipei	0.06	0.19
Spain	0.12	0.15
Slovak Republic	0.00	0.08
Russian Federation	0.02	0.08
Czech Republic	0.08	0.07
Portugal	0.03	0.05
Greece	0.04	0.04
Argentina	0.02	0.03

Table 1 (*continued*)

Poland	0.04	0.03
China	0.01	0.02
Mexico	0.01	0.02
Chile	0.01	0.01
Turkey	0.00	0.01
Romania	0.01	0.01

Source: OECD, Patent Database, September 2004.

Notes

1 Patents all applied for at the EPO, USPTO and JPO. 2000 figures are estimates.

2 Gross Domestic Product (GDP), billion 1995 USD using purchasing power parities.

Selected Environmental Indicators

(*Source*: Adapted from Environment Canada (2003) *Environmental Signals: Headline Indicators* www.ec.gc.ca/soer-ree/)

Environmental indicators provide a broad snapshot of the Canadian environment over the last several decades, covering nine broad areas: water use, wastewater treatment, air quality, acid rain, stratospheric ozone layer depletion, wildlife & wilderness, toxic substances, and non-hazardous solid waste.

Deteriorating	Mixed signals	Improving
Greenhouse gas emissions	Per capita municipal water use	Protected Areas
Non-hazardous solid waste	Air quality	Population covered by waste-water treatment
	Stratospheric ozone layer	Reduction in acid rain

Water use has continued to rise over the last twenty years, primarily as a result of population growth. Municipal per capita water usage, however, has slightly decreased over this period.

The treatment of *wastewater* has steadily improved since the mid-1980s, with major investments in the infrastructure of municipal wastewater treatment leading to a greater of the population covered. Nevertheless, it remains a core source of pollution to natural water areas and sources in Canada.

Air quality has remained relatively stable over the past fifteen years. The emission of precursor gases, a major source of airborne pollutants, has not seen an increase over this period. There are regional differences, however, with eastern provinces having significantly higher levels of air pollution than western provinces.

As a signatory to the Kyoto Protocol, Canada is committed to reducing its *greenhouse emissions* (GHG) to 6% below 1990 levels by 2012. On a per capita basis, Canada is one of the largest contributors to global GHG levels. GHG emissions have increased by 20% as a result of increased automobile travel and energy use.

Levels of *acid rain* have been steadily decreasing since the late 1980s, and have been below the national cap of 3.2 million tonnes since 1994. This progress is particularly evident in eastern Canada; however, further reductions in acid rain are necessary to prevent continuing damage to the environment in eastern parts.

The "thickness" of the stratospheric *ozone layer* above Canada has seen a steady decline since the late 1970s, in line with developments of the ozone layer. The Canadian ozone level was 6% below that of pre-1980.

Biodiversity has improved marginally in recent years with the designation of more areas as protected (6%) or strictly protected (10%). This still falls short of the United Nations' target of 12% of a country's total land area designated for the protection of habitat. Currently, 402 species are at risk in Canada. Of those species at risk that have been reassessed, the status of about 20 species has improved or no longer at risk while the status of just over 50 species has declined.

The release of *toxic substances* into the environment shows a mixed picture for the trend data available for 16 toxic substances from 1995 to 2000. While the levels of half of these decreased (such as a 35% decrease in mercury emissions), the levels of the other half either did not improve or worsened.

Levels of *non-hazardous solid waste* increased 10% between 1998 and 2000, reaching a level of almost 1000kg a person in 2000. Of this, however, almost 25% is recovered through waste diversion (recycling, reuse, composting).

(For Further details see Environment Canada (2003) *Environmental Signals: Headline Indicators* www.ec.gc.ca/soer-ree/)

Contributors

N. BRUCE BASKERVILLE has been since 2001 the senior performance management officer with the Planning and Performance Management Directorate of Corporate Services at the National Research Council of Canada. He has 20 years of experience in applied research and program evaluation and has been working on the development of an integrated planning and performance management solution for NRC. He has co-authored 12 peer-reviewed publication and is a Phd candidate at the University of Waterloo's Applied Health Sciences Program, specializing in program evaluation and behaviour change.

BERT BACKMAN-BEHARRY is a Calgary-based consultant with a focus on strategy development and implementation issues that bridge between the public and private sectors. He has worked extensively on innovation, business/organizational development and technology commercialization issues particularly related to information and communications technology and environmental technology.

FRANCOIS BREGHA is a principal of Stratos Inc., an Ottawa-based consultancy. Over the last fifteen years, he has advised several federal government departments on sustainable development issues.

DON DI SALLE is the director general of Corporate Services at the National Research Council of Canada. He has had extensive experience at NRC in policy development, service delivery and organizational design. He leads the development and implementation of major NRC corporate-wide business initiatives and services.

G. BRUCE DOERN is Chancellor's Professor in the School of Public Policy and Administration at Carleton University and holds a joint Research Chair in Public Policy in the Politics Department at the University of Exeter. He is also the director of the Carleton Research Unit on Innovation, Science and Environment (CRUISE). He is the author of several books on Canadian and comparative developments regarding science and technology, innovation, intellectual property, industrial, environmental and regulatory policy, and governance.

CAREY HILL is a PhD candidate in Political Science at the University of British Columbia. Her dissertation research is comparative and examines whether national standards matter for drinking water protection. Her teaching and research interests include Canadian and comparative public policy, urban politics, provincial politics, health policy, and environmental policy.

JEFFREY S. KINDER is a PhD candidate in public policy in the School of Public Policy and Administration at Carleton University. His teaching and research interests are in science, technology and innovation policy. He is co-author with Bruce Doern of *Government Science: Changing S&T Labs and Agencies* (forthcoming).

RUSSELL LAPOINTE is a doctoral student at the School of Public Policy and Administration at Carleton University. His dissertation is on the British Columbia treaty process. He obtained his masters degree at Simon Fraser University.

DÉBORA C. LOPREITE is a PhD Candidate in Public Policy in the School of Public Policy and Administration at Carleton University.

DAVID ROBINSON teaches public economics and game theory at Laurentian University. He is one of very few economists doing research on the economy of northern Ontario. He has conducted research on the northern Ontario economy for fifteen years. He has also published a book on game theory.

MIKE ROSENBLATT recently completed his PhD in public administration at Carleton University focusing on innovation in Canadian federal government labs. He continues to conduct research on innovation and science and technology policies. He is currently a sessional lecturer in the School of Public Policy and Administration at Carleton University.

STEPHAN SCHOTT is a natural resource and environmental economist who teaches in the School of Public Policy and Administration at Carleton University. His work has focused mainly on fishery economics, policy and management, sustainable electricity production and electricity markets, and experimental economics. His current subject of experimental research is the role of information disclosure in public and social dilemmas with Coady Wing (his co-author in the contribution to this volume).

ROBERT SLATER lectures in environmental and sustainable development policy at Carleton University to graduate and undergraduate students. He brings to his teaching practical knowledge derived from over 30 years experience as a senior manager of environmental issues in the Government of Canada and, currently, as president of an international consulting practice. He obtained his degrees from Imperial College and is a senior fellow at the International Institute of Sustainable Development.

JAC VAN BEEK is the director of Planning and Performance Management at the National Research Council of Canada. He has 20 years of experience in strategic and business planning with research-based organizations. He holds an MBA and is an adjunct professor of strategy at the University of Ottawa.

COADY WING is a graduate student in the School of Public Policy and Administration at Carleton University.

THE SCHOOL OF PUBLIC POLICY AND ADMINISTRATION at Carleton University is a national center for the study of public policy and public management.

The School's Centre for Policy and Program Assessment provides research services and courses in the evaluation of public policies, programs, and activities.

The Carleton Research Unit on Innovation, Science and Environment (CRUISE) is a research unit in the School devoted to research on Canadian and comparative policies and institutions dealing with innovation, science, and environment.